Echoing Helicon

Echoing Helicon

Music, Art and Identity in the Este Studioli,
1440–1530

TIM SHEPHARD

OXFORD
UNIVERSITY PRESS

OXFORD
UNIVERSITY PRESS

Oxford University Press is a department of the University of Oxford.
It furthers the University's objective of excellence in research,
and education by publishing worldwide.

Oxford   New York

Auckland   Cape Town   Dar es Salaam   Hong Kong   Karachi
Kuala Lumpur   Madrid   Melbourne   Mexico City   Nairobi
New Delhi   Shanghai   Taipei   Toronto

With offices in

Argentina   Austria   Brazil   Chile   Czech Republic   France   Greece
Guatemala   Hungary   Italy   Japan   Poland   Portugal   Singapore
South Korea   Switzerland   Thailand   Turkey   Ukraine   Vietnam

Oxford is a registered trademark of Oxford University Press
in the UK and certain other countries.

Published in the United States of America by
Oxford University Press
198 Madison Avenue, New York, NY 10016

© Oxford University Press 2014

Library of Congress Cataloging-in-Publication Data
Shephard, Tim, author.
Echoing Helicon : music, art and identity in the Este studioli, 1440-1530 / Tim Shephard.
pages cm
Includes bibliographical references and index.
ISBN 978–0–19–993613–7 (hardback : alk. paper)
1. Music—Italy—15th century—History and criticism.   2. Music—Italy—
16th century—History and criticism.   3. Music—Social aspects—Italy—History—15th century.
4. Music—Social aspects—Italy—History—16th century.   5. Studiolos—Italy.
6. Art and music.   7. Music in art.   8. Este family—Art patronage.
9. Este, Leonello d, 1407-1450.   10. Isabella dEste, consort of Francesco II Gonzaga, Marquis of
Mantua, 1474-1539.   11. Alfonso I dEste, Duke of Ferrara, 1476-1534.   I. Title.
ML290.2.S54 2014
781.5360945451—dc23
2013046865
9780199936137

This volume is published with the generous support of the AMS 75 PAYS
Endowment of the American Musicological Society, funded in part by the National
Endowment for the Humanities and the Andrew W. Mellon Foundation.

1 3 5 7 9 8 6 4 2

Printed in the United States of America
on acid-free paper

CONTENTS

PREFACE

I can trace the origins of this book to a moment more than ten years ago when, short of a topic for an undergraduate dissertation in music, a certain Professor Fallows presented me with a photocopy of Andrea Antico's print *Motetti nove e chanzoni franciose a quatro sopra doi*. That fascinating print led me along indirect paths to the court of Alfonso I d'Este, who ruled as Duke of Ferrara in the early sixteenth century, and at his court I encountered two large personalities: the composer Adrian Willaert and the painter Titian. Titian had been engaged to prepare a set of pictures for the duke's private study, one of which—the *Bacchanal of the Andrians*—was conspicuously musical. Not only did it feature singers, dancers, and instruments, but in the foreground of the painting was a notated song—possibly by Willaert, who began his Italian career in Ferrara. Why should notated music appear in a painting? What might music contribute to an interpretation of the picture? What might pictures tell us about the meanings attached to music? Why should a duke want such a musical image in his private apartment, and in his study in particular? These questions intrigued me, and prompted me to undertake postgraduate study in art history.

My chance to answer them came some years later as a doctoral student in music at the University of Nottingham, under the supervision of Philip Weller and with the financial support of the AHRC. In the course of writing a thesis on music and identity at Alfonso's court, I found myself inexorably drawn to the visual environment of his residence, and to that of his study (or *studiolo*) in particular. His *studiolo* seemed purposefully charged with musical messages, encoded in paint, and I wondered why. I looked for points of comparison and immediately came across the studiolo of Alfonso's sister Isabella, at the neighboring court of Mantua, finding its decoration to be equally loaded with musical significance. From there, I looked back to the previous generation and found musical elements also in the surviving decoration of a studiolo built by their uncle Leonello, who ruled Ferrara in the mid-fifteenth century. These connections were too serendipidous, and the rooms in question too interesting in their encoding of music, to ignore. They became the second half of my thesis, and from there I have developed them into the present book with the support of a Junior Research Fellowship at Worcester College, Oxford.

The material appearing in this book has been aired and tested at numerous conferences over the course of several years, including the annual conferences of the International Musicological Society, the Royal Musical Association, and the Association of Art Historians, several editions of the Medieval and Renaissance Music Conference, the music/bodies conference at Cork, and various research events at the Unviersity of Nottingham. I am grateful to everyone who responded to and commented upon my work in those fora. A large part of chapter 3 has already appeared as an article entitled "Constructing Isabella d'Este's Musical Decorum in the Visual Sphere," in *Renaissance Studies* 25 (2011), at 684–706. It was, of course, immeasurably improved by the close scrutiny of that journal's readers. I am grateful to *Renaissance Studies*, and its publisher John Wiley and Sons, for granting me permission to reuse the material here. A small part of chapter 4 has appeared within an article entitled "Finding Fame: Fashioning Adrian Willaert c.1518," in the *Journal of the Alamire Foundation* 4 (2012), at 12–35, and I am grateful to that journal and its publisher, Brepols, for allowing me to use it again.

Over the course of this book's long gestation many debts of thanks have been incurred, and it will be a pleasure to acknowledge them here. The first and largest is, of course, to my doctoral supervisor, Philip Weller, without whose open mind and astonishingly broad knowledge of Renaissance culture much of what I attempted in my thesis, and then again in this book, would have been impossible. Several other colleagues at Nottingham, and later at Oxford, have been especially generous with their advice, encouragement, and practical assistance, including Peter Wright, Dan Grimley, Paula Higgins, Sarah Hibberd, Nick Baragwanath, and Robert Saxton. Their support has been very much appreciated.

I am particularly grateful to a select group of Renaissance scholars who have read and commented on my work, or offered encouragement, critique, and advice at conferences. Their contributions have saved me from various errors, and prompted new ideas and avenues of investigation, as well as persuading me that there is an appetite for this type of research. They include Raz Binyamini, Bonnie Blackburn, Katherine Butler, Kathleen Christian, Lisa Colton, Anthony Cummings, Jeffrey Dean, Flora Dennis, Daniel Donnelly, David Fallows, Clare Guest, Jane Hatter, Matthew Hunter, Christian Leitmeir, Margaret MacIntyre, Melanie Marshall, Gabriele Neher, Katelijne Schiltz, Claudia Wedepohl, and Giovanni Zanovello. OUP's anonymous readers should also be included in this list, but of course I am unable to name them. Two further scholars, Gregorio Bevilacqua and Antonio Cascelli, were kind enough patiently to correct my translations from Italian, whilst Philip Weller and Eloise Aston generously helped me with Latin.

I extend special thanks to all those former inmates of the Postgraduate Room in the Department of Music at Nottingham with whom I shared my years as a doctoral student. They served as a kind and vivacious family whilst the majority of the work on this book was undertaken, and each has made a valuable contribution to it. They are Mark Clayden, Angela Kang, James Munk, Daphne Thorbjorg, Justin Williams, Katherine Williams, and, most importantly, Jan Butler and Dennis Leo.

Finally, my deepest appreciation is owed to my wife Bev, who through a constant process of discussion and debate has been through this whole book with me, and who deserves a medal for remaining patient and keeping me more-or-less sane. This book is dedicated to her, and to our daughter Elspeth who is much too young to have any idea what I'm talking about.

Echoing Helicon

Introduction

This book is about the roles assigned to music in the construction of courtly and princely identities. I examine this topic through the lens of visual culture—specifically, the visual culture associated with one particular room of the palace: the study, or *studiolo*. In the interests of practicability and coherence, I focus my investigation around the activities of three members of a single ruling family—the Este family—whose studioli, and musical interests, are well documented.

The book opens with a chapter setting out the context, and unpacking the concept of identity as it relates to both visual representation and music. My approach to identity is informed by modern theory, but is firmly rooted in the documented views of elite Italians who lived during the period under investigation. At the heart of the book are three substantial interpretative essays, dealing in turn with the studioli of Leonello, Isabella, and Alfonso I d'Este. These rulers all enthusiastically pursued musical interests, and all spent several years building and decorating studioli. In both respects, their activities unfolded to some extent in dialogue, and thus each chapter offers interesting points of comparison with the last. However, these case studies, spanning around a hundred years from the 1430s to the 1530s, also point to significant changes in the envisioning of music and musical identities in the courtly context. I am able to draw a range of conclusions about the role assigned to music in constructing the identity of each patron, and in the final chapter I elaborate on these to produce reflections on a selection of broader topics: the relationship between decorated space and musical meaning, the role of music-making in shaping identities, the concept of voice, and the imaging of the prince.

It will serve the reader well to understand at the outset that this book is not a catalog of the musical elements in the decoration of the Este studioli, and nor does it present a comprehensive account of the evidence for musical activities in these rooms. Such a brief lies well beyond the scope of this book as I have set it out above. Instead, in the three interpretative essays that lie at the heart of the book, I consider the musical elements of the decoration of the studioli, and other evidence about the patrons' musical interests, only as they seem relevant to the theme of identity. In this book, therefore, I am interpretative rather than descriptive, and selective rather than comprehensive, in my treatment of the subject matter.

I work from the premise that Italian rulers of the fifteenth and sixteenth centuries designed the visual environments of their palaces and castles with a view to presenting a favorable identity, tied in some way to contemporary ideals of princely and courtly behavior. In the case of studioli, such a premise is particularly easy to support, and is widely accepted in the literature. Music features frequently in the decoration of studioli, and was also among the most popular leisure activities of the people who built them. It seems reasonable to suppose, therefore, that music played a prominent role in the strategies of self-representation that Italian princes deployed in the decoration of their studioli. It may also be that this role, identified within the "fictive" space of visual culture, relates in some way to a prince's documented "real" musical interests. Over the course of this book, these hypotheses are tested repeatedly and, I hope, demonstrated to be correct.

The reader will readily discern from this summary that I am primarily interested in the musical activities of courtly amateurs, rather than those of the professionals in their employ. I am seeking to understand the relationships between princely music-making, palace decoration, and princely identities. In following this path, I am inevitably making a range of assumptions about the extent to which patrons were able to direct and control the painters who produced their decorations and the musicians who facilitated their musical entertainments. In the three cases here considered, these assumptions are strongly supported by the available evidence, and it is partly for that reason that I have chosen them. Nonetheless, in the course of this book I find several opportunities to make substantive points about individual musicians and painters working within the patronage of my protagonists, and to examine specific works from a fresh perspective. In particular, the musicians Pietrobono da Ferrara, Marchetto Cara, and Adrian Willaert, and the painters Cosmé Tura, Andrea Mantegna, Lorenzo Costa, and Titian feature prominently.

Alongside the charting of musical identities at court, this book also has a broader aim: to propose some new ways in which visual culture can be drawn into the discourse on music in the fifteenth and sixteenth centuries. Visual material has traditionally had an important place in research into performance practices and instrument design in the Renaissance. It has also featured in the guise of "composer iconography," helping to put faces to names. However, in many respects visual evidence is not especially well suited to addressing these kinds of questions. Artists were not always musical experts, and did not always set out faithfully to represent reality in any case; and some pictures of this period, particularly before the mid-sixteenth century, are difficult to pin to a specific context or person. The premise lying behind my use of visual material in this book is rather different, following a line closer to that of Richard Leppert (the *locus classicus* is Leppert, 1988) and, in the Renaissance sphere, Katherine McIver (see in particular McIver, 1997 and 2002). Whenever an artist undertook the task of representing music in any guise, the results inevitably encoded a range of assumptions and ideas about what music was and what it meant—those of the artist, but also (and more importantly for my purposes) those of the person paying for the image.

Approached in this way, it is possible to discern a more subtle and multifarious relationship between musical and visual culture. The inconvenient "inaccuracies" that make visual material such an unreliable source of practical information about music-making become interesting in themselves: music is distorted in visual sources not only as a result of the practical circumstances of an individual representation, but to reflect the conceptual and aesthetic aspects of musical experience. At the same time, visual representations do not only reflect ideas about music, they also prompt and perpetuate them: in their functions as interior decorations, book illustrations, and so forth, pictures form a meaningful backdrop for their owners' real-life musical activities. Visual sources may have a limited amount to tell us about the practicalities of professional musicianship in the Renaissance, but they have a great deal to tell us about how courtly and bourgeois amateurs (and amateurs, after all, made up the vast majority of musical participants) thought about their musical experiences, not least because those visual sources were themselves a component of them.

This approach informs the whole of this book. I take studiolo decoration to be both useful and used: the patron deploys it to address certain preoccupations, to inscribe particular ideologies upon the space that reflect positively upon their identity; once it is deployed, the patron continues to interact with it, to activate, manipulate, and even alter its meanings. The decoration thus exists in an interpretative and facilitatory relationship with the activities pursued in the room, and with the musical pastimes of the room's owner. It is in this effort of the decoration to intervene musically in the meanings of the space it inhabits that I intend to find the trace of the identity of its patron.

The Studiolo, Identity, and Music

The Studiolo "Type"

Several prominent characters of the Italian Renaissance built, in their palaces, a relatively small room to house studious pursuits. Modern scholarship, following the practice of some of those characters, generally terms those rooms "studioli." In the first survey of the subject, Wolfgang Liebenwein sought to establish the history and significance of the studiolo "type."[1] In conception, he found, the studiolo was tied to the *vita contemplativa*—the contemplative side of life, held in balance with the *vita activa* by the men judged great by the age. Among those who defined the concept for the Renaissance, the most important was Petrarch, whose studious *vita solitaria* was amply theorized by Petrarch himself, and who owned a famous studiolo with which it could be associated.[2]

Looking for physical predecessors for the studiolo, Liebenwein found antiquity somewhat barren, but established an important relationship with Cicero, Pliny the Younger, and Quintilian's views on the library and the villa—both rooms cast as venues for studious retreat. Given the close relationship between the first princely studioli in Italy and the humanist schools of Guarino da Verona and Vittorino da Feltre, where those authorities were held in particularly high regard, this insight is of considerable importance. Moving to the Middle Ages, Liebenwein pointed to the monk's cell and the monastic scriptorium as important forerunners for the scholarly and contemplative aspects of the studiolo type. Meanwhile, another aspect of the room that would mature rather later in the Renaissance—the cabinet or museum—finds its roots in the secular treasure-room. The first "true" studioli, for Liebenwein, are to be found at the

---

[1] Liebenwein 1988, especially 3–31 outlining the background to the studiolo "type." Other useful overviews of the studiolo include Boström 1987; Cieri Via 1988; Clough 1995; Thornton 1997.

[2] I am referring to Petrarch's *De vita solitaria* (translated as Petrarch 1924).

papal court in Avignon in the fourteenth century; the format was then taken up by the French kings.

Whilst Liebenwein's book deservedly remains the primary text on the subject, his attempt to define and describe the studiolo as a "type"—as if it were a new species of butterfly with a coherent, observable set of unifying characteristics—is difficult to take entirely at face value. His effort to determine evolutionary predecessors enjoying a linear relationship with the room inspires similar discomfort, although in the process he makes important and revealing connections. One of the unfortunate results of his typological approach is that Liebenwein is forced to exclude several Renaissance rooms that obviously fall within the topic, because they do not adhere closely enough to his set of unifying characteristics.[3] Several scholars have further objected that the word "studiolo," meaning literally "little study," was not used to label a room until the sixteenth century.[4] Among the terms more commonly applied to such rooms earlier in the Renaissance are "studio," "scrittoio," and simply "camerino." Nonetheless, few would dispute that the studiolo broadly framed, or "studiolo culture" as Stephen Campbell has called it, merits study as a coherent topic.[5] Apart from anything else, most of the famous studiolo builders of Renaissance Italy were related to one another, and created their studioli to similar ends in a dialogue of competition or emulation.

The best-known studioli of the Renaissance, and the ones most discussed in modern scholarship, are those that belonged to reigning despots. Leonello d'Este's room in the villa of Belfiore is often cited as the first, dating from the 1440s, and it was followed by those of Federico da Montefeltro at Urbino and Gubbio in the 1470s: these men had attended the schools of Guarino and Vittorino, respectively.[6] According to some scholars, the *Camera degli Sposi* built for Lodovico Gonzaga in Mantua, begun in 1465, is also to be thought of as a studiolo.[7] Although little is known about it, a studiolo was prepared for Ercole d'Este in Ferrara in the 1480s; but much more famous are those of Ercole's children, Isabella (in Mantua) and Alfonso (in Ferrara), whose efforts stretch into the sixteenth century.[8] Perhaps the best-known studiolo of the late Renaissance is that decorated by Giorgio Vasari for Francesco I de' Medici, Grand Duke of Florence, in the 1570s.[9] However, despots did not enjoy a

[3] See, in particular, Holberton 1987, 57.

[4] Clough 1995, 40; Thornton 1997, 18.

[5] Campbell 2003.

[6] Fullsome bibliography on these rooms will be provided when they are considered in detail later in the book.

[7] Clough 1995, 29–30.

[8] On Ercole's studiolo, see Tuohy 1991; and Tuohy 1996, 81–82 and 208–9. For bibliography on Isabella's and Alfonso's studioli, see the appropriate chapters of this book.

[9] On Francesco's studiolo see, among others, Berti 1967 and Bolzoni 1980.

monopoly: similar spaces were also created for minor nobles (for example Alberto Pio da Carpi), rich merchants (as Piero de' Medici), and, of course, popes (including Leo X)—as well as professional scholars.[10]

Princely studioli were usually prepared within the private apartment of the ruler, often in close association with a bedroom and a small chapel (although caution is required in defining the studiolo as a private space in the modern sense). They appear in urban palaces as well as suburban and rural villas, but they almost always enjoy some sort of relationship with landscape and the countryside. Leonello's studiolo was in a country villa, Federico's looked out from high in the castle wall over the surrounding countryside, Isabella's was next to a courtyard garden, and Alfonso's was decorated with painted land-scapes. Alongside the connection between the countryside and the contem-plative retreat of the hermit, in this respect the studiolo-builders also drew on the Roman senatorial preference for the villa and its life of literary leisure over the humdrum bustle of the city—as expressed, for instance, by Horace (*Satires* 2.6) and Pliny the Younger (*Epistles* 1.6, 1.9, 9.36). Guarino, who wrote a praise of his villa in imitation of Pliny's, had his students compare the virtues of the country and the vices of the city as an exercise in formal rhetoric.[11]

An ideal of literary leisure lies behind all the Italian studioli. Horace, Pliny, Petrarch, and Guarino were all alike in finding within their rural retreats the appropriate circumstances for communion with the Muses—that is, for writ-ing. Although, no doubt, few Renaissance despots seriously practiced their level of literary culture, the studiolo was a way of signaling that they were in touch with the ideal. Some princes, among them the noble students of Guarino and Vittorino who were versed in classical literature and the Liberal Arts, were genuinely literary in their interests. Importantly, the display of literary and scholarly pretensions had useful moral connotations. Princely leisure, follow-ing Roman senatorial as well as Petrarchan models, had to be seen to be useful rather than idle: not *otium* simply, but *otium honestum*.[12]

The studiolo also often housed a more genuinely recreational activity: that of collecting. Most such rooms were decorated with specially commissioned paintings and many contained (or purported to contain) books. For princes of a classicizing bent they were also sites for the display of *all'antica* medals and sculpture. Renaissance sources attest that the purpose of collecting, and

[10] On the studiolo belonging to Alberto Pio da Carpi, see Sarchi 2004; on various fifteenth-century Medici studioli, see Liebenwein 1988, 52–66. John Shearman (1993a, 195–99 and 202–3) has argued that the so-called Stanza della Segnatura was designed to house the library of Julius II, and after his death was turned by Leo X into a private *studio*.

[11] Grafton and Jardine 1982, 69.

[12] Vickers 1990.

of handling collections, was to offer "pleasure" and "relief," although it was also an opportunity to reveal good judgment, knowledge, and taste.[13] Taken together, the activities associated with the studiolo presented the spectrum of the prince's *vita contemplativa*, the counterpart to the *vita activa* displayed in the audience chamber and on the battlefield.[14] Within contemporary ideologies of rulership, this was an important role: the successful balance of the two was considered the mark of a great leader, and knowledge of the Liberal Arts was thought a necessary quality for good government.[15]

Given the studiolo's role in negotiating the relationship between princely ideals and princely realities, it is hardly surprising that a great deal was invested in their decoration. Fortunately, the survival rate for studiolo decoration (and for information about studiolo decoration) is relatively high, such that it is possible to describe some of the conventions. Wainscoting graced with intarsia decoration often played a prominent role: the intarsia documented for Leonello's studiolo is lost, but that from Federico's studioli survives largely intact. These wood-inlay decorations conventionally combine complex perspective scenes with symbols of the Liberal Arts, Muses, and Virtues, including a large number of musical instruments. Also prominent in Federico's intarsia, and present on the ceilings and floors of other studioli, are the ruler's devices and *imprese*, advertising the ruler's qualities through a sometimes abstruse language of symbols.[16]

In most studioli, on the walls above the wainscoting, often set into continuous wood framing, were paintings. Cicero, commenting on the decoration of his library, advised that the subjects chosen should correspond to the dignity of the room: thus, Bacchus, Mars, and Saturn are out; whilst Mercury, the Muses, Minerva, and Hercules are in.[17] A similar range of subjects were evidently considered appropriate for studioli—almost all classicizing, almost all carrying connotations of study and writing. Studioli were decorated for Federico and Ercole with panels showing the Liberal Arts personified; another of Federico's studioli was decorated with paintings of exemplary men, both ancient and modern; and the paintings made for Isabella's studiolo featured Apollo, Mercury, and Minerva. However, the most popular subject, found in Leonello's, Isabella's, and Alberto Pio's studioli as well as in the studiolo-like

[13] Holberton 1987, 57–58; Findlen 1994. On the significance of collecting for private display, see also Goldthwaite 1987, esp. 167–72.

[14] On the *vita activa* and the *vita contemplativa*, see Vickers 1985.

[15] See, for instance, Clough 1995, 19.

[16] On imprese see Lippincott 1990.

[17] Liebenwein derived this summary of Cicero's views on the decoration of a library from various comments in his correspondence, in particular *Epistulae ad Atticum* I.4; I.9; I.10; and *Epistulae ad Familiaris* VII.23. See Liebenwein 1988, 3.

Tempietto delle Muse in Urbino, and alluded to in Federico's intarsie, was the nine Muses. In them, the range of classical and literary associations courted by the studiolo-builders were most conveniently summarized and expressed. Further, by depicting the Muses on the walls, one might simulate and guarantee the kind of inspiring communion the room was designed to promote. It seems quite clear that these decorations were intended to make explicit the ideologies upon which the studiolo built, and to place them in direct association with the person and qualities of the ruler.

Identity and Self-Fashioning

During the Renaissance, selfhood and identity were often discussed and explained through dramatic analogies. Leonardo Bruni, for instance, a Florentine statesman and humanist of the early fifteenth century, wrote that "the same man can play many parts." His younger compatriot Leon Battista Alberti thought that people designed their appearance and actions with "wise artifice," through which they could "transform themselves" to appear favorably in different circumstances.[18] In the early sixteenth century, Baldassare Castiglione explained in great detail how to assume the role of the perfect man of the court; he even coined a term to describe the business of playing a carefully constructed role whilst appearing natural and at ease: *sprezzatura*.[19]

The dramatic analogy is particularly helpful in that it foregrounds a person's own agency in creating and manifesting their identity. An actor's job is not simply to have words put into his mouth by a playwright; he takes time to consider how to play his part, designing his gestures and facial expressions, determining the psychological and emotional content of his words, adapting his body to the parameters of his character, taking further instruction from a director, producer, and other actors in the play. In a treatise that was popular throughout the Renaissance, the Venetian patrician Francesco Barbaro advised his fellow Italians similarly to take affirmative action in constructing their roles, suggesting that they "rehearse...in front of a mirror."[20] Barbaro, Castiglione, and other Renaissance authorities describe the importance of consciously shaping every element of one's exterior demeanor, gesture, and

---

[18] On Renaissance identities, see especially Simons 1995, 267–77, with the further bibliography cited there. Simons offers these quotes from Bruni's *De militia* and Alberti's *Momus* at 270.

[19] The literature on Castiglione and identity is enormous and it would be pointless to list it all, but mention should at least be made of Rebhorn 1978.

[20] Kohl and Witt 1978, 203.

appearance so as to convey a positive impression of one's interior character and virtue.[21]

To reflect the idea that a person's identity—their role—can be self-consciously designed and constructed, it is now common to talk about Renaissance identities in terms of "self-fashioning." The term was introduced by Stephen Greenblatt to describe aspects of Elizabethan society (though it has since been adopted by many other scholars). To make a career in Elizabethan society, he argued, a man had to grasp the building blocks of his own identity, manipulating his image and his very character to political advantage. In more detail, "self-fashioning... describes the practice of parents and teachers; it is linked to manners or demeanor, particularly that of the elite; it may suggest hypocrisy or deception, an adherence to mere outward ceremony; it suggests representation of one's nature or intention in speech and actions."[22] Crucial for the use of this analytical tool in the discussion of art and culture is this last aspect—representation: self-fashioning "invariably crosses the boundaries between the creation of literary characters, the shaping of one's own identity, the experience of being molded by forces outside one's control, the attempt to fashion other selves."[23]

Renaissance observers were perfectly capable of noting and analyzing the performative aspects of one another's identities—although they sometimes did so with suspicion and distaste. In Poggio Bracciolini's treatise *De varietate fortunae*, for example, the powerful of the world are represented by masked actors, whom fortune eventually unmasks.[24] Among many incisive comments on contemporary noblemen in his *Commentaries*, Pope Pius II complained of Borso d'Este, Duke of Ferrara, that "He wanted to appear magnificent and generous—rather than genuinely to be so." In Pius II's analysis, Borso's construction of false greatness was achieved through his handsome appearance, his rich wardrobe, his refined conversation, his self-representation in public art, and his cultivation of flattering encomia.[25] Machiavelli, alongside some other contemporary writers on government, noted that the ruler should "seem

---

[21] See Shephard 2013c, 110–11.

[22] Greenblatt 1980, 3.

[23] Greenblatt 1980, 3.

[24] Fubini 2003, esp. 117.

[25] "Borsius egregio corpore fuit, statura plus quam mediocri, crine pulchro et aspectu grato; multiloquus auscultavit se ipsum dicentem, ut qui sibi magis quam auditoribus placeret. Multa in eius ore blandimenta commixta mendaciis. Magnificus ac liberalis videri magis quam esse cupiebat... Statuam sibi viventi in foro erexit, quae sedens ius dicere videretur; adiecti sunt et tituli, quos palpans adulatio excogitavit; nihil enim Borsio laude fuit dulcius.... numquam non gemmis ornatus in publicum prodiit." Text and translation in Pius II 2003, II.40.1 (1:360–63).

to possess" an appropriate range of princely virtues, because "Everyone sees what you seem, but few know what you are."[26]

As Pius II's analysis of Borso's public image would suggest, objects and representations could play an important role in the shaping and manifesting of identities—both those of the artists who created them and, more important for my purposes, those of the patrons who used them.[27] Like Cicero when discussing his library, Renaissance writers developed a sophisticated sense of the affinity between a room's decoration and furnishing, and the people inhabiting it. The principal theme is, of course, the appropriateness of a subject to the function of a room, amounting to a more-or-less coherent theory of the decorum of space.[28] But their thinking also went further, constructing an instrumental relationship between a room's decoration and its users. Paolo Cortese advised that painted decoration should feature "the lessons of history brought to life. For [by the sight of these paintings] either the appetite of the soul is aroused or the capacity for motion ... may be prompted by the striking life-like imitation, in the painting, of the thing represented."[29] This is evidently the point of the gallery of famous men in Federico's Urbino studiolo. Leon Battista Alberti even suggested that the instrumental relationship might extend from the soul to the body: "Wherever man and wife come together, it is advisable only to hang portraits of men of dignity and handsome appearance; for they say that this may have a great influence on the fertility of the mother and the appearance of future offspring."[30] Pictures, it seems, could be designed and deployed as tools capable of manipulating a person's character and even their physiology.

[26] "Deve adunque avere un principe gran cura che non gli esca mai di bocca una cosa che non sia piena delle soprascritte cinque qualità, e paia a vederlo e udirlo tutto pietà, tutto fede, tutto umanità, tutto integrità, tutto religione. E non è cosa più necessaria a parere d'avere, che quest'ultima qualità; perchè gli uomini in universale giudicano più agli occhi che alle mani, perchè tocca a vedere a ciascuno, a sentire a pochi. Ognuno vede quel che tu pari, pochi sentono quel che tu sei." Text Machiavelli 1891, 306; translation Machiavelli 1992, 61.

[27] Two classic and influential studies adopting this approach, one focused on artists and one on patrons, are Campbell 1996 and Starn 1989.

[28] On the decorum of space in Renaissance Italy, with an emphasis on Este spaces, see Rosenberg 1982.

[29] "nec enim dubium esse potest, cum homines aliquo picturae genere teneantur quo possint tamquam praesenti historiae eruditione frui, quin in his ex uehementi imaginum similitudine aut animi appetito praeparetur aut motrix euocetur uirtus." From Bk. 2, Ch. 2 of the De cardinalatu, first published in 1510—text and translation Weil-Garris and D'Amico 1980, 90–91.

[30] "Vbi vxoribus conueniant non nisi dignissimos hominum et formosissimos vultus pingas monent. Plurimum.n. habere id momenti ad conceptus matronarum et futuram speciem prolis ferunt." Text Alberti 1512, 140v; translation Alberti 1988, 299.

Music was also understood to be ethically potent, and indeed to enjoy a special capacity to shape the human soul. Castiglione noted that "Plato and Aristotle insist that a well-educated man should also be a musician; and with innumerable arguments they show that music exerts a powerful influence on us, and, for many reasons that would take too long to explain, they say that it has to be learned in childhood, not so much for the sake of its audible melodies but because of its capacity to breed good new habits and a virtuous disposition."[31] He had in mind Book 3 of Plato's *Republic* and Book 8 of Aristotle's *Politics*, both of which treat music's role in education in considerable detail; and Castiglione had no doubt also encountered the same ideas repeated more briefly by Cicero and Quintilian, whose purchase among the literati in Renaissance Italy was immense. Plato and Aristotle built on the Pythagorean idea that musical harmony can be described in terms of proportion, and that the same proportional mathematical system underlies the organization of both the heavens and the human soul. The relationship of similarity thus established between music and the soul could be used to explain its capacity to stir the emotions. Thus, Plato sought to establish which musical modes stirred which emotions, and to reject from his system of education those modes whose effects upon the human soul he considered deleterious. The ethical effects of music were understood, by some at least, to find purchase as a matter of course during contemporary musical performance. Marsilio Ficino, for example, reminded his readers that "song is a most powerful imitator of all things. It imitates the intentions and passions of the soul as well as words; it represents also people's physical gestures, motions, and actions as well as their characters and imitates all these and acts them out so forcibly that it immediately provokes both the singer and the audience to imitate and act out the same things."[32] Classical anecdotes concerning the ethical power and effects of music were told and retold by music theorists and were certainly also familiar among amateurs. Like objects and visual representations, then, music was commonly understood to have the capacity to shape a person's character and state of mind, and thus it could fulfill similar roles in the context of self-fashioning.

---

[31] "Platone ed Aristotele vogliono che l'om bene instituito sia ancor musico, e con infinite ragioni mostrano la forza della musica in noi essere grandissima, e per molte cause, che or saria lungo a dir, doversi necessariamente imparar da puerizia; non tanto per quella superficial melodia che si sente, ma per esser sufficiente ad indur in noi un novo abito bono ed un costume tendente alla virtù." Text Castiglione 1947, 118; translation Castiglione 1967, 95.

[32] "Memento vero cantum esse imitatorem omnium potentissimum. Hic enim intentiones affectionesque animi imitatur et verba, refert quoque gestus motusque et actus hominum atque mores; tamque vehementer omnia imitatur et agit, ut ad eadem imitanda vel agenda tum cantantem, tum audientes subito provocet." From Bk. 3, Ch. 21 of the *De vita libri tres*, first printed in 1489 and much reprinted thereafter—text and translation Kaske and Clark 1989, 358–59.

This analysis of identity has a number of points in common with modern critical theory, literary theory, sociology, and semiology. Whilst I do not mean to draw upon these intellectual resources in a heavy-handed, pervasive, or anachronistic manner, they do offer certain concepts that conveniently encapsulate or flesh out important facets of the relationship between music, art, and identity as it is found in the Renaissance sources.

First is the concept of "performativity," initially a part of J. L. Austin's literary theory, but since adapted for the discussion of identities by (among others) Judith Butler. A performative, in Austin's theory, is a verbal statement that in its utterance brings about the thing it describes: the classic example is "I now pronounce you man and wife."[33] Butler's gender theory configures identity as a construct that is inscribed upon the body through activities that are in themselves shaped by cultural codes.[34] She sees identity, therefore, as a performance, and the acts and gestures that produce identity as performative in the sense that they do not simply emerge from a preexisting identity, but actually bring into being the identity they describe. In her own words, such actions "are *performative* in the sense that the essence or identity that they otherwise purport to express are *fabrications* manufactured and sustained through corporeal signs and other discursive means."[35] She notes that this performance, although it may often entail the illusion of interiority, privacy, and intimacy, is inherently public—it relies for its functionality on "a decidedly public and social discourse."[36] This is distinctly similar to the dramatic account of identity described above, and also to the idea of self-fashioning. Further, and more importantly, Butler's concept of the performative neatly encapsulates the relationship between paintings or musical performances and their viewers or participants found in Cortesi, Alberti, Castiglione, and Ficino. It is a term that I will use in that sense several times over the course of this book, and I will often describe identity as a performance.

Second is the revival of the dramatic analogy found in the work of the sociologist Erving Goffman, and taken up from there by other scholars. Goffman's work provides useful points of comparison for the concept of self-fashioning, and supplies ways to think about the role of objects (such as those that might be found in a studiolo) within it. Goffman characterized the setting for social interactions as a stage upon which self (what I have termed "identity") is

[33] The classic formulation of Austin's performative is to be found in Austin 1962, 4–7.

[34] See, in particular, Butler 1990.

[35] Butler 1990, 136. Of course, Butler's use of the performative is somewhat different to Austin's, drawing also on Foucault's views on knowledge and subjectivity (on which see Foucault 1972).

[36] Butler 1990, 136.

constituted: its sets and props—the objects and décor of everyday life—serve the performer as the signs and prompts that facilitate his performance, and contribute to the constitution of his self. In Goffman's own summary, "there will be a team of persons whose activity on stage in conjunction with available props will constitute the scene from which the performed character's self will emerge, and another team, the audience, whose interpretative activity will be necessary for this emergence."[37] Rereading Goffman through a semiotic lens, R. S. Perinbanayagam calls the self a "system of signs," finding that, beyond the obvious semiotics of language, "time, space, clothing and other tangible objects are used to convey one's signification to another."[38] The assembling and design of the setting within which one performs an identity is, then, itself central to (and an aspect of) the performance. With reference to Austin's view of the performative in language, Perinbanayagam calls the operation of this system "doing self with things," characterizing it as a "composition...undertaken artfully."[39] This composition, constituted in "the assembly of individual signs into the maxisigns of the self," he finds to be identical to writing, so that "in assembling a self one constructs a text."[40] This formulation usefully describes and explains the activity of patrons in assembling about themselves collections of objects: furniture, paintings, antiquities, musical instruments, books, and others. It encapsulates my approach to the furnishing of a studiolo, and to the agency of a patron in constructing his identity.

Scholarship on Renaissance studioli has pointed repeatedly to a relationship between the studiolo and identity thought of in these terms. Stephen Campbell has observed that, "beginning with the aristocratic studioli of the fifteenth century, this...space was...the site where the cultivated self had been produced and put on display...The self could be constructed and revealed through the mute but richly equivocal language of painting and sculpture, defining the owner's 'personal space' even in his or her absence."[41] Dora Thornton has argued similarly that "It was not only the fact of owning a study, but also the nature of its decoration and contents which indicated an individual's credentials, and many of the characteristic things found in the room subtly suggested ways in which an individual related to the wider social world."[42]

---

[37] Goffman 1969, 223.

[38] Perinbanayagam 1990, 320.

[39] Perinbanayagam 1990, 317. The essay is entitled "How to do self with things."

[40] Perinbanayagam 1990, 318.

[41] Campbell 2003, 303. His subsequent monograph on Isabella's studiolo (Campbell 2004) develops the connection at length. Other studiolo studies adopting a similar approach include Starn 1989; Findlen 1994, esp. 293–345; Clough 1995; Thornton 1997, esp. 1–7; and Campbell 2000.

[42] Thornton 1997, 1.

The familiarity with the *studia humanitatis* and the Liberal Arts that a studiolo served to advertise was configured as a tool of self-fashioning also by
its fifteenth-century enthusiasts. In a treatise on education that enjoyed wide
circulation in Renaissance Italy, Pier Paolo Vergerio explained the importance
of an education "in the circle of the Muses":

> Parents can provide their children with no more lasting resources, no
> more dependable protection in life than instruction in honorable arts
> and liberal disciplines. With such an endowment, children can usually
> overcome and bring distinction to obscure family origins and humble
> homelands.... But although it is fitting that everyone ... desire to edu-
> cate their children correctly, ... it is particularly fitting that those of
> lofty rank, who cannot say or do anything in secret, be instructed in
> the principal arts in such a way as to be held worthy of the fortune and
> rank they possess.... Nor is there any more firm or solid rationale for
> ruling than this: that those who rule be judged by all to be the worthi-
> est to rule.[43]

The self-fashioning value of such an education, he argues, is so great as to create from a pauper a man of rank and substance. It is even an essential component of the identity of a prince.

Whilst identities could undoubtedly be seen in performance in a studiolo,
the question of for whom the performance was staged is a complex one. The
studiolo was usually situated within the prince's private apartment, suggesting that access was severely limited, and that it was intended as a space where
the prince could avoid observation. The category "private" certainly pertained
in the Renaissance: both Alberti and Filarete observe a careful distinction
between public and private spaces when discussing architecture, characterizing the private by restricted access, relaxed rules, and the pursuit of "delight."[44]
However, the category is problematic, as Vergerio observes when he notes, in

---

[43] "Neque enim opes ullas firmiores aut certiora praesidia vitae parare filiis genitores possunt
instructos, quibus rebus praediti et obscura suae gentis nomina et humiles patrias attollere atque
illustrare consueverunt.... Verum cum omnes homines deceat ... eos esse qui recte erudire suos
liberos studeant ... praecipue tamen qui excelsiore loco sunt, quorumque nihil neque dictum
neque factum latere potest, decens est ita principalibus artibus instructos essel, ut et fortuna et
gradu dignitatis quam obtinent digni habeantur.... Nec est ulla certior aut stabilior regnandi
ratio quam si hi qui regna obtinent, ab omnibus dignissimi omnium regno iudicentur." Text
and translation Kallendorf 2002, 4–5. For some useful remarks on the aspirational character of
humanist expertise both for Federico and for the scholars he patronized, see Clough 1973; and
Falvo 1986, 114–24.

[44] Alberti 1988, 19–20, 189, 292–94; Filarete 1965, 19.

the passage given above, that "those of lofty rank... cannot say or do anything in secret"—intentionally recalling Pliny the Younger's famous *Panegyric to Trajan*:

> One of the chief features of high estate is that it permits no privacy, no concealment and, in the case of princes, it flings open the door not only to their homes, but to their private apartments and deepest retreats; every secret is exposed and revealed to rumour's listening ear.[45]

Alberti similarly acknowledged the tension between privacy and princely visibility, advising that "in [the palace of a prince], even private quarters must have a regal character, as though public, since there is no part of a royal household into which the crowd will not spill."[46] The prince was visible even in his privacy, and therein lurked problems. For Vergerio, as presumably for at least some of the studiolo-builders, the solution to the problems lay in the visible pursuit of the *studia humanitatis* (whether in practice or in appearance).

Castiglione treats the subject of access to the prince's private apartment under the topic of showing and receiving favor. It is an honor that should never be presumed, and thus an invitation was a political act: "The courtier will never attempt to make his way into the chamber or private quarters of his master uninvited, even though he possesses considerable authority himself."[47] He goes on to explain why the prince might judge the audience for his private identity so carefully: "when princes are by themselves, they enjoy the liberty of saying and doing just what they please, and so they do not want to be seen or overheard by anyone in a position to criticise."[48] Castiglione's solution to the problem of princely visibility was the restriction of access to private space: the prince could maintain control over every aspect of his performance.

The studiolo was a primary venue for such visible privacy—its decorations frequently designed specifically to articulate and manifest the virtues of the contemplative side of the prince's life, advertising his *otium* as *honestum*. Cecil

---

[45] Pliny 1969, panegyric no. 83. See also Welch 2002 on Giovanni Pontano's distinction between public magnificence and private splendor.

[46] "quae in his etiam singulorum receptus naturam sapiant principum necesse est: quae quidem plurimorum sint, quando nusquam in regum domibus non superfluit multitudo." Text Alberti 1512, 62v; translation Alberti 1988, 120.

[47] "Non cercherà d'intromettersi in camera o nei lochi segreti col signor suo non essendo richiesto, se ben sarà di molta autorità." Text Castiglione 1947, 166; translation Castiglione 1967, 127.

[48] "spesso i signori, quando stanno privatamente, amano una certa libertà di dire e far ciò che lor piace, e però non vogliono esser né veduti né uditi da persona da cui possano esser giudicati." Text Castiglione 1947, 166; translation Castiglione 1967, 127.

Clough has brought together documentary evidence showing that the studiolo of Federico da Montefeltro was used to discuss the duke's most secret affairs.[49] The studioli of Leonello, Isabella, and Alfonso d'Este were demonstrably on the tour for the most famous or important guests.[50] One might conveniently characterize the room as a space to entertain a "public" who were of sufficient stature or intimacy to merit "private" reception. In recognition of this fact, Dora Thornton has considered at length the importance of visitors to the efficacy of a studiolo, discussing the courtly studiolo's "conviviality."[51]

Music in the Studiolo

Written references to music-making that locate it unequivocally in one or another space of the palace are rare, beyond those concerning sacred music placed in a sacred context and those reporting musical entertainments over dinner.[52] Music rooms are documented for a few nobles, including Ercole I d'Este, but they appear to have been primarily for storing musical instruments, and few would wish to argue that secular music-making in the palace was restricted to them.[53] No doubt for this reason, most scholars have paid no more than cursory attention to the presence and role of music in the studiolo.[54] However, the available indirect and nonwritten evidence strongly suggests that studioli were used as venues for musical performance, undertaken both by professional musicians and, most particularly, by noble amateurs.

[49] Clough 1995, 40. Thornton (1997, 120–21) disagrees, however, preferring to see Federico's studioli as the venues for less formal gatherings.

[50] See chapter 2 of the present study on the visit to Leonello's studiolo of Ciriaco d'Ancona (also Thornton 1997, 120). On visits to Isabella's studiolo, see Fletcher 1981, 53; Kolsky 1984, 54; Brown 1986; Brown 2004, 283. On visits to Alfonso's studiolo, see the correspondence published in Hope 1971; Goodgal 1978; and Hope 1987.

[51] Thornton 1997, 106–25.

[52] For a selection of references concerning the performance of music at dinner, see Shephard 2010a, 109n81. See also Messisbugo 1992.

[53] On Ercole's music room ("camera de la musica" or "camera dali istrumenti"), see Lockwood 1984, 145; and Tuohy 1996, 82–83. On the phenomenon of the music room and the location of musical instruments within the house, see also Dennis 2006, 232–35; and Dennis 2012.

[54] The exceptions include Iain Fenlon on Isabella's studiolo (Fenlon 1981; Fenlon 1997); Camilla Cavicchi on Leonello's studiolo (Cavicchi 2007); and Emmanuel Winternitz, Nicoletta Guidobaldi, and Robert Kirkbride on Federico da Montefeltro's studioli (Winternitz 1942; Guidobaldi 1994; Guidobaldi 1995; Guidobaldi 1996; Kirkbride 2008, 138–44). In addition, Flora Dennis (2006, 234) mentions a later-sixteenth-century Venetian phenomenon of "music studies" (*studi di musica*).

Figure 1.1 Vittore Carpaccio, *A Monk and Three Musicians in a Room*, ca. 1475–1522, pen and ink on paper rubbed with chalk, British Museum, London. © British Museum.

There can be no doubt that music fits the recreational model of the studioli. In its mathematical and astronomical guise, it numbered among the Liberal Arts, and was thus a pursuit appropriate to the prince's studious leisure. In the form of song, musical composition and performance were tied inextricably to poetic texts, whose place in the studiolo few would question. Certainly music served the ends of pleasure and relief, and indeed Castiglione cast it as the most obvious and characteristic mode of courtly relaxation: "during our leisure time we can find nothing more worthy or commendable to help our bodies relax and our spirits recuperate, especially at Court."[55] Even as uncompromisingly scholarly a commentator as Angelo Decembrio, writing probably in the 1450s, could concede that the ideal library (a room closely related to the studiolo) might contain not only books, but "an instrument for drawing up horoscopes or a celestial sphere, or even a lute if your pleasure ever lies that way: it makes no noise unless you want it to."[56] Visual depictions of studies sometimes accord with Decembrio's suggestion.

[55] "niuno riposo di fatiche e medicina d'animi infermi ritrovar si po piú onesta e laudevole nell'ocio che questa; e massimamente nelle corti." Text Castiglione 1947, 116; translation Castiglione 1967, 94. For an interesting discussion of contemporary views on the value of musical leisure, see Kirkbride 2008, 138–43.

[56] "Intra bibliothecam insuper horoscopium, aut sphaeram cosmicam, citharamue habere non dedecet, si ea quandoque delecteris: quae nisi cum volumus, nihil instrepuit." Text and translation Baxandall 1965, 196 with n35.

Figure 1.2 Lorenzo Lotto, *Portrait of a Gentleman in His Study*, 1528–30, oil on canvas, Galleria dell'Accademia, Venice. © Bridgeman Art Library.

A drawing by Vittore Carpaccio (probably of ca. 1500 or slightly later) shows three figures playing musical instruments, including lutes, in a room that Dora Thornton interprets as a study (Figure 1.1). Lorenzo Lotto's *Portrait of a Man in His Study* (ca. 1527–28) features a lute resting against the back wall of the room (Figure 1.2). The studiolo is even physically suited to the performance of music on a small scale. Its small size and wooden wainscoting would have provided a convenient, intimate, and resonant space for one or two musicians, and accommodated four or five. Alberti recommended the coffered wooden ceiling, with which many studioli were equipped, as particularly appropriate for musical venues: "wherever people are to be heard reciting, singing, or debating, [stone] vaulting will not be suitable, because it reflects sound, whereas a composite timber ceiling will be, because it resonates."[57]

The weight of these various arguments has led a few scholars to consider the performance of music in studioli inevitable and almost certainly characteristic. Iain Fenlon has argued for music-making in the studiolo of Isabella d'Este; John Shearman has located Leo X's instruments and musical enthusiasms within his studiolo; Alessandra Sarchi has proposed Alberto Pio da Carpi's

[57] "Locis quidem omnibus quibus vox aut recitantium aut canentium, aut dispitantium audienda est: testudinata haud vsque conueniunt quae vocem retundant: contignata conveniunt quae sonora sint." Text Alberti 1512, 68r; translation Alberti 1988, 131. This advice seems to be somewhat at odds with the later view of Sebastiano Serlio, who advocated brick vaulting in spaces designed for music—see Moretti 2010, 44.

studiolo as a space for musical entertainments; Robert Kirkbride has supported the idea that music was played in Federico's studioli; and Laura Moretti has discussed a room modeled on an ancient study that was designed to house Alvise Cornaro's musical entertainments.[58] In her survey of Renaissance study rooms, Dora Thornton also argues in favor of music's place therein.[59]

A further clue as to the importance of music in the studiolo is found in the fact that music—in notation, instruments, performance, or as symbol—is among the most characteristic features of studiolo decoration. Indeed, it is that circumstance that makes this book possible. Among the most explicitly musical studiolo decorations were those made for Federico, whose two studioli, in his palaces at Urbino and Gubbio, were graced by two similar but distinct decorative programs.[60] In Urbino, portraits of exemplary men, both ancient and modern, appear above wainscoting decorated with *trompe l'oeil* cupboards and the theological virtues in intarsia; in Gubbio, paintings of the seven Liberal Arts (among them music) appear above similar intarsia cupboards. The contents of the fictive cupboards in both studioli constitute an inventory of tools appropriate to the pursuit of the Liberal Arts, apparently mixed freely with those appropriate to the Muses and to the Virtues (Figures 1.3 and 1.4).[61] We find the armillary sphere and astrolabe of Astronomy or Urania; the dividers, set square, and plumb bob of Geometry; any number of books that might be associated with either Rhetoric or Grammar; and a large collection of musical instruments and even notated music that relate primarily to Music as a Liberal Art, although also to the Muses.

The number and range of musical objects is in fact quite astonishing.[62] In the Gubbio *intarsie* there are percussion instruments, including a tabor and a tambourine; stringed instruments, including two lutes, a cittern, a harp, a rebec, and a fiddle; wind instruments, including two cornettos, a horn, and a pipe; and a portative organ.[63] In Urbino, several songs are also to be found,

[58] Fenlon 1981, 88 (repeated in Fenlon 1997, 363–64); Shearman 1993a, 203 (although he later revised this view, locating Leo X's musical entertainments instead in the *guardaroba* of the same apartment—see Shearman 1993b, 32); Sarchi 2004, 133; Kirkbride 2008, 143–44; Moretti 2010.

[59] Thornton 1997, 120–23.

[60] On Federico's studioli, see Remington 1941; Clough 1967; Cheles 1986; Fabiański 1990; Clough 1995; Raggio 1996; Raggio 1999; Kirkbride 2008. I have given references to music-focused studies of Federico's studioli in a previous note. For a convenient summary of Federico's patronage see Clough 1973.

[61] The objects together with their possible significance are identified and cataloged in Cheles 1986, 58–82.

[62] Musical motifs are common in Italian Renaissance intarsia in general, though few secular decorations survive as complete as those of Federico. For a range of indicative examples, see Reese 1965; and Winternitz 1967, plates 47–55.

[63] As identified in Winternitz 1942, 106–8.

Figures 1.3 and 1.4 Francesco di Giorgio Martini and Giuliano da Maiano, *Studiolo* from the Ducal Palace in Gubbio, ca. 1478–82, intarsia, Metropolitan Museum, New York. © The Metropolitan Museum of Art.

with legible text and musical notation.[64] The equipment lies about as if caught up in an ongoing process of regular use.

It is very tempting to take their presence as evidence for the performance of music in the room, and I think it likely; indeed, Vespasiano da Bisticci reports of Federico that "there wasn't an instrument that His Lordship did not have in the house."[65] But caution is prompted by an interpretative confusion: it is difficult to tease apart the instruments' symbolic function from their "snapshot" character with any confidence. For all its assertion of scholarship, the intarsia decoration entails an ambiguity: the floor-to-ceiling decoration fictionalizing the presence of Liberal Arts paraphernalia more or less precludes the actual presence of such objects stored in the room.[66] Irrespective of their literal reality, the musical instruments and other objects constitute a fashioning of Federico's identity. They operate in a performative mode: by asserting the duke's liberal arts credentials, they effectively make them real.

Federico's use of the medium of music to demonstrate his credentials went further. He left a concise statement of the message he intended his studioli to convey in a song, notated in intarsia on the wall of his Urbino room. The text reads: "Federico, the greatest leader of all Italians, outdoors and at home, he fights wars and cultivates the Muses."[67] Music is here chosen as the vehicle for expressing the successful balance of the active and the contemplative that characterized a great prince. The studioli, we presume, manifest and facilitate primarily the domestic, contemplative side of this equation. The classical reference point for Federico's formula was, in fact, explicitly musical: in an anecdote popular among humanists of the fifteenth century, Homer tells that Achilles relaxed after battle with a song.[68]

Federico's self-congratulatory song brings us to the heart of the relationship between music and the studioli. He and every other studiolo builder saw the "cultivation of the Muses" as the activity that most effectively defined the room: Stephen Campbell has called the Muses the "definitive studiolo subject." The Muses, of course, were inextricably tied to music. The connection was a natural one for the classicizing Renaissance, as indeed for the medieval authorities on which Renaissance musical thought often relied. Guido of

[64] These include *Bella gerit*, discussed below, *O rosa bella* and *J'ay pris amour*—on these see Guidobaldi 1995, 49–73.

[65] "non era istrumento che la sua signoria non avessi in casa." Guidobaldi 1995, 11.

[66] This disjunction is noted also in Thornton 1997, 120–21. The *trompe-l'oie* effect would only really work if the room was almost empty—certainly not with anything up against the walls, as it simulates the entire wall space from the floor to above head height.

[67] "Bella gerit musasque colit Federicus omnium maximus Italicorum Dux foris atque domi." Text and translation Fenlon 1997, 363.

[68] As, for instance, Vergerio: Kallendorf 2002, 84–87.

Arezzo, for example, a medieval authority with long-lasting influence, stated
as the purpose of his music-didactic *Micrologus* to induce the Muses to return
to the school-room.[69] Elsewhere we find the etymology of the word "music"
traced to a common origin with the word "muse," with the support of no less an
authority than Plato. Guarino, for instance, wrote in a letter to Leonello that
"you are living proof that the Muses rule not only musical instruments but also
public affairs."[70]

Bartolomeo Ramis de Pareia, a Spanish music theorist active in Bologna,
Rome, and perhaps Florence from 1472, aligned the Muses explicitly and in
some detail with the system of musical modes. In his *Musica Practica* of 1482,
Ramis proceeds thus on the general authority of Hesiod, as a source on the
origins of music, and on the specific recommendation of Martianus Capella
and Macrobius:

> to demonstrate this still more fully...through that from which music
> has originated, just as it is approved by Hesiod, we will arrange the
> nine Muses...so that the one who recounts wars let us give to Mars
> and thus to the Phrygian tone [etc.]...And so we will arrange all of the
> Muses in their proper places according to Martianus and Macrobius,
> just as we will assign a verse to each through which her connection to
> music will be shown.[71]

His view, or something very like it, was a commonplace: the widely read Italian
theorist Franchino Gafori, for instance, included a more compendious consideration of the same topic in his *De Harmonia Musicorum Intrumentorum Opus*
completed in 1500, drawing on such diverse authorities as Ovid, Diodorus
Siculus, Homer, Augustine, and (again) Hesiod.[72]

---

[69] The first words of the treatise, part of a prefatory verse, are "Gone from school are the
Muses; there may I hope to induce them, / Unknown yet to adults, to unveil their light to the
young ones!" Babb 1978, 57.

[70] Quoted in translation in Grafton and Jardine 1982, 53. Plato links *Mousai* and *mousika*
twice (that I know of): in *Alcibiades* 1.108c and *Cratylus* 406a. This etymology is explored also
in music theory, for instance Jacobus of Liege's *Speculum Musicae* I.11 (ca. 1300, but with lasting
influence)—the relevant passage is translated in Godwin 1993, 131–32.

[71] "Quod si adhuc idem certius probare libet auctoritate et comparatione per id a quo musica
traxit originem, ut Hesiodo placet, musas novem filias Iovis et memorie taliter disponemus, ut
eam que bella narrat Marti tradamus, et sic tono phrygio...Et sic unamquamque musarum
locis debitis collocabimus secundum Marciani et Macrobij auctoriates. Sic et unicuique versum
imponemus per quem convenientia cum musica denotetur." From Bk. 3, Ch. 3 of *Musica Practica*.
Text Ramis 1983, 112; translation Ramis 1993, 112.

[72] Gaffurius 1977, 197–200.

In antiquity the Muses appear very often as musicians, both in written and in visual sources. Their copious traffic with ancient poets is most characteristically configured in musical terms, partly because ancient poetics, either in practice or as a conceit, recognized no meaningful distinction between music and poetry.[73] Thus, it is in the Muses' song that poets find their immortality, and, in one of the most pervasive poetic conceits, through their song that poets find inspiration. The Muses' song acts, in this context, as a repository of cultural memory, as well as the means by which the body of poetic subject matter could be communicated to mortal mouthpieces.[74] Hesiod's is the archetypical exposition of this conception of the musical Muses, in the proem to the *Theogony*, a work that was certainly familiar in Renaissance Ferrara:[75]

> From the Muses of Helicon let us begin our singing, that haunt Helicon's great and holy mountain, and dance on their soft feet round the dark-violet spring and the altar of the mighty son of Kronos. And when they have bathed their gentle skin in Permessos, or the Horse's Fountain [i.e., the Hippocrene spring], or holy Olmeios, then on the highest slope of Helicon they make their dances, fair and lovely, stepping lively in time. From there they go forth, veiled in thick mist, and walk by night, uttering beautiful voice, singing of Zeus who bears the aegis, and the lady Hera of Argos, ... and the rest of the holy family of immortals who are for ever.
>
> And once they taught Hesiod fine singing, as he tended his lambs below holy Helicon.... And they told me to sing of the family of blessed ones who are for ever, and first and last always to sing of themselves.
>
> ...Come now, from the Muses let us begin, who with their singing delight the great mind of Zeus the father in Olympus, as they tell of what is and what shall be and what was aforetime, voices in unison....
>
> They were born in Pieria to Memory ... in union with the father, the son of Kronos; oblivion of ills and respite from cares....
>
> ...Whomsoever great Zeus's daughters favor among the kings that Zeus fosters, and turn their eyes upon him at his birth, upon his tongue they shed sweet dew, and out of his mouth the words flow

---

[73] On this aspect of ancient poetics, see, in brief, the introduction to Nagy 1996.

[74] For a recent study of this aspect of ancient poetry(/song), see Wheeler 2002.

[75] Hesiod's *Theogony* was printed in Ferrara as early as 1472 (Mottola-Molfino and Natali 1991, 3:436), and the Aldus edition of Hesiod was dedicated to Battista Guarini (heir to his father Guarino in the intellectual life of Ferrara—Benvenuti 1979, 100). Hesiod's work was drawn upon by Alberti in a text dedicated to Leonello d'Este, and apparently also by Guarino when designing Leonello's painted Muses—see Campbell 1997, 41–42 and n62.

honeyed; and the peoples all look to him as he decides what is to pre-
vail with his straight judgments....

Such is the Muses' holy gift to men. For while it is from the Muses
and far-shooting Apollo that men are singers and citharists on earth,
and from Zeus that they are kings, every man is fortunate whom the
Muses love...he soon forgets his sorrows and thinks no more of his
family troubles, quickly diverted by the goddesses' gifts.[76]

The poet himself, in response, conventionally conceives of his poetic utterance as song. In the time of Hesiod, Homer, and the older lyric poets the conception was perhaps literally meaningful, reflecting a performance practice
as well as (in an improvisatory tradition) a compositional practice. Ovid and
Virgil wrote their poetry down, but found the idea no less appealing: Virgil,
for example, begins his self-consciously archaizing *Aeneid* with it—"Arms and
the man I sing..."

The Muses' musical aspect informed by far the greater proportion of their
depictions in the fifteenth century.[77] Most obvious, and for good reason, are
the so-called *Tarocchi di Mantegna*—neither tarocchi nor by Mantegna, but
a series of images constituting some sort of didactic card game, or simply an
iconographic catalog.[78] The full set of nine Muses with Apollo given to Master
E was most likely printed in Ferrara in the 1460s, but the designs enjoyed an
extremely wide circulation, offering models for a number of subsequent representations.[79] Also pervasively musical, and in some respects indebted to the
Tarocchi, are the Muses painted by Giovanni Santi for the Tempietto delle
Muse in the ducal palace at Urbino, and those painted for Alberto Pio's studiolo in Carpi (which feature music notation).[80]

The case of Federico's studioli, and the prevalence in studiolo decorations
of the subject of the Muses, demonstrate unequivocally that, irrespective of
the likelihood of actual musical performance in studioli, music enjoyed a close
and vital relationship with the studiolo phenomenon. That relationship could
extend from concept, through decoration, to the announcement and manifestation of the prince's identity. Although it is important and extremely likely

[76] Hesiod 1988, lines 1–113. On the significance of this passage, see Havelock 1986, 19–23
and 79–82.

[77] On the depiction of Muses in north Italy during the fifteenth century, see Lippincott 1987,
58–64; Anderson 1991; Sarchi 2004.

[78] On the *Tarocchi* see Lippincott 1987, 58–67; and Mottola-Molfino and Natali 1991, 2:431–
37 with the bibliography given there.

[79] See, for instance, the derivative images given in Mottola-Molfino and Natali 1991, 2:438–40.

[80] Mottola-Molfino and Natali 1991, 1:136–37; Sarchi 2004.

that musical performances did take place in studioli as a matter of course, this conceptual conclusion is the only one essential to the rest of this book.

The Protagonists

The Este family ruled Ferrara from the middle of the thirteenth to the end of the sixteenth century—an exceptionally long tenure for an Italian dynasty.[81] At times they also held Modena and Reggio. However, Este power, like all despotic power in Renaissance Italy, was always contingent and often contested. To begin with, Ferrara had previously been a commune, and the communal government remained a factor to consider in city politics under their rule. At the same time, Ferrara was technically a part of the Papal States, and therefore held in fief to the Pope, whilst Modena and Reggio ultimately belonged to the Holy Roman Emperor. Feudal obligation was both a boon and an inconvenience for the Este. It offered them an avenue to legitimacy, through the conferring of titles such as Marchese and Duke, but it also placed some restrictions on their diplomatic hand, as the displeasure of one or other overlord could (and sometimes did) have serious consequences. Further, like all dynasties, the Este had to contend with rifts in their own ranks, arising from factionalism and the usual disputes over legitimacy and the succession. Finally, despite ruling a prosperous and relatively substantial territory, the Este were on the wrong side of the divide between big and small on the Italian stage. Their resources were considerably greater than those of the other small states, such as Mantua, Urbino, and Monferrato, but vastly inferior to those of the big five—Naples, the Papal States, Florence, Venice, and Milan. Este territory bordered three of these five, placing them in a potentially (and sometime actually) precarious position.

In the end, the Este ruled at the sufferance of multiple parties: their subjects, their feudal overlords, their more powerful neighbors, and the various bastard branches of their own family. Although Ferrara was a military power and several of the Este were very capable commanders, very few of their delicate negotiations and relations with these parties could be pursued successfully through war. Alongside the similar regimes in Mantua and Urbino, the Este learned to entrench and exercise their power by more subtle means.[82]

[81] For an overview of the origins and early history of the Este rule, see Dean 1987. The standard account of the Este and their patronage in the fifteenth century is Gundersheimer 1973; this should be supplemented by the old but still useful studies of Edmund Gardner: Gardner 1904 and Gardner 1906.

[82] These brief comments on diplomacy in Renaissance Italy are indebted to Mattingly 1955, esp. 55–120.

Much in Italian politics, for example, rested on ties of kin, and throughout the fifteenth and sixteenth centuries the Este pursued marriage arrangements with several illustrious dynasties. Marriage was a useful way to form a tangible relationship with a larger power—for example, Naples or Rome—and consequently to enjoy their protection; but it could also form bonds of mutual support among the smaller states—the Este built family connections with Mantua and Urbino, for example. Another important strategy for securing bonds of friendship was to offer services as a *condottiere*, or mercenary commander, to one of the five larger states. Relations with states outside Italy were also central to Italian diplomacy, partly because the balance of power that generally pertained among Italy's various players could only be tipped one way or another with outside help, and partly because Spain, France, and the Empire all claimed territorial interests on the peninsula.

Alongside, and intertwined with, these diplomatic strategies, Este power relied heavily on what we might call the theatre of rule.[83] A dynasty that could demonstrate that they had all the trappings of power was generally presumed to have the force to back it up. In the case of the Este's subjects, this was a matter of inspiring awe and wonder, matching up visibly to conventional notions of princely virtue, and producing occasional gestures of magnanimity; but among elites across Italy, it was more a question of showing that they belonged in the club. Este princes had, by one means or another, to build a reputation among their peers on the Italian stage as princes worthy of the name. This was a complex business, involving several interlocking sets of ideals and standards, and it proceeded on several fronts. Foreign ambassadors and dignitaries, resident and visiting, had to be favorably impressed at home; travelling representatives of the regime had to impress abroad; retainers moving from employer to employer between courts had to tell stories of admirable lifestyle and accomplishments; correspondence flying all across Europe had to convey an appropriate image of the ideal prince; literary men had to be co-opted into writing and distributing favorable reports and assessments; and artists and musicians had to be employed to create suitable monuments and images of the regime. It is here that questions of identity arise, and here that the carefully controlled visibility of the studiolo had an important role to play.

For the Este, the fifteenth century began with the larger-than-life figure of Niccolò III—a man whose bastard offspring reputedly numbered in the thousands, and whose progeny would rule the duchy for the entire century. Niccolò worked hard and successfully to bring stability and a sense of legitimacy to the Este rule in Ferrara, and handed on a much more conventional

---

[83] A helpful overview of this topic can be found in Welch 1997, 211–39.

despotic state than he had inherited. He was also responsible for bringing the humanist Guarino da Verona to Ferrara, and thereby instating Ferrara as one of the premier centers of learning in Italy. He was succeeded in 1441 by his illegitimate son Leonello—the first of the protagonists of this book—a man who, although trained as a *condottiere*, demonstrated an interest in and a flair for classical scholarship under the tutelage of Guarino.[84] A popular ruler and an able politician, in his short reign Leonello adopted a role as a mediator and peacemaker on the Italian stage, and made a marriage connection with the powerful Aragonese kingdom of Naples. He was also a noted patron of artists and scholars of various kinds, playing host to Leon Battista Alberti and receiving the dedication of his *De re aedificatoria*.

Leonello was succeeded in 1450 by his brother Borso, another of Niccolò III's bastards, despite the objections of Leonello's own legitimate son, also named Niccolò. Borso, educated at the court of the King of Naples, had been a trusted lieutenant of Leonello, and enjoyed a long and popular reign. It was he who persuaded the Emperor to make the lordship of Modena and Reggio into a duchy, in 1452; and after much cajoling, in 1471, extracted the title of Duke from the Pope for Ferrara. Dying childless (perhaps as a matter of dynastic policy) in 1471, Borso left the duchies to his half-brother, a legitimate son of Niccolò III, Ercole I, who nonetheless had to see off a challenge from Leonello's son Niccolò before he could take secure possession. Ercole was already forty when he took the reins of power and had behind him a career as a courageous and uncompromising, if not especially successful, *condottiere*. Like Borso, he spent formative years at the court of Naples, and he married a daughter of the ruling Aragonese line, Eleonora d'Aragona, in 1473. Following an ill-advised war with Venice in the 1480s, Ercole was responsible for the massive Northward expansion of the city of Ferrara known as the *addizione*—a considerable feat of design and engineering (both physical and social). His reign stretched some way into the upheavals that assailed Italy from the mid-1490s, beginning with the French invasion of 1494. Although leaning in principle towards France, he steered a carefully neutral path through the diplomatic maneuvers of those years, opting to play the role of peacemaker rather than that of combatant.

After a century of sideways successions, Ercole managed to establish primogeniture, and was succeeded in 1505 by his first son, Alfonso I. Ercole had also played a careful diplomatic game as he placed his other children in marriages and careers. His first daughter, Isabella, married the Marchese of Mantua, Francesco Gonzaga, in 1490; and Alfonso married first Anna Sforza, daughter

[84] On Leonello, see the biographical sketches in Gundersheimer 1973, at 104–20, and Gardner 1904, at 44–66.

of the Duke of Milan, in 1491, and then (after Anna's death) Lucrezia Borgia, daughter of Pope Alexander VI, in 1502. These two, Isabella and Alfonso, are the remaining protagonists of this book.[85] Both ultimately turned out to be able statespeople, and played major roles in the unfortunate dramas of the Italian Wars, which dominated their adult lives.

At her marriage at the age of sixteen, Isabella took on a ruling position, Marchesa of Mantua. She proved herself to be a vigorous patron, a connoisseur in the arts, and a leader in women's fashion, and she was keen to advertise these accomplishments throughout elite Italy. During the war following the League of Cambrai, her husband suffered the ignominy of capture and imprisonment in Venice, during which time she won praise for her activities as regent. Later, when Ferrara was under direct threat, she served as a diligent lobbyist on behalf of her natal dynasty.

Alfonso was an unruly youth, whose inappropriate japes were reported as far afield as Venice—a source of understandable concern for his father.[86] However, following his marriage to Lucrezia Borgia, whom he seems genuinely to have liked and respected, and particularly after the death of his father, he seems to have turned readily to the serious business of running his state. Early on, he developed a considerable reputation as an expert in the military arts, and in particular in the use of artillery. These accomplishments served him well in a reign punctuated by frequent military campaigns, in the course of which the city of Ferrara came under direct threat more than once. Alfonso was a successful commander and reputed heroic, on the whole enjoying the acclaim of his subjects. However, he was also an enthusiastic patron of scholars, artists, and musicians, keeping at his court the likes of Antoine Brumel, Celio Calcagnini, and Dosso Dossi. His contemporaries remarked on his curious mechanical hobbies: founding canon, and turning wood at the lathe (to make, among other things, musical instruments).

Leonello, Isabella, and Alfonso provide the center points of the three case studies at the heart of this book. Their activities as studiolo builders and as musicians were inevitably shaped by the different times and circumstances of their reigns. Leonello's studiolo responded to his education in the circle of the early humanists, and his reputation as a man of culture. Isabella's engaged with the particular challenges of being a ruling woman, whilst providing a focus for her efforts as a connoisseur. Alfonso's offered relief and respite from his labors in the field, and gave vent to his more sensual vision of antiquity. For

---

[85] The standard biography of Isabella remains Cartwright 2002 (first published in 1915); for Alfonso, Gardner 1906 gives a helpful overview.

[86] See Shephard 2013c.

all of them, their patronage projects, although certainly enjoyable, formed a part of the careful and often implicit negotiations with subjects and peers that ensured their continuing positions of power in the palace, in the city, and in Italy at large, through the construction and presentation of appropriate princely identities.

2

Leonello and the Erotics of Song

...Calliope, who is chief among them all;
for she even attends august kings.

Hesiod[1]

The Belfiore Studiolo: Muses and Music

The villa of Belfiore, a country retreat to the north of Ferrara, was begun by Marchese Alberto d'Este in the 1390s and continued by his successor, Niccolò III. Niccolò's son Leonello, who became Marchese in 1441 and hoped to spend more time at the villa, added a new south-facing apartment.[2] Within the new extension he had built a studiolo, whose decoration would occupy him until his death in 1451 and be brought to completion only by his own successor, his brother Borso.[3] Between 1449 and 1453 wainscoting with intarsia decoration was prepared and installed in the room: though no trace or evidence survives, it is easy to imagine that musical motifs of some kind were featured, as they were in the studioli of Federico da Montefeltro.[4] Principal among the decorations, however, was a series of painted panels depicting the Muses.

Information on the program for the paintings, its conception, and dating is found primarily in a letter written to Leonello in 1447 by the humanist Guarino da

---

[1] Hesiod 1988, lines 80–81.

[2] On Belfiore and the building of Leonello's apartment, see Eörsi 1975, 15. The information in this paragraph is derived from there.

[3] On the decoration of the Belfiore studiolo see Eörsi 1975; Boskovits 1978; Cieri Via 1988, XVIII–XX; Mottola-Molfino and Natali 1991; and Campbell 1997, 29–61. The studiolo in Belfiore was neither the first nor the only such room used by Leonello—see Liebenwein 1988, 46 (he discusses the Belfiore studiolo at 46–49).

[4] The same observation is made in Cavicchi 2007, 130–31n6. For an overview of the importance of intarsia decoration to Renaissance studioli, see Thornton 1997, 53–60.

30

Verona, who had been called to Ferrara in 1429 to serve as Leonello's tutor, and had established there a school of considerable fame.[5] Leonello, it seems, had written to his former tutor and mentioned that he intended to have panels of the Muses made for his studiolo. Guarino responds with praise for the initiative, a brief scholarly explication of the Muses, and instructions on how each one should be depicted.

After some slight equivocation, Guarino declares that there should be nine Muses, and identifies them by their standard names. Only a few of the resulting paintings survive, and those are sometimes difficult to pick out with confidence. Their identifications were first proposed systematically by Anna Eörsi and subsequently revised, very sensibly, by Miklos Boskovits. Boskovits accepts five surviving paintings into the canon of the studiolo, all depicting enthroned women: a *Thalia* by Michele Pannonio (Budapest, Szépművészeti Múzeum); two panels now in the Pinacoteca Nazionale, Ferrara, depicting (according to Eörsi) *Erato* (Figure 2.1) and *Urania*, perhaps by Angelo da Siena; and two panels painted largely or entirely by Tura, one of *Terpsichore* (Milan, Museo Poldi-Pezzoli) and an *Allegorical Figure* (Figure 2.2) in the National Gallery, London, whose identity is disputed.[6]

Guarino's terms are of considerable interest for what they reveal about his recreational ideal. The project is "noble and truly splendid," but precisely because it is "not stuffed with pointless or licentious figures."[7] The Muses are to be understood as personifications of arts which were arrived at by human endeavor; this is reflected in their etymology, for "μῶσθαι means *seek* in Greek, so that Μοῦσαι means *seekers*."[8] The scheme, then, can only be admitted if it is useful and decorous, and because the Muses can be shown (if here spuriously) to exemplify the thirst for study and knowledge. He is strangely reticent on the subject of poetry, usually the natural preserve of the Muses, and his often bizarre interpretations of individual Muses suggest a rather forced emphasis on the themes he was so careful to establish.

However, our suspicions are raised by the considerable disjunctions, discussed at length by Stephen Campbell, between Guarino's prescriptions and the paintings eventually produced.[9] The alterations to the scheme, presumably undertaken with Leonello's direct participation or at least with his agreement,

[5] Text and translation of the letter are published in Baxandall 1965, 186–87 and 201–2. For a detailed discussion of Guarino's views on painting, see Baxandall 1963 and Baxandall 1965. For a more general assessment of Guarino's school, see Grafton and Jardine 1982.

[6] Eörsi 1975, esp. 23; Boskovits 1978, 473–75.

[7] "praeclaram vereque magnificam"; "non vanis aut lascivis referta figmentis." Text and translation Baxandall 1965, 186 and 201.

[8] "Μοῦσαι enim graece indagare dicitur; μῶσθαι igitur indagatrices dicantur." Text and translation Baxandall 1965, 186 and 202.

[9] Campbell 1997, 40–51.

Figure 2.1 Angelo Maccagnino and Cosmé Tura?, *Erato*, ca. 1450, tempera on panel, Pinacoteca Nazionale, Ferrara. Reproduced by permission of MiBAC—Pinacoteca Nazionale Bologna, Archivio fotografico.

Figure 2.2 Angelo da Siena and Cosmé Tura?, *Euterpe*?, ca. 1450, tempera and oil on panel, National Gallery, London. © The National Gallery, London.

point up certain differences of emphasis and aim. For example, Guarino stipu-
lated that Erato, who "attends to the bonds of marriage and true love," should
"hold a boy and a girl one to each side of her, setting rings on their fingers
and joining their hands."[10] The surviving painting convincingly identified as
Leonello's *Erato* is populated by no children, and the Muse's distinctly seductive pose suggests that something other than true love and decorous union is at
hand. Evidently Leonello did not entirely share his old tutor's preoccupations.
In fact, Campbell shows that the original scheme was conservative in its moral
caution even for Guarino, and may reflect the scholar's particular vulnerability
to censure around 1447 on the subject of poetry, which, according to some
commentators, was both useless and degenerate.[11]

By November 1447 the painter Angelo da Siena, identified elsewhere by
Guarino as among the best of the age, was at work in the studiolo. In 1449
Ciriaco of Ancona visited Ferrara and saw Angelo at work, with two of the
Muses complete: Clio and Melpomene (neither of which survive).[12] Leonello
died in 1451 leaving the project unfinished, but it was apparently carried
forward without interruption by his successor, Borso. Angelo is still listed
as painter of the studiolo in 1452, and logic has led scholars to suppose that
Michele Pannonio became involved in the project upon Angelo's death in
1456.[13] Between 1459 and 1463 Cosmè Tura appears in the court records as
"depintore dello studio," and it is presumed that the Muses still unaccounted
for were completed by him or under his supervision.[14] The villa of Belfiore was
razed in 1483 in the reign of the next ducal incumbent, Ercole I, during a war with
Venice, and the fate of the paintings is uncertain from that point.

Several of the surviving paintings have been substantially overpainted.
Although all agree that the alterations were carried out by Tura, or under his

---

[10] "Erato coniugalia curat vincula et amoris officia recti; haec adulescentulum et adulescen-
tulam utrinque media teneat, utriusque manus, imposito anulo, copulans." Text and translation
Baxandall 1965, 202.

[11] Campbell 1997, 40–44. The influence of Guarino and his program of teaching on the marchese is perhaps generally overstated: Anthony Grafton and Lisa Jardine strike a wise note of caution when they remark that he began his course with the humanist at the age of twenty-two and
pursued it for six years—by preference Guarino liked his pupils to start very much earlier and stay
much longer (Grafton and Jardine 1982, 61). The primary source for Leonello's own literary out-
look has traditionally been Angelo Decembrio's dialogue *De politia litteraria*, in which Leonello
is given a well-informed, rather austere, Ciceronian, humanist voice (see Gundersheimer 1973,
104–20; and the modern edition of the dialogue, Decembrio 2002). However, some scholars
have questioned the extent to which Decembrio's Leonello accords with other evidence of the
marchese's interests—see, for example, Campbell 1997, 18. On the background to the dialogue
see, most conveniently, Perry 1986, esp. 614–18; and Celenza 2004.

[12] Eörsi 1975, 15.

[13] See, for example, Eörsi 1975, 16; Boskovits 1978, 381.

[14] Eörsi 1975, 15.

supervision, opinions differ concerning their date. Thomas Tuohy has argued that the changes were effected in the 1480s at the behest of Ercole I.[15] On the basis of style, Stephen Campbell prefers the 1460s and the reign of Borso.[16] Fortunately, the precise resolution of this problem is not particularly important to my arguments. For the purposes of this study, I have assumed that the first versions of the paintings, visible only in X-ray photographs, reflect the instructions for the project established by Leonello, and that the alterations and overpainting took place under Borso and after the death of Angelo da Siena. The majority of the panels have also been cut down, removing the inscriptions that once appeared at the foot of each Muse and are preserved in one copy of Guarino's letter.[17] Michele Pannonio's *Thalia* retains its inscription and presumably indicates the original appearance of its companion pictures.

Perhaps for reasons of moral caution, Guarino's proposed Muses are unusual in the extent to which they suppress the nine's traditionally musical attributes. The program, as far as we can tell, incorporated two explicitly musical Muses, alongside the collateral musical motif of Clio's trumpet. Euterpe was to be a music teacher:

> Euterpe, discoverer of the pipes, depict making the gesture of one teaching to a musician carrying musical instruments; her face should be particularly cheerful, as the origin of her name makes clear.[18]

Melpomene a singer:

> Melpomene devised song and vocal melody; therefore she must have a book in her hands with musical notation on it.[19]

Neither instruction has been firmly identified with a surviving painting, and the Melpomene is certainly lost, but they serve at least to establish the currency of music as a symbol in the room.

Evidence also points to a practical connection between Leonello's studiolo and music. When Ciriaco visited he found there an organ, which he described

---

[15] Tuohy 1991.

[16] Campbell 1997, 31–38. Campbell contests Tuohy's view, presuming it to be incompatible with his own; I am not sure this is the case.

[17] The text of the longest version of Guarino's letter is published in Eörsi 1975, 22.

[18] "Euterpe tibiarum repertrix chorago musica gestanti instrumenta gestum docentis ostendat; vultus hilaris adsit in primis, ut origo vocabuli probat." Text and translation (slightly amended) Baxandall 1965, 187 and 202.

[19] "Melpomene cantum vocumque melodiam excogitavit; eapropter liber el sit in manibus musicis annotatus signis." Text and translation Baxandall 1965, 187 and 202.

with considerable enthusiasm. Commissioned by Leonello (who could play the organ) in 1447, the instrument was "new and miraculous," worthy to be numbered among the marchese's "royal and precious ornaments."[20] In an inscription on its base, recorded by Ciriaco, the organ names its maker and locates itself within the room's decorative scheme:

> Pieridians [i.e., Muses], note with miraculous song the new organ that Costantino, following Apollo, has made.[21]

Ciriaco further described the organ as "Melpomenean" (Melpomenea organa), but any attempt to associate the instrument directly with the painting of Melpomene in the studiolo is immediately disappointed: for Guarino, as we have seen, she sang from a book. The organ may not have been the only instrument kept in the studiolo: when Angelo Decembrio admitted that one might keep a lute in a library, in his discourse De politia litteraria, he placed the concession in the mouth of Leonello himself.[22]

Music-making seems to have been one of the activities associated with the villa of Belfiore since its inception. The now lost fresco decoration of the villa, described in some detail by Giovanni Sabadino degli Arienti in his De Triumphis Religionis of 1497, depicts the diversions of several generations of the Este court in the villa gardens and the countryside nearby. One fresco depicted the rural leisure of Alberto d'Este and his court:

> Having finished the hunt we see then, located in a flowery meadow, the dinner-tables prepared and around them they [the courtiers] scatter themselves on the grass, with the servants kneeling so as to serve conveniently, so tasty an invitation the picture gives to whoever sees these scattered diners, there being on one side on a dais the prince Alberto dressed in gold brocade, having on his head a long purple cap [reaching] down to his back, in the style of that time. They having eaten one sees a limpid, flowing source and several wanderers, and young men and ladies dancing to the sound of lutes and pipes and to the sound of a harp played by a lady, and other women and maidens who weave garlands of flowers and herbs to ornament their blond tresses.[23]

---

[20] Cavicchi 2007, 136–37; Peverada 1994, 3–9. The quotations from Ciriaco's description given here and hereafter are translated from the text given in Cavicchi 2007.

[21] "Organa Pierides nova miro cernite cantu quae Constantinus alter Apollo dedit."

[22] I quote the relevant passage in chapter 1.

[23] "Finita la venatione se vedono poi, posti in uno fiorito prato, le mense parate et intorno a quelle li scombenti sopra l'herba, con li servitori genuflessi per comodo servire, che saporoso

Another, somewhat similar fresco described by Sabadino dates from the reign of Ercole I, later in the fifteenth century.

The musical Melpomene made for the studiolo is attended by one of those moral disjunctions between plan and realization noted above.[24] In the program, Guarino envisaged her singing from notated music in a book. The medium would most likely be the mensural notation associated at that time primarily with polyphonic music written by musicians associated with the church—a compositional practice that intersected, in its theoretical statements at least, with music taught as a Liberal Art at the universities. Presumably, for Guarino, the symbol of the music book carried appropriate connotations of study and mathematical rigor, or of sacred rather than secular music. Following his visit to Belfiore, Ciriaco wrote a description of the resulting painting:

> Melpomene wears a golden tunic and a red cloak from the shoulders and plucks a cithara with her left hand, her god-like face turned to her father in Olympus, moving with a certain dignified and becoming liveliness so that the strings seem to accompany her harmonious hymn with a tuneful sound, and she seems to shape song with her rosy lips.[25]

Song read from music notation has become unwritten song delivered to the accompaniment of the "cithara"—a style with appropriate classical associations, but also, as we will later see, one which existed in a crucial ideological and technical relationship with secular musical practice at Leonello's court.

---

invito duona la pictura a chi vede li discombenti mangiare, existendo da uno canto in desia il principe Alberto vestito di brocato d'oro, havendo in capo una purpurea bireta lunga sino al dorso, ala fogia de quel tempo. Mangiato che hano si vedeno ad uno limpido fonte reducti et al.cuni pelegrini gioveni e dame danzare al suono de cythare e tibie et al. suono de una arpa sonata da una dama, et al.tre donne e donzelle che tesseno girlande de fiori e de herbette per ornarse le bianche trezze." Text Gundersheimer 1972, 68.

[24] Eörsi registers this disjunction at 26–27, citing Sabbadini's suggestion that, after writing the letter, Guarino changed his mind on the advice of Teodoro Gaza (teacher of Greek at the University of Ferrara during Leonello's reign). She does not discuss its significance from a musical perspective.

[25] "Altera vero aurea unita & ab humeris purpureo amicta paludamento manu levem pulsando citharam heroidea facie in olympum ad parentem versa honesta gravique quadam alacritate ut chordae melodemati concordem peana cantu perbelle quidem modulari & roseis labiis vocem formare visa." Text and translation Baxandall 1965, 188 with n10.

Euterpe's Seductive Harmonies

The *Allegorical Figure* at the National Gallery attributed to Cosmè Tura (Figure 2.2) has been identified most recently by Jaynie Anderson and Stephen Campbell as Leonello's *Calliope*.[26] Both scholars put forward quite different reasons for the indentification, however, and theirs are not the only opinions on the table. Eörsi thought the panel showed Erato, on the basis of its proximity to the iconography of Venus (leaving her with two Eratos in the studiolo), whilst Anderson acknowledges the possibility that the figure was Euterpe in its earliest version.[27] The latter identification finds its basis in the National Gallery's technical report on the painting, in which it was revealed that the chair-back once looked rather like a row of pipes, such as one finds on an organ.[28] As this interpretation would require the muse to be actually sitting on the organ, it is not attractive, and a classical fluted niche-back is perhaps a more plausible reading of the X-ray evidence.

Like some of the other surviving Muses, Tura's painting was substantially altered not long after it was finished, and has been cut down so that it no longer bears its inscription. The technical examination found that several key aspects, including the ornate throne, the figure's drapes, and details in the landscape, were altered after the painting had lain dormant, half-finished, for months or perhaps years.[29] Whilst the finished painting is agreed to be largely or entirely Tura's, the author of the earlier underdrawing, revealed by X-radiography, is by no means obvious.[30] It seems to me most likely that Tura took up a painting left unfinished at Angelo da Siena's death in 1456.

I hope to demonstrate that the figure in the National Gallery painting is indeed Euterpe, though with no reference to an organ. In the lower right corner of the panel, integrated into the background landscape, is a cave-like grotto in which a blacksmith hammers at his forge (Figure 2.3). This striking feature, not immediately identifiable with any muse, is one of the standard elements of the iconography of *Musica*, the Liberal Art. During the fourteenth and fifteenth centuries, Musica frequently has as her attribute a hammer (or hammers) and an anvil, often operated by a man, a connection still proposed by Cesare Ripa in his *Iconologia* at the end of the sixteenth century.[31] Among several depictions in fifteenth-century Italy, we find two Florentine cassone panels: one by Giovanni

---

[26] Anderson 1991, 176–80; Campbell 1997, 38–40.

[27] Eörsi 1975, 23; Anderson 1991, 179.

[28] Dunkerton, Roy, and Smith 1987, 20.

[29] Dunkerton, Roy, and Smith 1987, 20–30.

[30] Dunkerton, Roy, and Smith 1987, 30–32; X-ray at 10.

[31] Ripa 1976, 366–68. Numerous examples from the fourteenth and fifteenth centuries are listed in Gibbons 1968, 93–94.

Figure 2.3 Angelo da Siena and Cosmé Tura?, *Euterpe?*, detail. © The National Gallery, London.

dal Ponte and dating from ca. 1435, the other by Francesco Pesellino (and workshop) and dating from ca. 1450. Both panels depict the full range of Liberal Arts accompanied by their mortal representatives, including Musica attended by a man hammering on an anvil. Another example is to be found in the left-hand chapel in the Tempio Malatestiano, which is decorated with a complete set of Liberal Arts and Muses in relief (Figure 2.4). (Eörsi has shown that Guarino's instructions to Leonello concerning the depiction of the Muses were followed rather more literally to create the Muses in the Tempio, whose creation is almost exactly contemporaneous with the decoration of Leonello's studiolo.)[32]

[32] Eörsi 1975, 46–48; also King 1988. Interestingly, but misleadingly, the *Tempio*'s Musica is mislabelled "Euterpe" in Anderson 1991 (fig. 82). For a complete and convincing exposition of the identities and layout of the *Tempio* reliefs, with illustrations, see King 1988.

Figure 2.4 Agostino di Duccio, *Music*, 1456, bas-relief, Tempio Malatestiano, Rimini.
© Mary Evans Picture Library.

The reason for the association is easy enough to divine. For the fifteenth century, the blacksmith's resounding hammer functioned paradigmatically as a reference to the invention of music.[33] Beginning with Boethius, the primary authority in musical writing (whose works were owned by Leonello in Latin and French), and supported by Guido of Arezzo, most music theorists of the Middle Ages and the Renaissance found an opportunity to reference, either in passing or in detail, the story of Pythagoras and the blacksmith.[34] It was, for hundreds of years, the standard account of music's origins. In the words of Tinctoris, writing at the court of Naples, in his *Liber de arte contrapuncti* of 1477:

Three of these [concords]...Pythagoras found first of all, because they stand together in proportional ratio. Through a certain divine will, while passing by a mechanic's workshop, he recognized that these three concords were produced by the blows of the hammers. Having examined their weights, he discovered that the diatessaron was produced in a sexquitertia proportion from the hammer weighing twelve pounds as compared to that weighing nine; and, since that hammer of nine pounds compared to that which was six was sexquialtera proportion, it produced the diapente [etc.].[35]

A second, parallel tradition told the same story in a biblical register: in place of Pythagoras, Jubal (identified in Genesis 4:20 as "the father of all who play the harp and flute") makes the discovery, and the blacksmith is Tubal Cain, his

[33] On music's blacksmith-related creation myths in the Middle Ages and Renaissance, see Beichner 1954; McKinnon 1978, esp. 1–18; and Slim 1990 (detailing several visual depictions).

[34] Boethius gives the story in his *De musica* I.10—English trans. Boethius 1989, 18. The 1436 inventory of the Este library records the following: "Libro uno chiamado el scrito de Boetio," and "Libro uno in francexe chiamado Boetio"; they are numbers 154 and 233 in Cappelli's transcription (Cappelli 1889, 22 and 27). A "Boecio in franxexe" was copied for Leonello in 1447 by Biagio Bosoni (Bertoni 1918, 101). For an overview of Boethius's reception among Renaissance music theorists, see Palisca 1990. Guido entitles the last chapter of his *Micrologus* (chapter 20) "How the nature of music was discovered from the sound of hammers"—English trans. Babb 1978, 82–83.

[35] "Quarum tres, hoc est diatessaron, diapente ac diapason, qua ratione proportionali constarent primus omnium Pythagoras invenit. Fabrorum etenim officinam quodam nutu divino praeteriens, malleorum ictibus istas tres concordantias effici cognovit. Hinc pondus eorum examinans, malleo duodecim ponderum existente ad eum qui novem erat relato, diatessaron ex sexquitertia proportione fieri perpendit. Quom malleus iste novem ponderum ad eum quod sex erat relatus fuit proportio sexquialtera diapente reddidit..." Text Tinctoris 1975, 2:14–15; translation Tinctoris 1961, 18. It is important to note that most writers did not use the Pythagorean story to preface a lengthy consideration of Pythagorean cosmic harmony, as one might expect: in

brother.[36] This version is transmitted in full by Johannes Gallicus, a resident of
the court of Mantua from the 1440s and a student of Vittorino da Feltre, in his
pedagogical treatise *De ritu canendi vetustissimo et novo* of ca. 1458–64.[37]

Euterpe is among the most explicitly musical muses, alongside Melpomene
and Terpsichore, and is usually the sister most closely identified with music.
Noting this, Eörsi calls her the "heir of Musica."[38] As Jaynie Anderson has
observed, at the time Leonello planned his studiolo the Muses were a relatively
unusual subject and lacked a clearly defined iconography, unlike the Liberal
Arts.[39] In such circumstances, it would be perfectly natural for a painter to use
the conventions associated with the Liberal Arts to inform his depiction of a
Muse, and in fact it was only later in the Renaissance that a clear and consistent
distinction was made between them.[40] The conflation of the two groups was
present already in antiquity, as in this from Diodorus Siculus, whose *Library
of History* was known in Italy at least from 1406 (and whose discussion of the
Muses is a conceivable source for Guarino's view of Euterpe):

> To each of the Muses men assign her special aptitude for one of the
> branches of the liberal arts, such as poetry, song, pantomimic danc-
> ing, the round dance with music, the study of the stars, and the other
> liberal arts.[41]

Of course, on the basis of the disjunction between Guarino's Melpomene
and the Melpomene described by Ciriaco, we know for certain that a match
between the instruction and the painting is not a necessary precondition of
a correct identification. Nonetheless, a specific justification for including this
attribute of Musica's can be found within Guarino's letter. It lies in the inscription provided for the painting of Euterpe—the only part of the instruction

fact, some (such as Tinctoris—see Tinctoris 1961, 14) specifically distance themselves from such
theories, which they consider out of date, and most others note the subject only in passing.

[36] I quote from the New International Version. On the Jubal story, see Beichner 1954; and
McKinnon 1978, 3–10.

[37] On Gallicus, see Schrade 1953, 317–20; McKinnon 1978, 12–13; Palisca 1990, 259–63.
Slim (1990, 167–68) notes several other authors who transmit the Jubal story in full, including
Johannes's pupil Niccolò Burzio, whose work appeared in print, and Martin Agricola, as well as
several outside the field of music theory.

[38] "l'erede di Musica che trovava posto anche fra le sette Arti Liberali." Eörsi 1975, 38.

[39] Anderson 1991, 165–66.

[40] On the close connection between Muses and Liberal Arts in Late Antiquity and the Middle
Ages, see Ettlinger 1967; on their conflation in the fifteenth century in Federico da Montefeltro's
Gubbio study, see Fabiański 1990, 200–201 and 206–7.

[41] Diodorus Siculus 1935, 4.7.3. On knowledge of Diodorus Siculus in the Renaissance, see,
in brief, Robathan 1932.

that the artists couldn't very well ignore—which reads: "Tibia concentus hac praemonstrante figurat" (This teacher formed the harmony of pipes), reaching beyond the classical view of Euterpe as the muse of lyric poetry to her archaic role as player of the double *aulos*. It is harmony, and Pythagoras's mathematical-mystical theory of harmony in particular, that lies behind the inclusion of music among the Liberal Arts; and it is towards the invention of harmony and its theorization that the blacksmith motif specifically points. By foregrounding Euterpe's role as the originator of harmony, Guarino made her conflation with Musica a logical and obvious strategy.

The blacksmith scene is not the only indication that Tura's muse is Euterpe. The figure courts a certain licentious air, strongly divergent from Guarino's conception. As I have noted, Eörsi identified her as Erato, prompted by the shell-niche and dolphins which seem to reference Venus's marine birth. Rather like Angelo da Siena's *Erato*, her dress has already come undone at the abdomen, and she holds a suggestive branch of ripe cherries. In this respect, Tura's muse is again strongly consonant with a musical identification.

Whilst the idea of a seductive muse is one that Guarino appears to have wished to avoid, some other Renaissance thinkers acknowledged a natural and obvious connection between music and love. In his *Complexus effectuum musices*, written at the court of Naples around 1471, Johannes Tinctoris lists as the seventeenth in his catalog of music's characteristic "effects," "Amorem allicere" (to attract love). As he points out, his assertion enjoys antique support:

> So Ovid advises girls desirous of attracting men's love to learn singing. Indeed, in *Ars amatoria* he says:
>
> > "Song is seductive: girls should learn to sing (her voice,
> >
> > And not her face, has many a girl's procuress been)."
>
> That is why poets record that when Orpheus strummed sweetly on his lyre, many women were fired with love for him.[42]

Tinctoris's taxonomy of musical effect was not a purely intellectual exercise: as Castiglione would later observe, "the words of songs are nearly

---

[42] "Unde Ovidius puellis amorem virorum allicere cupientibus praecipit ut cantare discant. Enimvero in tertio libro *De arte amandi* sic inquit: *Res est blanda canor: discant cantare puellae / (Pro facie multis vox sua lena fuit)*. Hinc est quod cum Orpheus liram dulcissime pulsaret, multas mulieres eius amore incensas a poetis traditum est." Text and translation Cullington 2001, 81 and 64. Further examples of the Renaissance discourse on musical seduction, alongside examples of the moralizing counter-discourse, can be found in the next chapter of this book.

always amorous."[43] Closer in time to our case, the peripatetic musician and
writer Ugolino Pisani, who visited Leonello's court in 1437, complained of
the many musicians he knew "who neither enjoy nor use music for its own
sake, but instead for the pleasures of women or parties to be gotten from
singing, where they go hither and thither every day in order to get into bed."[44]
It is in this connection, of course, that music appears as a tool of seduction
in the Taurus scene in the Salone dei Mesi in Palazzo Schifanoia. The pipe
(*tibia*) with which Guarino wanted Euterpe equipped enjoyed particularly
rich erotic associations (in which capacity it appears in the hands of women
in the Schifanoia scene), as the morphologically suggestive instrument of
the lusty satyrs.

Noting this Muse's erotic charge, Campbell argues that the painting pointedly adopts a somewhat inflammatory position within contemporary debates
surrounding the propriety of poetry—one contrary to the intentions of
Guarino.[45] He argues, justly, that the marine motifs have the effect of bringing the figure into alignment with the identity of the Sirens.[46] The feminine
person and beautiful voice of the Siren conveniently encapsulate a range of
moral concerns over verse: seductive beauty of surface, concealing content
that is at best vacuous, at worst licentious and degrading.[47] The Sirens' position and utility within the tradition *contra* poetry pivots upon their appearance at the beginning of Boethius's *Consolation of Philosophy*. We find a poet,
grief-stricken at his misfortune and abandoned by reason, receiving laments
by dictation from elegiac Muses. Philosophy arrives to save him and dismisses
these "poeticas Musas" (Muses of poetry), labeling them "scenicas meretricu-
las" (theatrical tarts) and "Sirenes."[48] Instead of clothing its subject in the garb

[43] "perché il piú delle volte cantando si dicon parole amorose." Text Castiglione 1947, 158;
translation Castiglione 1967, 121.

[44] "Sicut Rubinetus et multi quos cognosco, qui non utuntur nec delectantur cantu propter
ipsam virtutem sed propter voluptates consequendas ex ipso cantu vel mulierum vel commessa-
tionum, ut faciunt quottidie huc illuc discumbendo." From the marginal annotations in Pisani's
copy of the works of Aristotle; text and translation Perry 1986, 619.

[45] Campbell 1997, 40–51.

[46] Campbell 1997, 39–40. Although the canonical classical authors almost unanimously
render the Siren as half woman half bird, the tradition giving them instead the tail of a fish was
extant in antiquity and was dominant by the late Middle Ages. New philology notwithstanding,
the standard Siren of the Renaissance was associated with fish, not birds, and was more or less
synonymous with "mermaid." See Holford-Strevens 2006, 29–37. Of course, the dolphin is not,
strictly speaking, a fish, but it was considered as such in the period in question.

[47] The universal applicability of these moral paranoias, and their inevitable association with
the female body, is discussed in Lichtenstein 1987.

[48] Boethius 1973, 1.26–41. This section of Boethius's text and its Renaissance reception are
discussed in detail in Panizza 1990. Boethius's patchy popularity among humanists of the fourteenth and fifteenth centuries is outlined in Grafton 1981, 410–11.

of philosophical and useful respectability, a siren-muse seems to clarify the painting's statement in favor of poetry's degenerate potential.

If the Sirens could be invoked to condemn poetry, they might be employed even more obviously and successfully against music.[49] A convenient example may be drawn from Petrarch's *De remediis utriusque fortunae*, completed in 1366 and widely circulated throughout the fifteenth century.[50] In the course of dialogue 23, "De cantu et dulcedine a musica" (On the sweetness of music), the Sirens are marshaled as evidence of music's ability to deceive:

> JOY: I am charmed by songs and sounds.
> REASON: Also wild animals and birds are tricked by song.... The Sirens, too, are believed to deceive by song.... there is nothing more suited for deceit than the voice.[51]

Both the muse's seductive appearance generally and its Siren-like qualities specifically, therefore, lend further support to its identification as Euterpe, the musical muse.

In fact, the Sirens' associations were not uniformly negative. From a classical author close to Guarino's heart, the Sirens received a rationalization designed precisely to counter the musical problem put forward by Petrarch. In Cicero's *De finibus bonorum et malorum* we read that:

> Apparently it was not the sweetness of their voices or the novelty and diversity of their songs, but their professions of knowledge that used to attract the passing voyagers; it was the passion for learning that kept men rooted to the Sirens' rocky shores.[52]

This argument, in fact, serves to bring the Sirens into precise alignment with the humanist's initial, pedagogic, interpretation of the Muses. Whilst the

---

[49] A wealth of examples (though, I think, not the one I am about to use) can be found in Austern and Naroditskaya 2006.

[50] Conrad Rawski (1967, 13) describes the *De Remediis* as "one of the basic books of the early Renaissance." The complete Latin text (not to speak of compilations and translations) survives in well over a hundred manuscript copies, and about thirty printed editions (the first of 1474). On the transmission and reception of the *De Remediis*, see Rawski 1967, 8, 13–15, and n13 and n88, with the further references given there.

[51] "Gaudium: Cantibus sonisque permulceor. / Ratio: Et fere cantu falluntur et volucres illud mirabilius...Ad hec sirenes cantu fallere creditum....et ad summam nihil ad fallendum voce aptius." Text and translation Rawski 1971, 306 and 308–9. It is worth noting that, writing in a different mode, Petrarch was able to use the Sirens to a different (though equally seductive) end: in canzone 167 Laura is "questa sola fra noi del ciel sirena" (this Siren of heaven who alone is amongst us). For a wide-ranging exploration of the problem of the Siren for music-making women in the early modern period, see Calogero 2006.

[52] Cicero 1931, 5.18. This view evidently proceeds from an unusually literal reading of Homer.

painting diverges significantly from Guarino's instructions, as one might expect from a prince such as Leonello the points of divergence are far from philologically indefensible.

A second rationalization may be even more directly pertinent to Tura's figure, drawing the Muses and Sirens into musical alignment. The system of celestial harmony, derived ultimately from the mathematical theory of harmony symbolized by the blacksmith, was usually demonstrated by assigning to each planet a Muse or a musical interval; but according to a Platonic view it was attributable instead to the Sirens. Giorgio Anselmi revived this alternative perspective for the fifteenth century in his *De musica*:

> it is not a single mode that all the heavens sing, with the blessed spirits who inhabit them, but, diverse as they are, one which is as varied as it is harmonious.... These spirits preside according to their ranks, and the whole force of harmony flows forth from them, owing to their correspondence with the spheres.
>
> These are in truth the spirits which Socrates in the *Republic* of Plato called Sirens, each sitting, as he said, upon one ring. "Siren" in fact means a singing god, but he actually meant to signify spirits, as ceaseless in their song as the spheres are in their motion. Our theologians more correctly call these spirits angels.[53]

Anselmi, a citizen of Parma (at times within Este territory) of good family, who studied in Pavia and worked in Ferrara, was not a professional musician.[54] His treatise, composed in 1434, is written accessibly in dialogic form.[55] We know for certain that music treatises circulated at Leonello's court: archival records show that during the 1430s Leonello himself had a singing tutor

---

[53] "Non est autem unus modus idem, quem celi omnes felicesque hi spiritus [qui] in his insident decantant; sed pro illorum diversitate tam diversus quam consonus. Supersedent autem spiritus hi secundum suos ordines, et per eorum ad spheras congruentiam, quatenus omnis harmonie vis redundet. Sunt vero spiritus quos Socrates in Republica Platonis Syrenas nominavit, cum singulas orbibus singulis insidere dixit. Interpretatur vero Syren deus canons per pius incessantes a cantu spiritus, sicut spheras a motu significari voluit. Nostri vero theologi melius spiritus hos angelos appelant." Text Handschin 1948, 131; translation Godwin 1993, 149–50. On the Platonic Sirens, see Holford-Strevens 2006, 22–23; and Calogero 2006, 140–46. Campbell mentions the involvement of Sirens in the harmony of the spheres very briefly (1997, 39), but does not offer a fifteenth-century reference, much less locate the idea in Ferrarese territory.

[54] On Anselmi's life, see Handschin 1948, 124; Anselmi 1961, 7–19; Palisca 1985, 8. Anselmi practiced in Ferrara, and later in Modena, as a doctor of some renown. Massera (Anselmi 1961, 14) hypothesizes that he was invited to Ferrara in 1420 by Niccolò III himself, who later conferred upon him honorary citizenship.

[55] Palisca (1985, 8) suggests that the *De musica* was a university textbook, and that Anselmi taught in the faculty of arts and medicine at the university of Parma.

("regole de canto") copied for his use.[56] As a local authority, it is quite possible that Anselmi's work was known at court, and his Platonic source (*Republic* 10.617 B 4–7) would certainly have been familiar.

The dolphins, alongside their role in associating Tura's muse with the Sirens, offer a final clue pointing to a musical interpretation of the painting. In order to substantiate his assertion that "wild animals and birds are tricked by song," Petrarch, in continuation of the passage quoted above, reports that:

> even the fish are touched by the sweetness of music. You know the story of Arion and the dolphins...after such great danger the harper was first brought to shore unharmed, sitting on the back of the swimming fish.[57]

The story of Arion and the dolphins was well known in the Renaissance, and Arion's name found a regular place in the lists of ancient "inventors" of music given conventionally in the introductions to Renaissance music treatises. His feat is told in full in Ovid's *Fasti* (II.79–128), a work found in the 1436 inventory of the Este library and familiar throughout the Renaissance.[58]

In sum, the symbolic vocabulary of Tura's painting prompts the identification of the figure as a very musical Euterpe, despite the absence of the musical instruments Guarino assigned her. She is given as an attribute the scene of a blacksmith at the forge referring to the discovery of harmony, borrowed from Musica. She is given a seductive appearance, in accordance with a conventional view identifying music as a tool of seduction, which could unexpectedly (via Cicero) be brought into alignment with Guarino's view of Euterpe as a teacher. Her erotic charge suggests an association with the Sirens, whose role was primarily musical, and who were brought into musical association with the Muses by a music-theorist sometimes resident in Ferrara via the Pythagorean science of harmony. Even the jewel-encrusted dolphins adorning her throne constitute a reference to a well-known myth about the invention and power of music. The musical connection in general is most appropriate to the muse Euterpe.[59] Further, the several references to harmony, and specifically to Pythagoras's discovery of the mathematics of harmony, are exactly aligned with the inscription

[56] Lockwood 1976b, Document 2.

[57] "musica quoque dulcedine pisces tangi. Nota tibi Arionis ac delphinis est fabella...Astipulantur imagines enec illic ubi e tanto periculo incolumnis primum appulsus est natantis piscis tergo insidens fidicen." Text and translation Rawski 1971, 306 and 308–9.

[58] See number 187 in Cappelli's transcription of the inventory (Cappelli 1889, 24).

[59] The only other plausible identification, in light of the musical elements, would be Melpomene, but to argue in favor of Melpomene would involve suggesting that Ciriaco, who saw a quite different painting in situ that he thought represented Melpomene, got his facts wrong.

suppliedbyGuarinotoaccompanyandexplicateapaintingofEuterpe.The more seductive elements, however, point to the influence of a prominent aspect of Leonello's own musico-poetic vision, to which I will now turn.

Eros as Ovidian Muse

Guarino came up with a rather unusual idea for the depiction of the chief of the muses, Calliope, in Leonello's studiolo:

> Calliope, the seeker out of learning and guardian of the art of poetry, also provides a voice for the other arts; let her carry a laurel crown and have three faces composed together, since she has set forth the nature of men, heroes and gods.[60]

Evidently the humanist was no painter: "three faces composed together" is not an obvious visual strategy, particularly at almost life-size. Nonetheless, his assertion that Calliope offers a "voice" is interesting, and full of musical possibilities. The idea derives from the etymology of Calliope's name, correctly identified by Diodorus Siculus as composed of "kale" (beautiful) and "ops" (voice).[61]

The "voice" supplied by Calliope is further explored in the inscription provided by Guarino for the painting, which reads "Materiam vati et vocem concedo sonantem" (I grant to poets their raw material and resounding voice).[62] The terms in which this motto configures Calliope and her relationship with poets are striking and revealing. In particular, Guarino's choice of the word "vates" to connote "poet" is loaded. The earliest word for poet, tied explicitly to the poet's supposed mystic or prophetic role, *vates* fell out of use in Hellenistic times to be revived by Virgil and his Augustan successors.[63] Leonardo Bruni explains it thus in his letter on the study of literature of ca. 1424, in the course of advocating the wisdom of the ancient poets and conferring upon Virgil the term's honor:

> The wisest of the ancients tell us that the divine mind dwells in the poets, and that they are called *vates* because they speak not so much

---

[60] "Calliope doctrinarum indagatrix et poeticae antistes vocemque reliquis praebens artibus coronam ferat lauream, tribus compacta vultibus, cum hominum, semideorum ac deorum naturam edisserat." Text and translation Baxandall 1965, 202 and 187.

[61] Diodorus Siculus 1935, 4.7.4.

[62] Text and translation Campbell 1997, 38.

[63] The basic reference on this subject is Newman 1967. See also Pasco-Pranger 2000, with intervening bibliography.

of their own accord as through a divine inspiration, in a kind of higher mental state.[64]

The Augustan poets used the word and its associations as one among a range of loaded and obvious references to Archaic poetry (Homer and Hesiod), designed to serve as the markers of a newly virtuous and "useful" Latin poetics—embodied in Virgil's *Aeneid* and *Georgics*, for example, and Ovid's *Fasti*.[65] Guarino appears to have had something almost identical in mind, and no doubt he was aware that in invoking Archaic poetics he was also recalling the Augustan invocation.

As some familiarity with ancient poetics would lead one to suspect, "vates" is a word not devoid of musical connotations. In offering a catalog of music's extraordinary effects, a standard feature of the Renaissance music treatise, Ramis is able to adduce biblical evidence that music facilitates vatic theophany: "when Eliseus, disciple of the great Elias, the founder of the Carmelites, wished to prophesy, he summoned a musician to play."[66] Approaching through the classical tradition one might easily arrive at the same conclusion. Appeals to vatic status went hand-in-hand with the conceit of framing poetry as song among the purposeful archaisms of the Augustans, and, as they so frequently make clear, the prototypical prophet-poets—Apollo, Orpheus, Musaeus— expressed themselves in song. These, and the "divine" effects of their song, constituted the genealogy of musical invention cited so frequently by fifteenth-century music theorists.

The *Calliope* from Leonello's studiolo apparently does not survive—and even if it did, there is little reason to suppose that it would have followed Guarino's instructions. Nonetheless, it has long been recognized that the humanist's conception is preserved in a strange three-faced head on the reverse of a portrait medal made for Leonello by Pisanello (Figure 2.5).[67] As the precedent set by the paintings for the studiolo might lead us to expect, the

---

[64] "Nempe mentem divinam inesse poetis sapientissimi veterum tradidere vatesque inde nuncuparunt, quod non tam ex se quam concitatione quadam animi afflatuque divino loquerentur." Text and translation Kallendorf 2002, 114–15.

[65] According to Guarino's son Battista, his successor at the University of Ferrara, Guarino's program for the teaching of Greek relied precisely on a detailed realization of the archaising relationship between Virgil and Homer/Hesiod—see Kallendorf 2002, 282–83. The subject is therefore one with which Leonello would also, very likely, have been closely acquainted.

[66] Ramis 1993, 43.

[67] See Lippincott 1990, 67–68. Previously it had been argued that the image stood for Prudence—see the bibliography cited in Lippincott 1990, n75. For a helpful introduction to the subject of the Renaissance medal, see Scher 2000.

Figure 2.5 Pisanello, portrait medal of Leonello d'Este, ca. 1441–43, Münzkabinett, Staatliche Museen zu Berlin. Photograph by Lutz-Jürgen Lübke.

program has undergone substantive alteration: the head is not that of a female Muse, but that of a male child—a Cupid or Eros.

Together, this strange hybrid and the erotic *Euterpe* suggest that Leonello may have entertained a personal conception of the muses that combined their features with those of Eros. This hypothesis is apparently confirmed by a second medal by Pisanello, made in 1444 to commemorate the marchese's second marriage (to Maria of Aragon), which also serves to reveal the character of his Erotic muse as musical. On the reverse of the medal we find Eros holding a

Figure 2.6 Pisanello, portrait medal of Leonello d'Este, 1444, Victoria and Albert Museum, London. © Victoria and Albert Museum, London.

scroll bearing musical notation; immediately to the left a lion (leone, Leonello) peers closely at the music, his mouth open—evidently he is singing (Figure 2.6).[68] There can be little doubt that Eros is here literally fulfilling the function of a poetic muse: the ensemble recalls several ancient configurations of

---

[68] On this medal see Mottola-Molfino and Natali 1991, 2:33, with further bibliography; and Waddington 2000, 27–29.

the mechanism of divine inspiration. Propertius, for instance, places his muse squarely in the role of music pedagogue: "now my Muse teaches me a different harp";[69] Pindar similarly claims that "the Muse stood by me as I found a newly shining way to join to Dorian measure a voice of splendid celebration";[70] and at the very origins of written poetry we hear that the Muses "taught Hesiod fine singing."[71] These examples call to mind the fact that Guarino characterized Euterpe as a music-teacher. The medal serves to illustrate the mechanism by which Calliope's "voice" was supplied to her vatic supplicants.

Leonello was himself a poet. Presumably, therefore, Eros appears in the 1444 medal in the guise of his personal muse (or rather his muse appears in the guise of Eros), in an arrangement that identifies the mechanism of the marchese's inspiration, and of his poetic performance, as musical. This combination of factors suggests that the choice of the Muses as the subject for his studiolo decoration was one with a personal significance, perhaps explaining the divergences from Guarino's instructions. The studiolo Muses were intended to function literally in facilitating his poetic efforts—a visual counterpart to the hymn or prayer invoking divine aid (most often that of the Muses) that prefaced classical poems in the archaic and Augustan traditions.[72]

Leonello's vatic Eros certainly took his muse in a different direction to that envisaged by Guarino, but strictly speaking it was not a departure from the Augustan vision. Ovid was an ambiguous figure for Guarino: according to his son Battista, whose treatise on education is taken largely to preserve Guarino's approach, only the *Fasti* was admitted to his classroom; the student "will take pleasure in Ovid's other works when they shall read them on their own."[73] Guarino's Virgilian "vates" signaled austerity and severity of purpose. In the *Fasti*, a similar poetics prevails; however, elsewhere Ovid uses the word playfully. In a pointedly self-contradictory moment of satire, Ovid claims for himself the title "vates" in the proem to his *Ars Amatoria* (Art of Love), whilst at one and the same time relinquishing the validation of the elevated subject and citing his experience as the source of his inspiration.[74] Experience in love is configured as a form of divine communication. It seems that Ovid's less serious vatic poetics enjoyed considerable popularity at the Este court: Leonello's

[69] Propertius 1990, 2.10.10.

[70] Pindar 1997, Olympian Ode 3.3–6.

[71] Hesiod 1988, line 22.

[72] Something similar is noted in Cieri Via 1988, XVIII.

[73] "Reliquis eius operibus cum per se ipsos legent indulgebunt." Text and translation Kallendorf 2002, 288–89.

[74] On vatic poetics in Ovid, see Ahern 1990 and Pasco-Pranger 2000. The contradiction lies in claiming the title "vates," which specifically involves divine inspiration, whilst admitting to being inspired by experience.

library boasted not one, but several copies of the *Ars amatoria* and its counterpart, the *Remedio amoris*.[75]

Ovid's erotic *vates* finds particularly suggestive, and musical, expression
in the poems that open each book of the *Amores*, a collection in which the
poet is constantly poking fun at Virgil's epic and its Homeric models. In I.i,
in response to Eros's intrusion into his poetic world, Ovid makes a pretense of
putting up a fight to preserve his austere heroic credentials, only to be hope-
lessly enslaved by a shot from Eros's deadly bow (I.i.21–25):

> I had uttered this complaint, when forthwith he opened his quiver and
> selected arrows which had been made for my destruction. He strongly
> bent his curving bow on his knee and said "Take this, bard [*vates*], as a
> subject for your poems." Alas! that boy had unerring arrows…[76]

It immediately becomes clear (as Eros himself indicates by calling his poet
"vates") that the arrow has become the means of transmission, and the sign, of
a new kind of divine inspiration: Eros takes on the role of muse, as he does on
Leonello's medal. Eros's triumph at once brings about a Venusian transformation
of the more conventional manifestation of Ovid's muse (I.i.26–30), analogous to
that visited by Leonello upon Guarino's original versions of Euterpe and Erato:

> I am on fire, and Love reigns in my once empty heart.
>   Let my work rise in six feet and fall again in five. Iron wars with your
> metre, farewell. Garland your golden brow, my Muse, with myrtle from
> the sea-shore, for you are to be measured off in eleven foot lengths.

Amores II.i is similar, and again close to our case. Here, poets of the heroic
mode are ridiculed, for their reward is tragedy, whereas the poet of love is
rewarded by a beautiful girl. Once again, Ovid is *vates*, and now he acknowledges openly that his songs are given him by Eros himself (II.i.37–38):

> And fair ones, turn hither your beauteous faces as I sing the songs
> which rosy Love dictates to me!

In the medal, Leonello's muse has undergone an identical metamorphosis, so
that the marchese sings from Eros's songbook.

---

[75] See numbers 28, 72, 122, and 126 of the 1436 inventory as transcribed by Cappelli (Cappelli
1889, 14, 17, and 20).

[76] Throughout this section I have used Ovid 1973 for Bk. I of the *Amores*, and Ovid 1914 for
Bk. II.

The similarities between Ovid's poetics and Leonello's are profound, and it is difficult to imagine that the student of Guarino did not intend them. Few more philologically astute (or, at the same time, more obvious) subversions of the humanist's original scheme can be possible. Through this comparison, the approach to the Muses suggested by the evidence from the studiolo, and confirmed by the medals, is brought vividly to life as a central aspect of the personal aesthetic of an active and sophisticated poet. Leonello's muse was Eros, and the poetry Eros gave him came with a tune.

Leonello's Musical Poetics

Leonello's two surviving sonnets do much to enhance our picture of Leonello the poet, and draw us even further into the world of his Erotic muse. In one, the marchese envisages an encounter with Eros in the sanctuary of the Muses. Its characters and themes are by now familiar and expected:[77]

Batte il Cavallo su la balza alpina,	The Horse strikes the mountain rock,
E scaturir fa d'Helicona fonte,	And makes the fountain spring from Helicon,
Dove chi le man bagna, e chi la fronte,	Where one bathes his hands, and another his brow
Secondo che più honore o Amor lo inchina.	According as honor or Love inclines him more.
Anch'io m'accosto spesso alla divina	I, too, often approach the divine
Acqua prodigiosa de quel monte:	And wondrous water of that mountain;
Amor ne ride, che'l sta lì con pronte	Thereat laughs Love, who lurks there with, ready,
Le sue sagitte in forma pellegrina;	His darts, disguised as a pilgrim;
E mentre il labbro a ber se avanza e stende;	And whilst my lips to drink I advance and extend;
Ello con il venen della puntura	He with the venom of the dart
Macola l'onda e venenosa rende;	Marks the stream and renders it venomous;
Sì che quell'acqua, che de sua natura	So that that water, which by its nature
Renfrescar me dovrebbe, più 'maccende,	Should refresh me, the more inflames me,
E più che bagno, più cresce l'arsura.	And the more I bathe, the more the burning grows.

---

[77] This sonnet is published in Gardner 1904, 53, in transcription and translation. I have used his translation, somewhat altered. Gardner transcribed the poem from Baruffaldi 1713, 21. Note

This sonnet reads like a Petrarchan rewriting of *Amores* I.i. The poet, inno-
cent and unsuspecting, seeks inspiration in the haunt of the Muses; but Eros,
sneering and unstoppable, unexpectedly diverts him from his higher purpose
to erotic "burning."

Leonello's other surviving verse recounts a second dispute with Eros, this
time involving a conversation. In a reversal of a standard poetic trope, Amor
has made Leonello blind, and mocks him as he attempts to find his way by
hearing and touch alone:[78]

Lo Amor me ha facto cieco, e non ha tanto	Amor has made me blind, and does not have
De charità, che me conduca en via,	Enough charity, to lead me on the road,
Me lassa per despecto en mea balia,	But leaves me in contempt and at his mercy,
E dice: hor va tu, che presciumi tanto.	And says: now go you, that presume so much.
Et eo perche me scento en forze alquanto,	And I, because I hear more acutely,
E stimo de truovar che man me dia,	And think to find what hands give me,
Vado, ma puoi non sciò dovo me sia,	Go, but cannot know where I am,
Tal che me fermo dricto in su d'un canto.	Such that I stop directly in a corner.
Allora Amore, che me sta quatando,	Then Love, who assails me,
Me mostra per desprezzo, et me obstenta,	Shows me scorn, and hinders me,
Et me va canzonando en altro metro.	And sings rudely of me in a different meter.
Ne'l dice tanto pian, ch'eo non lo senta:	He spoke so softly, that I didn't hear:
Et eo respondo così borbottando:	And I respond similarly muttering:
Mostrame almen la via, che torna endietro.	At least show me the road home.

The reference to the "meter" of Eros's scorn signals a continuing and
self-conscious link between love's torment and the act of writing (or delivering)
verse. Further, Eros's "different meter" should probably be read as another reference to the beginning of the *Amores*, where Ovid bids farewell to the "meter"
appropriate to "iron wars," abandoning himself to the new meter dictated by
Eros: "Let my work rise in six feet and fall again in five," rendering tangible the
connection already implicit between Leonello's verse and his images. Eros,

that these surviving poems are in the vernacular, despite the fact that Decembrio, in his *De politia litteraria*, has Leonello scorn the vernacular in favor of Latin (on which see Gravelle 1988,
372–75).

[78] Text Baruffaldi 1713, 21. This sonnet was not published by Gardner.

and his Ovidian poetics, was evidently a primary aspect of Leonello's personal aesthetic.

Noting that Leonello was himself a poet, Lewis Lockwood points out that at his court music functioned, among other things, as a style of poetic delivery.[79] The implication, to be developed here at more length, is that at least some of Leonello's poetry was performed as song, and was probably designed as such. The aspects of Leonello's poetic self-imaging discussed thus far appear strongly to confirm this view, and even to propose the Belfiore studiolo as the natural venue for such performances. His muse, who in the medal we find literally dictating songs to the poet-Prince, relied at least on an archaizing conceit configuring poetry as song, and there are almost overwhelming reasons to suppose that at Leonello's court that conceit was in fact a reality.

The performing practice Lockwood has in mind is one in which secular verse is sung or declaimed to the accompaniment of a stringed instrument(s), usually *lira da braccio* or lute. Singer and accompanist were often one and the same person, and the music they used was semi-improvised, based on melodic and rhythmic formulae (or formulaic melodies) linked to the metrical and rhyming structures of the verse. The practice is extremely difficult to document musically, for the obvious reason that it was very rarely notated; nonetheless, collateral evidence suggests that throughout the fifteenth century it was a favored musical style in Italy among those of a classicizing bent. Nino Pirrotta, for instance, repeatedly pointed out that some humanist writers appear to accord it higher status than the notated polyphonic music of the period.[80]

Lockwood's account of Leonello's documented musical interests offers much to support his assessment, and equally to further my own argument.[81] Archival records reveal that during the 1430s Leonello had both a songbook ("libro de canto") and (as I have mentioned) a singing tutor copied for his use, and that at least by 1437 he was a competent lutenist.[82] In that year is recorded the copying of a collection of Leonello's "cantione et soneti" (songs and sonnets)—undoubtedly "cantione" is not meant to refer to musical compositions,

---

[79] Lockwood 1984, 64–65. For example, musical settings of two stanzas from a poem written at Leonello's court survive in a manuscript probably made at court shortly after Leonello's death—see Fallows 1977 and Lockwood 1984, 109–18.

[80] On this style of musico-poetic performance, see Bertoni 1929; Rubsamen 1943; Kristeller 1947; Haraszti 1955; Rubsamen 1957; Pirrotta 1972; Pirrotta 1972a; Lockwood 1975; Pirrotta and Povoledo 1982; Pirrotta 1970; Prizer 1986; Pirrotta 1994; Gallo 1995, 69–112; Fallows 1995, esp. 254–55; Haar 1999; Abramov-van Rijk 2009.

[81] See Lockwood 1984, 46–47 and 64–73. Lockwood's account of music at Leonello's court should be supplemented by the brief comments in Gallo 1995, 72–74.

[82] The entries are published as Documents 1 and 2 in Lockwood 1976a. See also Lockwood 1984, 46.

but to poetry written to be sung.[83] The marchese explained his interest in a letter to Guarino, probably dating from his student years: "occasionally as I turn away from books, I then give myself over to singing and lute-playing for the relaxation of the spirit and as a pastime."[84]

The exact role and status of music in Leonello's education and in the humanist cultural mood of his court is difficult to establish with absolute clarity. Guarino has little directly to say on the subject; and though Vittorino da Feltre gave music a place in his curriculum, he admitted it on the one hand as a mathematical and astronomical subject, and on the other as part of a philosophy of education that was somewhat broader than Guarino's.[85] However, the practices and attitudes of Guarino's contemporaries, as well as those espoused by his antique models, suggest that the omission is one of record rather than one of practice.

Guarino's sometime teacher in Padua, Pier Paolo Vergerio, included several comments on music in his *De ingenuis moribus et liberalibus adulescentiae studiis liber* (The Character and Studies Befitting a Free-Born Youth) of 1404, the most widely distributed treatise on education of the fifteenth century.[86] Having established early on that "among the Greeks, [no one]...was...considered liberally educated unless he knew how to sing and play the lyre,"[87] he later locates music in more detail within his system. Under the heading "De otio et vacatione" (On Leisure and Relaxation) he declares that, "Nor will it be unseemly to relax the mind with singing and playing the lute, as we mentioned above."[88] By way of authority, he adduces the fact that "This was the custom of the Pythagoreans," but he places more weight on a Homeric precedent: "and it was once a celebrated fact among the archaic heroes that Homer depicted Achilles withdrawing from battle and resting this way."[89] Meanwhile, Quintilian's *Institutio oratoria*, an account of Roman education that enjoyed great influence over the practice of the humanist educators, gives the subject of music even greater prominence.

---

[83] Lockwood 1984, 46–47.

[84] "interdum me ad lirbos revoco, porro cantui et fidibus laxandi animi gratia temporis quicquam concedo." Text and translation Lockwood 1984, 46 and n3.

[85] On music in Vittorino's curriculum, see Woodward 1906, 19–20; and Gallico 1981. For a comprehensive and illuminating attempt to get at Guarino's views on music, see Gallo 1995, 69–74: his findings throw considerable weight behind the readings put forward here. Also of considerable value, and drawing many of the same conclusions, is MacCarthy 2010, 25–58.

[86] Published in transcription and translation in Kallendorf 2002. The sections here quoted are at 52–53 and 84–85. On Guarino and Vergerio, see Woodward 1906, 26–36; and Gallo 1995, 72–73, who reports that Leonello gave Guarino a copy of the treatise.

[87] "Ars vero musicae...magno quondam apud Graecos honore habebatur, nec putabatur quisquam liberaliter eruditus nisi cantu et fidibus sciret."

[88] "Sed nec erit quidem cantu fidibusque laxare animum; qua de re superius est habita nobis mentio."

[89] "Nam et Pythagoreorum mos hic erat et fuit quondam priscis heroibus celebre, ut Achillem Homerus inducit a pugna redeuntem in hac re solitum acquiescere."

Although he concedes that it is not central to the orator's art, Quintilian argues strongly and at length that it is necessary and important.[90]

The kind and conception of music to which Quintilian, and his fifteenth-century imitators, mean to refer is frequently clarified: its validity derives from its association with poetry and poetics. Quintilian, courting the vatic implications of the combination, notes that "Orpheus and Linus, to mention no others, were regarded as uniting the roles of musician, poet and philosopher."[91] Shortly after, he embarks upon a lengthy proof of the assertion that "the art of letters and that of music were once united." His view is reprised in particularly explicit terms during Leonello's reign in an oration delivered by Gregorio da Città di Castello in Naples, probably on the occasion of the reopening of the University by Alfonso of Aragon (to whose court Leonello's brothers Ercole and Sigismondo were attached):

> poetry is called music, and is consecrated to the Muses.... the poet should not only have a command of the theory of music but should also be skilled in practice, for how else will he exercise many of the skills that pertain to poetry?[92]

It is no doubt with precisely such a "literary" music, and with such humanist and antique justifications in mind, that Decembrio saw fit to allow a lute into his, and by implication Leonello's, ideal library.

In light of such evidence and such modes of thought, it seems very likely that a lute (or a lira da braccio) was likewise to be found in the Belfiore studiolo, and that improvised musical performance was integral to Leonello's very conception of his poetry. The images with which his studiolo is associated responded to and bolstered, indeed are utterly integrated with, the musical poetics of his leisured identity. His hybrid muse brought him song both in conceit and in practice.

Pietrobono, Companion of Princes

Already by the time he became Marchese, Leonello had in his employ a well-favored young Ferrarese musician named Pietrobono, who was to become

---

[90] On the influence of Quintilian on the early humanist educators, see Woodward 1906, 8–10, and many further comments dotted through his first two chapters; also Grafton and Jardine 1982.

[91] Quintilian 1920, 1.10.9. Quintilian considers music at 1.10.2–33.

[92] "poetica musica dicitur et Musis est consacrata: ...poetam non solum musicae rationem, sed etiam usum habere oportet; quo modo enim tam multa exercebit, quae pertinent ad poetam?" Text and translation Gallo 1995, 102–3.

fifteenth-century Italy's most famous exponent of the improvisatory perform-ing style.[93] This Pietrobono, who appears to have had exceptional facility on both lute and lira da braccio, seems more than any other musician of the century to have embodied the humanist musical vision. Consequently, his talents were widely praised in writing and oration, often in very striking terms.[94] Although most of the lauds date from after Leonello's death, it was under Leonello that the characteristic shape of Pietrobono's career and accomplishments was estab-lished, together with his reputation, and the humanist praise must therefore exist in a close relationship with Pietrobono's role as defined at Leonello's court.

A pamphlet by Aurelio Brandolini, which probably began life as an oration delivered in Naples in 1473, is devoted in its entirety to Pietrobono's qualities. Following his praise of the lutenist, whom the court of Naples made several attempts to poach, Brandolini addresses King Ferdinand of Aragon thus:

> It would hardly have been worthy of you, O greatest king, to have any other Muse:
>
> this one was worthy of no one other than you.[95]

Brandolini's formulation strongly recalls Hesiod's claim that Calliope "attends august kings," which is followed, in the *Theogony*, by a list of the benefits a king might expect from the relationship. It configures Pietrobono as himself a Muse fit for kings, taking over Calliope's role. This view of the lutenist points to the possibility that he had already played an analogous role in Ferrara for Leonello. Perhaps the marchese's conception of his Muse developed in cor-respondence with the man who was in reality his principal secular musician.

---

[93] On Pietrobono under Leonello, see Haraszti 1949; Pirrotta 1966; Lockwood 1975; Lockwood 1984, 46 and 69–70; Prizer 1986; and Gallo 1995, 86–97. A second musician of standing in Leonello's retinue, named Niccolò Tedesco, appears to have had similar skills—see Lockwood 1984, 47.

[94] On the humanist praise of Pietrobono see, most importantly, Haraszti 1949; Pirrotta 1966, 139–61; and Gallo 1995, 86–97. The list of lauds includes Antonio Cornazano's vernacu-lar "Laudes Petri Boni Cythaiste" from his *Sforziade*, describing a banquet held in Cremona in 1441 (Pirrotta); Paolo Cortese in the course of his *De cardinalatu libri tres* of 1510 (Pirrotta); Lodovico Carbone's doctoral oration, delivered in Ferrara in 1456 (Gallo); Aurelio Brandolini's multi-part "Musica Lippi," which probably began life as an oration delivered in Naples in 1473, when Pietrobono visited as part of a Ferrarese delegation (Gallo); Filippo Beroaldo's eulogy "ad Petrum Bonum Citharedum," probably written in 1473 when the delegation passed through Bologna (Haraszti and Gallo); verses by Paolo Emilio Boccabella, perhaps written in Bologna in or slightly after 1474 (Gallo); a eulogy written by Battista Guarino, perhaps near the beginning of Borso's reign (Gallo); and Johannes Tinctoris's brief mention in his *De inventione et usu musicae*, written in Naples in the 1480s (Gallo).

[95] "Haud alia tu dignus eras, rex maxime, musa: / hic quo non alio te nisi dignus erat." Text and translation Gallo 1995, 132–33.

In the only laud dating from within Leonello's reign, Pietrobono is described
in terms that promote, if not directly confirm, this suggestion. Describing a
(possibly fictional) performance at a banquet in Cremona in 1441, Antonio
Cornazano frames the lutenist in "high triumph" (alto triumpho), as one
"endowed with music by the heavens" (che in musica le stelle havean dot-
ato), even calling him a "god." Recalling Tura's Euterpe and her blacksmith,
he asserts that the harmonies of the heavens are subject to his understanding ("soa comparation nullo reservo, e l'armonie che i ciel fano suspendo").
Looking forward to the treatment of Eros's muse-like inspiration in Leonello's
sonnets, he describes the effect of Pietrobono's performance as a burning in
the heart ("ni accender fiama in cor, ch'el la non sia"). He concludes his opening praise by ascribing to Pietrobono the feats of the mythical musicians, com-
paring him to Apollo, Orpheus, Amphion, and others.

Not unexpectedly, Cornazano is joined in this comparison by almost every
other writer on Pietrobono. The practice of equipping visual representations of
such ancient musicians with the modern tools of Pietrobono's trade (lute, lira)
made it possible to envisage a literal continuum between Pietrobono's performance and antique poet-musicianship.[96] Brandolini even argues that the name
Pietro was a corruption of "Pheobus."[97] All are quite comfortable with the
implication that Pietrobono was therefore a poet, rather than simply a musician: in fact, the word chosen by Brandolini and Filippo Beroaldo to convey
this compliment is precisely "vates," bringing to mind Guarino's inscription
for Calliope. Ludovico Carbone, in his doctoral oration delivered in Ferrara in
1456, fleshes out the vatic theology, explaining that Pietrobono is "inflammari
quasi divino numine afflatum" (afire like one inspired by a divine power).[98]
Cornazano's various references to the heavens carry an identical implication.

As these vatic lauds might lead one to expect, humanist commentators
found in Pietrobono an embodiment of the integration of music and poetry
advocated within classical poetics. Cornazano's account of his performance
in 1441 is full of the suggestion that the narrative of Pietrobono's songs is conveyed not only through words, but through his playing on the *cetra* (probably
meaning lute or *chitarino*). Most explicitly, he describes him "giving with sound
most vivid words" (dando col suon vivissime parole). Beroaldo similarly claims
that "From the singing strings he produces resounding words" (Exprimit hic

[96] There are many examples in a variety of media, but Laurence Witten has described and published a convenient corpus of woodcuts dating from the fifteenth and sixteenth centuries showing Apollo or Orpheus playing the lira or viola da braccio (Witten 1975).

[97] Brandolini's complete pamphlet in praise of Pietrobono is given in transcription and translation in Gallo 1995, Appendix (114–35); it is discussed at 90–97. I have followed the text and
translation given there.

[98] Gallo 1995, 89.

Figure 2.7 Giovanni Boldù, portrait medal of Pietrobono, 1457, Ashmolean Museum, Oxford. © Ashmolean Museum, University of Oxford.

fidibus resonantia verba canoris). In the extraordinary skill of Pietrobono's playing, the ideal of the complete unification of poetry and music, which lies behind Leonello's musical muse, is achieved.

A medal made by Giovanni Boldù in 1457 (Figure 2.7) supplies an imagining of Pietrobono that is extremely suggestive in this light. The obverse carries a portrait of the musician, together with the motto "ORPHEUM SUPERANS" (surpassing Orpheus). On the reverse, Pietrobono is subjected to a kind of mythological reframing: he is presented as a classicizing, winged nude youth, seated on a pedestal, caught in the act of playing the lute.[99] Evidently the aim is partly to substantiate the comparison to Orpheus and, by extension, other ancient divine musicians, popular also in the written lauds—a realization of Cornazano's claim that the lutenist was a god. But neither Orpheus, nor Apollo, nor any of their musical cohorts is conventionally equipped with wings. The figure may be meant to recall Mercury, whose wings are usually attached to his sandals; but the wings and the beauty of the body resonate more strongly with Eros, who sometimes appeared in the fifteenth century as a beautiful youth rather than as a child.[100] Whether or not the medal can be linked directly to Pietrobono's role at Leonello's court, this choice of depiction may reflect a general association of the lutenist with amorous subject matter. In the 1441 performance described by Cornazano, Pietrobono (whose music, we must remember, set the heart aflame) sings a series of songs detailing the romantic adventures of contemporary nobles, before accompanying couples in an "amorous" dance.[101] The subject matter is appropriate to the matrimonial setting, certainly, but the implication is that it suits this musician's skill especially.

In sum, the description and depiction of Pietrobono during and shortly after Leonello's reign reveal strong synergies between his identity and that of Leonello's personal Muse (as evidenced in words and images associated with the marchese's studiolo). The proximity suggests that Pietrobono's role within Leonello's patronage may have been as an embodiment of or symbol for the prince's Muse—a role validated by Hesiod and later attributed to Pietrobono in a different context by Brandolini. Such a conclusion should not be unexpected. As Leonello's principal secular musician working within the idiom of sung poetry, it was Pietrobono's professional business to facilitate the marchese's own efforts in the field: in other words, it was his job to fulfill the function of a musical Muse. In this respect, Pietrobono's role, together with the studiolo with which it was so closely integrated, was an aspect of Leonello's performance of literary humanism. Perhaps he constitutes the final element in the princely subversion of Guarino's poetics: the scholar can write of his Muse, but the ruler can have one on staff.

[99] On this medal, see Hill 1984, 1:416–18; and Guidobaldi 1998. (NB, however, Guidobaldi is in error in giving the inscription on the pedestal as "primus inventor:" Hill reads it correctly as "OMNIVM PRINCEPS"—that is, roughly, "of all, the first," or "preeminent.")

[100] There can be no question that the proposed composition is a plausible one for the fifteenth century: cf. the medal discussed in Hill 1984, 1:296, probably made in Parma around 1490, in which Eros (this time a child) is depicted similarly, seated on a rock playing the lute.

[101] "Allor, retracto in altro adoperarse, / hebbe el cerchio amoroso a ballo spinto / e gli portici voti a copie sparse."

3

Isabella and the Decorum of Voice

> After all, one could perhaps put up with the conduct of men. But the women -! That is another thing that the women are keen about—to have men of education living in their households on a salary and following their litters. They count it as one among their other embellishments if it is said that they are cultured and have an interest in philosophy and write songs not much inferior to Sappho's.
>
> Lucian[1]

Making Isabella's Studiolo: A Summary

Of all the studioli of the Renaissance, that of Isabella d'Este is perhaps the most exhaustively studied.[2] Her first studiolo was established shortly after she became Marchesa of Mantua, in a small tower of the Castello di San Giorgio. Correspondence with her Mantuan secretary in 1491, beginning before she had even moved to Mantua, concerned the arrangement of the room and its decoration with arms and devices by the painter Luca Liombeni. Immediately beneath her studiolo in the Castello she prepared a second room of similar character, known as the *grotta*, which became the principal home of her large collection of antiquities.[3]

Whilst on a visit to Ferrara in 1495, Isabella requested a scale drawing of her studiolo from her Mantuan secretary, presumably to discuss revisions to the room with her natal family and their artists.[4] The new plan, involving marble

---

[1] Lucian 1921, On Salaried Posts in Great Houses 36.

[2] Studies that treat Isabella's studiolo comprehensively and in detail include Verheyen 1971; Lightbown 1986, 186–209 and 442–44; Liebenwein 1988, 80–102; Campbell 2004. The physical environment of Isabella's studiolo and grotta is comprehensively treated in Brown 2005. The studiolo has been studied from a musical perspective in Fenlon 1997. My summary of the physical history of the room draws on these sources.

[3] On the grotta and Isabella's antiquities, see in particular Brown 1976; Brown and Lorenzoni 1977–78.

[4] Liebenwein (1988, 81–83) notes that during this visit Isabella would have been able to inspect a new apartment made for her mother. The year before, she had visited the Montefeltri, giving her an opportunity to examine the studies in Urbino and Gubbio (Brown 2005, 45).

surrounds for door and window and new painting by a certain "Bernardino picture da Padua," was enacted in 1496. Egon Verheyen suggests that Bernardino's
work was on the ceiling, because part of Isabella's plan appears to have been to
prepare the walls of the studiolo for a sequence of large canvases. Isabella's
room was reorganized once more around 1504–5, when the installation of a
new ceiling necessitated certain other alterations.[5] At some later point, probably in the 1510s, a new project was begun to prepare a fresh suite of rooms
connected to a courtyard garden on the ground floor of the Corte Vecchia.
These rooms were completed in 1522, and the studiolo and grotta moved into
two of them, now alongside a third room called the Scalcheria and two smaller
rooms. The paintings were carried over from one studiolo to the next, and the
antiquities from one grotta to the next, but the new rooms were outfitted with
new wainscoting to above waist height. The older grotta had been equipped
with intarsia-decorated wainscoting featuring architectural scenes and musical instruments, and it is possible that the wainscoting of the new room was
decorated with similar designs. The scenes showing musical instruments and
notated music currently installed in the Corte Vecchia grotta almost certainly
originate from somewhere in the new apartment, but it is impossible to be sure
where.[6]

Andrea Mantegna, whose close association with the Gonzaga spanned
three generations of marchesi, supplied the first of the studiolo's famous canvases (all now in the Louvre)—the *Parnassus*, installed in 1497.[7] A purchase
of varnish made in June 1502 by an agent of Isabella on Mantegna's behalf
has been taken to indicate that his *Pallas Expelling the Vices from the Garden
of Virtue* was then about finished. Meanwhile, negotiations with Giovanni
Bellini, Pietro Perugino, and Leonardo da Vinci were pursued without much
success. Towards the end of 1502 discussions with Perugino reached a break-
through. In November, Isabella sent him written instructions on the subject
for his proposed painting and a sketch, and remained in frequent contact until,

[5] Verheyen 1971, 13 and n28.

[6] On the notated music in Isabella's intarsia, Ockeghem's puzzle-chanson "Prenez sur moi,"
see among others Fallows 1992; Fenlon 1997, 362–63 and 366–67; and Mengozzi 2008, with
further bibliography. On the instruments depicted in Isabella's intarsie, see Fenlon 1997, 362–
63. On the intarsie of the earlier grotta, see Brown 2005, 49–50; on the uncertainties surrounding the origins of the intarsie currently in the newer grotta, see ibid., 156–58.

[7] Good summaries of the assembling of Isabella's large pictures, each to a limited extent dis-
placing the last, can be found in Verheyen 1971; Lightbown 1986, 186–91; Christiansen 1992,
420–24; Brown 2004. The Parnassus was reworked in the early 1500s, probably by Lorenzo
Leonbruno who decorated rooms adjacent to the studiolo and grotta in the new Corte Vecchia
apartment. The changes largely involved the background landscape and the heads of Apollo and
some of the Muses, and appear to have been made in the interests of bringing the painting up to
date with new priorities in tonal finish—on this see Christiansen 1992, 421.

after several delays, the *Combat of Love and Chastity* was delivered in 1505. Further unsuccessful negotiations were undertaken, this time with Francesco Francia and probably Fra Bartolomeo. A more felicitous exchange began in 1504 with Lorenzo Costa through his then employers, the Bentivoglio of Bologna: Isabella sent instructions and a drawing, as well as other details, in that year, resulting in the *Coronation* in about 1506–7. Shortly before his death in 1506, Mantegna was working on a third painting for Isabella, a *Comus*, but it was never finished. Negotiations to employ Costa as his replacement in the post of court artist began towards the end of the year, and some time after his employment began—scholarly opinion varies from 1507–15—Costa apparently took over the subject left unfinished by Mantegna, producing the *Comus* as it survives today. With this painting, the studiolo reached a state of temporary completion. Plans were made in 1515 for a painting by Raphael that never materialized, but the next and last additions to the scheme were the so-called *Allegories of Vice and Virtue* painted for Isabella by Correggio in about 1529.

From the correspondence it is clear that it was Isabella's regular practice to send written instructions to her artists on the subject and content of the paintings they were to produce. Sometimes she also sent a drawing, to be absolutely sure the artists understood what she wanted. Detailed evidence for the nature of the instructions and the way in which they came about is limited, but helpful, implicating a scholar at court named Paride da Ceresara. An instruction written by Paride for Perugino survives, and a letter of 10 November 1504 refers to him as "vui, che ogni dì haveti ad fare nove inventione" (you, who every day have to make new inventions).[8] Unfortunately, the letters in which Isabella requested the instructions do not survive, and thus it is difficult to assess the extent to which she herself determined the content of her paintings. However, her correspondence with artists subsequent to the sending of an instruction often implies that she had a detailed understanding of their content, and was keen in effect to take ownership of them. Importantly, the evidence concerning the design of these paintings indicates clearly that Isabella's subjects were not determined at the outset of the project as a coherent program, but were created over the course of several years as foils to her changing priorities, even though she may always have envisioned five, six, or more works.

It is well established that Costa's *Comus* was based on a passage from Book 1 of the *Eikones* (Latin: *Imagines*) of the elder Philostratus.[9] In this text, written in the third century A.D., an aristocratic man of letters walks with a young friend through a gallery of pictures in a villa near Naples. As they look at each picture

---

[8] Brown 2004, Document 66.

[9] On the Comus and its relationship to Philostratus see, most recently, Campbell 2004, 205–19, esp. 208–15.

in turn, he explains to his companion how to read and interpret the content. It is a moot point as to whether or not the pictures ever really existed: for the Renaissance the idea that they might have done was enough to make the text immensely attractive.[10]

A translation of the *Imagines* into Italian was made for Isabella by a Greek scholar resident in Mantua named Demetrios Moscos.[11] A dedicatory letter addressed to Isabella, preserved in both surviving copies of the translation, identifies the grotta as the text's natural habitat: "Ecco ti mo di philostrato le Icone…digne della sua aurea Grocta" (Here for you the *Icone* of Philostratus…worthy of your golden Grotto).[12] In 1515 and 1516 Isabella wrote to Ferrara attempting to retrieve the translation, which had been lent to her brother Alfonso; at that time, she claimed, Alfonso had had it for "several years." From a later letter we know that the translation was commissioned for her by Mario Equicola, her tutor and a prominent humanist, who joined her court in 1508.[13] It therefore seems reasonable to date the translation around the time the *Comus* was finished—perhaps ca. 1511, as Maria Reina Fehl suggests.[14]

However, Isabella's encounter with Philostratus must have begun before Moscus or Equicola arrived at court. Someone, probably Paride (who could read Greek), was already employing the text on Isabella's behalf by 1506 when Mantegna was working on his *Comus*. Furthermore, the paintings set into the wall, the mythological subjects, the didactic aspect, and Isabella's stated aim to own works by the full spectrum of famous artists active in the Italy of her day all bespeak the project's more fundamental debt to Philostratus's approving description of his friend's villa.[15]

An inventory of the items in Isabella's studiolo and grotta was compiled shortly after her death, as part of a complete survey of the Gonzaga patrimony carried out in 1540–42.[16] Although evidently many of the items listed were likely not there forty years earlier, and probably also some others had been removed, it supplies a useful picture of the material surroundings of Isabella's leisure. (It lists no musical instruments, but these were often kept in a dedicated store room, and in any case Isabella's musical interests appear to have faded in her later life.) In the grotta we find a huge array of collectables, almost all distinguished by their precious material or their antique provenance, as

[10] On Philostratus in the Renaissance, see Webb 1992.
[11] Isabella's translation is studied in Fehl 1974b; Fehl 1985; and Koortbojian and Webb 1993.
[12] Text Koortbojian and Webb 1993, 262–63.
[13] See Koortbojian and Webb 1993, n1.
[14] Fehl 1985, 123–24.
[15] See in particular Philostratus's introduction to the *Imagines*.
[16] The inventory is published with commentary, annotations, and glossary in Ferrari 2001.

Figure 3.1 Andrea Mantegna, *Parnassus*, 1497, tempera and gold on canvas, Musée du Louvre, Paris. © RMN-Grand Palais (Musée du Louvre) / Stéphane Maréchalle.

well as a number of rich chests and caskets to contain them. Included were pots of various kinds, statuary in bronze and marble, bas-reliefs, medals and ancient coins, cameos and carved semi-precious stones, glassware, and a few objects from the natural world. Also present were some items of more practical value: clocks, mirrors, a writing desk with inkwell and pens, a chair, and devotional books. The contents of the studiolo were similar, but with an emphasis on display rather than storage. Together with the paintings there were more statues, reliefs, and vases; among the practical items were a mirror, an inkwell, four ivory chairs, and an astrolabe.

Alongside the well-known *impresa delle pause* depicted in several places in her apartment, the painted decoration of the studiolo featured a profusion of musical elements. In the *Parnassus* (Figure 3.1) we find Apollo accompanying a chorus of Muses on the lyre, as well as Mercury holding a syrinx, the invention of which was credited to him by some ancient sources. Perugino's *Combat of Love and Chastity* features an ensemble of satyrs on a hill at the right, playing the tambour and pipe—traditional Bacchic instruments. In Costa's *Comus*, in a garden of delight presided over by Comus and populated by various mythical personalities, music-making abounds, including players of the flute, horn,

Figure 3.2 Lorenzo Costa, *Coronation*, ca. 1505, oil and tempera on canvas, Musée du Louvre, Paris. © RMN-Grand Palais (Musée du Louvre) / Stéphane Maréchalle.

syrinx, lyre, *lira da braccio*, and psaltry; in the distance to the right, other musicians approach by sea on dolphins (recalling the dolphins of Leonello's *Euterpe* and the story of Arion). The much later paintings by Correggio deploy music to celebrate Minerva and to torture a satyr.

Also pervasively musical is the *Coronation* (Figure 3.2). In this work, at the center of a clearly delineated and guarded grove, a lady, normally taken to stand for Isabella herself, is being crowned by a cupid. They are flanked by a pair of musicians, one playing a lira da braccio and the other a lyre, who closely resemble the angelic musicians familiar from Costa's altarpieces: they seem to perform a generic celebratory role. Within the grove together with Isabella are four men who represent different pursuits familiar from Isabella's court and suited to her studiolo, two of whom are musicians. At the front of the grove on the left is a turbaned man holding a monochord (an experimental instrument designed to demonstrate musical proportion), who must be Pythagoras. On the right, a similarly attired man turns his ear to listen as he alters the tuning pegs of a more conventional stringed instrument: he is Aristoxenus, inventor of a sensory theory of harmony set in opposition to Pythagoras's mathematical model.[17] The arrangement has usually been taken as an allegorical representation of Isabella's court, perhaps even of her studiolo specifically, and this seems a valid interpretation. When considering the *Coronation*, it is worth bearing in mind that it was effectively a gift from a neighboring court, required to undertake a slightly different spectrum of tasks from those paintings made within Isabella's own court. No doubt Paride's invention took that fact into account: interestingly, Isabella specifically praised its "gallantry" (*gallantaria*).[18] The choice of music, both as a Liberal Art (Pythagoras) and as a practice (Aristoxenus), as the most prominent activity in Isabella's "grove" is, of course, telling.

Voice and Decorum

In her time Isabella was hailed, with a vigor hardly matched for other contemporary women, for her learning, her taste in fashion and the arts, and her musical accomplishments. However, recognition in such categories—during her lifetime more usually accorded to men—was not without its potential pitfalls. When placed in relation to women, each could be subject to suspicious and moralizing as well as acclamatory readings.

Isabella's reputation as a literata with classicizing interests, evident in her dealings with poets, scholars, and artists, was open to just such negative readings. Lisa Jardine has shown that classical learning, as professed by Isabella's contemporaries Cassandra Fedele, Laura Cereta, and Alessandra Scala, could be a dangerous accomplishment for a woman—constituting, for one fifteenth-century moral critic, evidence of incest.[19] Their learning was acceptable only if it could be distanced from the action of philology by, effectively, turning them into personifications of scholarship. As Stephen Kolsky has argued, Isabella's actual learning was very likely rather below the level reached by women such as Fedele, and her classical interests were perhaps closer to a courtly lifestyle choice than to a philological pursuit; but it was through her reputation, rather than her reality, than Isabella was most widely known and judged.[20]

---

[17] In the summary offered by Nicola Vicentino in his *L'Antica musica ridotta alla moderna prattica* of 1555, "Aristoxenus, who depended solely on sense, denied reason, whereas the Pythagoreans, in contrast, governed themselves solely by reason, not sense." Vicentino 1996, 6.

[18] In fact, in the quality of its allegory and the structure of its praise the painting is directly comparable to extra-Mantuan literary "gifts," including those of Niccolò da Correggio (discussed at some length in Gerbino 2009, 21ff) and Ariosto (Orlando Furioso XIII.59–60).

[19] Jardine 1985, esp. 813.

[20] Kolsky 1984, 59–60.

It is important to acknowledge that none of the scholars discussed by Jardine shared the exceptional social status enjoyed by Isabella, but several factors suggest that neither she nor her rank were beyond the reach of conventional moral concerns. Recent research suggests that both Isabella's mother Eleonora d'Aragona and her sister-in-law Lucrezia Borgia, as successive duchesses of Ferrara, operated to a significant extent with the caution and reserve advised for women of the lesser wealthy and noble classes in behavior manuals (such as those studied exhaustively by Ruth Kelso), restricting their cultural agency largely to the field of religion.[21] Further, Rose Marie San Juan has shown with particular clarity the extent to which Isabella was evidently aware of moral difficulties in designing the decoration of her private apartments.[22] Finally, several scholars have noted that Isabella and her ladies-in-waiting were indeed criticized on moral grounds on more than one occasion.[23]

Isabella was also known to her contemporaries for her interest in poetry, particularly that associated with Petrarch and the Petrarchan revival. She was an early purchaser of the Aldus edition of Petrarch's works, and corresponded with such literary figures as Pietro Bembo and Niccolò da Correggio. Although poetry itself sometimes came under fire in the Renaissance, these activities were perhaps easy enough to defend;[24] but Isabella appears also to have been herself a poet. Many years ago, Alessandro Luzio published a letter in which Isabella appears to ask a literary correspondent for his reaction to her own work; since then, occasional attempts have been made to identify poetry attributable to her.[25] A significant body of research has grown up around the subject of female authorship in the Renaissance, cataloging the various difficulties, both practical and moral, to which it was often subject. Ann Rosalind Jones, in particular, has uncovered the strategies adopted in the verse of women-poets a generation or two younger than Isabella operating in varying social contexts (including Pernette du Guillet, Catherine des Roches, and Tullia d'Aragona) to counter the legal, physical, and verbal silence imposed upon women by fifteenth- and sixteenth-century writers on women's education and conduct.[26] Meanwhile, a generation earlier than Isabella, the Florentine matriarch Lucrezia Tornabuoni (wife of Piero I de' Medici, often

[21] See in particular Gundersheimer 1984; Zarri 2006; and Kelso 1956. For remarks in this vein on the musical activities of Eleonora and Lucrezia, see Shephard 2015.

[22] San Juan 1991.

[23] See in particular Jones 1981; and Regan 2005.

[24] On the discourse contra poetry in Renaissance Italy, see, for instance, Campbell 1997, esp. 40–51.

[25] On Isabella as a poet, see Luzio 1887, 51–68; and Gallico 1962a, with an attempt to identify poems attributable to her.

[26] See in particular Jones 1986; and Jones 1990.

called *de facto* ruler of Florence), apparently a more active poet than Isabella whilst of nearly comparable social standing, was known to contemporaries not primarily for her (lost) sonnets, but for her more conventionally virtuous sacred and devotional verse.[27]

Whilst a degree of musical accomplishment was relatively common among Italian noblewomen, Isabella's interests went beyond the conventional (as her contemporaries frequently acknowledged).[28] She was well trained as a singer, benefitting from the tuition of her father's chapelmaster Johannes Martini, and was proficient on several of the stringed instruments associated with elite entertainment, including lute and lira da braccio. Like many at the Italian courts, she particularly valued the practice of singing verse to the accompaniment of a lute or lira, and she was praised by contemporaries for her skill in so doing. In a letter written to her in 1502 by Bernardo Accolti (l'Unico Aretino), himself a famous musician, Isabella is complemented for both her taste and her practical accomplishments in this vein:[29]

> Where do music, song, liberality, plays and Tuscan compositions (which perhaps you cannot judge) flourish with wondrous novelty in a woman of such nobility and intelligence, that [she] not only can judge those things but also perfectly compose and perfectly recite to viola or lute?

Some indication of the occasions and locations for Isabella's own musical performances can be gleaned from the surviving evidence. At home in Mantua, her court and her patronage centered on her private apartment—in particular the studiolo and grotta. As we have seen, the decoration of both rooms featured music prominently, a fact that has led Iain Fenlon and others to propose them as characteristic venues for her music-making.[30] In these rooms, which were private in the rather restricted sense described in chapter 1 above,

---

[27] See Tornabuoni 2001, in particular the introductory essay. Lucrezia, however, took the opportunity presented by her sacred themes and narratives to address limitations upon the status accorded contemporary women.

[28] On Isabella as a musician, see Prizer 1999. Isabella was relatively conventional in the fact, if not the extent and insistence, of her musical accomplishments: on other Italian noblewomen-musicians of the fifteenth century the fundamental text is Brown 1986, esp. 64–74; see also Bryce 2001, esp. 1094–102; and Shephard 2015.

[29] "Ove fiorisce el suono, el canto, la liberalità, le comedie, gli spectaculi e le tusche compositioni di quali forse non sai dar iudicio con novo miraculo in donna e di tanta alteza e di tanta inventute, quelle non solo iudicando ma perfectamente componendo e perfectamente in viola o leuto recitandole?" Text Prizer 1999, 32–33.

[30] Fenlon 1981, 88; repeated in Fenlon 1997, 363–64.

Isabella would have been attended by her *donzelle*, as well as her paid retainers, but she also received important guests.[31] The marchesa also occasionally performed for fellow nobles of both sexes at foreign courts, for example in Milan, Naples, and Ferrara, most often for an extremely small gathering, but on one documented occasion for a larger group at a banquet.[32]

Isabella's activities as an amateur musician effectively set the parameters for her music patronage: it has been noted that she patronized only music that she was herself interested in performing. In the fifteenth century, the practice of singing verse to the accompaniment of a stringed instrument was usually unwritten and partly improvised; and performers who pursued it successfully, such as Serafino Aquilano, could win immense fame at the Italian courts. During Isabella's lifetime, and partly at her encouragement, out of the older practice grew a similar, but written, genre known as the *frottola*.[33] The term is misleading, as is the designation "genre" (although both are used conventionally in the musicological literature), as the poetic forms involved were various: strambotti, barzellette, capitoli, canzoni, and others, spanning a range from bawdy to courtly Petrarchan.[34] The development of the frottola is connected closely with Isabella's court, and with the musicians active there, in particular Bartolomeo Tromboncino and Marchetto Cara. Both men served as composers as well as singer-lutenists, with the dual purpose of providing entertainment and facilitating Isabella's own music-making.

Poets from across Italy, as well as from the Mantuan court, sent verse to Isabella for Tromboncino and Cara to set, and for her to sing. It appears that Isabella saw performance as song as the inevitable fate of all suitable verse, and many of her literary correspondents understood and shared her view. In 1493, for example, she wrote to the aristocratic poet Niccolò da Correggio, with whom she carried on a lengthy literary exchange, asking to borrow his lira da braccio; she received in reply both the lira and a *capitolo* to sing to its accompaniment.[35] When Pietro Bembo sent her a substantial file of his poems in 1505, he did so in the hope that "alcun mio verso sia recitato et cantato da Vostra Signoria" (some of my verse [might] be recited and sung by Your Ladyship).[36]

---

[31] Fletcher (1981, 53) notes a visit of the Duke of Bourbon in 1509, and Kolsky (1984, 54) mentions a visit of Venetian ambassadors in 1515. Brown (2004, 283) notes several visitors whose role was to help further Isabella's decorative plans.

[32] For a conspectus of Isabella's specifically documented performances, see Prizer 1999, 25–30.

[33] On Isabella's frottola, see in particular Rubsamen 1943; Gallico 1962b; Gallico 1965; Prizer 1980; Prizer 1985; Prizer 1986; and Prizer 1991. On the relationship between the frottola and earlier improvisatory practice, see in particular Gallico 1965; and Prizer 1986.

[34] A useful guide to these and other relevant verse types is Elwert 1973.

[35] Prizer 1999, 22.

[36] Text Prizer 1999, Document 5.

The echoes in this practice of the classical view ascribing music and poetry a single identity—as invoked by Leonello—are tangible. In fact, Isabella might easily have thought of her frottola as yet another demonstration of her well-known "insatiable desire for antiquities." As I noted in relation to Leonello, the performance style of song to the accompaniment of a single stringed instrument lent itself well to equation with the practice of ancient poet-musicians such as Apollo and Orpheus: such a conflation played a central part in their iconography. The connection was so endemic that at least by the 1520s it was possible to refer to this performing idiom as "singing in the style of Orpheus."[37] Logically enough, this idiom was often adopted when ancient characters had to sing in the course of a theatrical performance—several examples feature Tromboncino, who appears to have specialized in the area.[38] At the same time, writers of classical tastes tended to use the terms "ad lyram" and "ad citharam" to refer to what in the vernacular would undoubtedly be the lute or the lira da braccio.[39] Isabella's musical recreation benefitted from just such an antique projection: Mario Equicola claimed in his *De mulieribus* that "whenever she returns from political or economic business to her natural ways, she takes up the *cithara*."[40] In an extension of this equivalence, other writers asserted that Isabella's music-making was like that of Orpheus and Amphion.[41] Isabella's musicians sometimes played explicitly to the idea, diverting from the classicizing Petrarch and his modern imitators to set real classical verse by, for instance, Horace, Ovid, Virgil, and Propertius.[42] Perhaps Isabella numbered her musical efforts among the classicizing treasures on display in her grotta and studiolo, to be seen alongside the bronze statue of "Apollo with his instrument" listed in the inventory of the contents of the grotta compiled just after her death.[43]

Nonetheless, such a pastime could engender moral uncertainties as potent as those sometimes attracted by scholarly and poetic interests. A growing body of recent scholarship has exposed and explored the difficulties and limitations that could attend women's musicianship during the later sixteenth century, and a much smaller amount of published work has brought a similar approach to bear on the study of Isabella's own period.[44] Prominent social commentators

---

[37] "cantando al modo d'Orfeo." Messisbugo 1992, 41.

[38] Examples can be found in Rubsamen 1943; Pirrotta and Povoledo 1982; Lockwood 1984; Prizer 1985, esp. 10–21; and Gerbino 2009, 17–19.

[39] Pirrotta and Povoledo 1982, 23ff.

[40] "siquid autem ab oeconomicis politicisque resipiscit negotiis citharam sumit." Equicola, *De mulieribus* (Ferrara, 1501), 4o, f.b2v. Text Kolsky 1984, 55.

[41] As, for example, Tebaldeo and Trissino. See Prizer 1999, 32, 34, and Document 6.

[42] Rubsamen 1943, 7 and n18; Prizer 1999, 38–43. See also Gerbino 2009, 21–23.

[43] "un Apollo col suo instrumento." No. 172 in the inventory as published in Ferrari 2001.

[44] The classic account of the decorum of female musicianship and musical performance in Renaissance Italy is that given in Kelso 1956, 52–53 and 228. See also, from among the more

contemporary with Isabella repeatedly connect music with seduction, and particularly with feminine powers of attraction. Paolo Cortese, for instance, in his 1510 *De cardinalatu*, notes (without restricting his comments to one sex or the other) that:

> many, estranged from the natural disposition of the normal sense, not only reject it [music] because of some sad perversion of their nature, but even think it to be hurtful for the reason that it is somehow an invitation to idle pleasure, and above all, that its merriment usually arouses the evil of lust.[45]

Pietro Aretino explained similarly, but directing his comments specifically at women, that "I suoni, i canti e le lettere che sanno le femmine [sonno] le chiavi che aprono le porte della pudicizia loro" (Music, songs, and letters are among the accomplishments of women that are the keys to open the door to their modesty).[46] Pietro Bembo cautioned his daughter Elena along slightly variant lines that playing musical instruments "è cosa da donna vana e leggiera" (is a thing for silly and superficial women).[47]

Such views of music could facilitate an association of musical activity with vices to which women were conventionally thought susceptible: most obviously vanity and sexual incontinence. In some circumstances, the application of such moral perspectives could result in a curtailing of women's freedom to pursue musical interests, and in most circumstances the pursuit of such interests left open the possibility of censure.[48] Particularly vociferous on this subject are many of the surviving Renaissance conduct books, which, whilst presenting an ideal rather than necessarily a detailed reality, are useful in establishing the tenor and parameters of contemporary views. Summarizing the findings of

recent literature concerned with Isabella's period, Lorenzetti 1994; Bryce 2001; Lorenzetti 2003, esp. chapter 4; and Shephard 2015.

[45] "multi a communium sensuum natura auersi non modo eam praua quadam nature peruersitate respuunt, sed eam etiam inutilem esse opinantur. Proptereaque ea quedam sit ignauae uoluptatis inuitatrix, maximeque eius iucunditate soleat libidinum excitari malum." Cortese, *De cardinalatu libri tres* (Castel Cortesiano 1510), fol. 72v. Text and translation Pirrotta 1966, 148 and 152. I have spelled out abbreviations and updated punctuation. As I will later discuss, and as Cortese points out at some length elsewhere in the same passage, it was also possible to take an entirely positive moral view of music. However, as Cortese also unintentionally makes clear, such a position needed justification.

[46] Letter published in 1537, given in Einstein 1948, 1:94. Recent studies considering the close association between music and erotic love in Renaissance Italy include Dennis 2010; Shephard 2010c; and Shephard 2015.

[47] Letter of 10 December 1541. The letter is widely published and discussed, most recently in Feldman 2006, at 105 and n2.

[48] For a more detailed presentation of the evidence relating to this point, see Shephard 2015.

her extremely large survey of such books, Ruth Kelso describes a reluctance to concede that women of good social standing can perform music at all. If they are allowed to sing and play, it is in private, preferably alone, as a counterpart to spinning and weaving in the battle against idleness, and always tempered by proper and prudent judgment of the occasion. Public performance, entered into unwillingly, should be undertaken "in a low voice" and "with reverence and shame," or else (in the case of the lady of the court in particular) in the company only of other noblewomen.[49] Addressing the question of courtly women directly, Castiglione was certainly aware of the need to divert censure along precisely the moral lines I have outlined. He preferred women to engage in music "very circumspectly," and if they must perform to wait to be "coaxed a little, [beginning] with a certain shyness, suggesting the dignified modesty that brazen women cannot understand."[50] He further advises that a woman performing music or dance "wear clothes that do not make her seem vain and frivolous."[51]

Isabella and her female attendants certainly provoked censure on more than one occasion, although I am not aware of any instance in the surviving documentation that can be connected specifically and incontrovertibly with music.[52] For example, in early 1502, Isabella and several of her attendants and courtiers went to Ferrara for the lengthy celebration of the marriage of her brother Alfonso to Lucrezia Borgia. In May, after the wedding was over, Isabella was surprised and displeased to receive a letter from Rome giving a biting critique of her behavior. Her detractors protested that "she was not well dressed, that she put on airs during the celebrations, and many other things, that she wanted to appear a boy."[53] Isabella's position at the forefront of clothing taste suggests that her correspondent did not mean her clothing was not fashionable, rich, and impressive.[54] The decorum of dress was a hotly contested area in fifteenth and sixteenth century Italy, with infringements of established codes even attracting fines under

[49] Kelso 1956, 53 and 228 (as is her usual practice Kelso is summarizing many sources, rather than quoting one in particular).

[50] "faccia con riguardo, e con quella molle delicatura che avemo detto convenirsele...quando ella viene a danzar o far musica di che sorte si sia, deve indurvisi con lassarene alquanto pregare, e con una certa timidità, che mostri quella nobile vergogna che è contraria della imprudenzia." Text Castiglione 1947, 306–7; translation Castiglione 1967, 215.

[51] "Deve...vestirsi di sorte, che non paia vana e leggiera." Text Castiglione 1947, 307; translation Castiglione 1967, 215.

[52] For further instances not discussed here, see Regan 2005, 60–62 with n25.

[53] "non era ben conza, che magnava nella festa et multe altre cose, che voleva parere pucto." Letter of 5 May 1502, in which Mario Equicola reported to Margherita Cantelma on a critical letter sent to Isabella from Rome (no longer extant). Text and translation Prizer 1985, 6 and n17.

[54] A quantity of information on Isabella's dress and her interest in fashion can be found in Welch 2005, 245–73.

some circumstances (although this form of censure evidently would not apply to a marchesa).[55] Messages about status, dynasty, affiliation, and moral character had to be conveyed successfully in a variety of situations through visual appearance. Perhaps it is appropriate in this case to call to mind Castiglione's concern that a woman's dress should not make her "seem vain and frivolous." The complaint that Isabella "wanted to appear a boy" is somewhat more cryptic, and is difficult to interpret with confidence. Certainly, it is true that women who were culturally active in fifteenth- and sixteenth-century Italy were sometimes praised in terms that configured them as male, either explicitly or implicitly—that is, they were praised for embodying virtues and accomplishments usually thought masculine.[56] Perhaps such favorable rhetoric could be turned to the ends of attack, as Castiglione implies when he warns women off "manly exertions" in their music-making and dancing.[57]

Voice and Legitimacy

In a classic essay, Rose Marie San Juan argued persuasively that Isabella adopted moralizing strategies in the painted decorations of her studiolo to counterbalance social concerns over the morality of literary ability and classicizing interests in women.[58] As San Juan describes, the most important exhibit in the studiolo from everyone else's point of view was Isabella herself, and it was immensely important that she live up to the demands of courtly feminine decorum even whilst challenging the limits assigned to her agency.[59] Her private spaces were frequently required to play a public role in the reception of visiting statesmen, and traps lurked in the ambiguity of decorous standards thus provoked. As the studiolo was quite possibly a venue for her own music-making, it seems, in light of the potential moral difficulties detailed above, that music should be added to San Juan's list. In fact, a detailed study

[55] See, for instance, Welch 2000.

[56] See, for example, the various examples and relevant discussion scattered throughout Jardine 1985; and LaMay 2002.

[57] "non voglio ch'ella usi questi esercizii virili cosí robusti ed asperi." Text Castiglione 1947, 306; translation Castiglione 1967, 215.

[58] San Juan 1991, 72–74. Something similar had been proposed briefly already in Elam 1981, 24.

[59] San Juan 1991, 71–72. Cf. an excerpt from a letter to Isabella, written by Equicola on behalf of Margherita Cantelmo (though it concerns the grotta rather than the studiolo): "Non e per questo ad me se leva il desyderio de essere nella sancta grocta, nel conspecto venerando de la diva imagine di quella, la quale in terra meritamente adoro" (Not for this reason is removed my desire to be in the sacred grotta, to be in the venerated sight of the divine image of she whom on earth I rightly worship)—text and translation Kolsky 1989, 233.

reveals that music was given a surprising priority: the images that Isabella and her supporters built around her as the manifestation of her identity evidence a clear concern with the uncomfortable associations of her favored pastime.

The most explicitly musical example, and the first one chronologically, is the *Parnassus* by Mantegna (Figure 3.1). My reading of the painting is a little different from that offered by other scholars, although plentiful and varied interpretations are already available. Some have stressed its humor, some its edifying message, and some have sought to tie it at a perhaps improbable level of detail to classical prototypes, both literary and visual.[60] Most recently, Stephen Campbell has argued that the painting aims at a productive and multivalent intertextuality. He views the *Parnassus* as making reference to the origins of poetry, through the Hippocrene spring, through the employment of Greek rather than Roman source-material (both visual and literary), and through Plinian motifs suggestive of the fecundity of nature.[61]

The "subject" of the painting, it is usually assumed, is the story of Mars and Venus, but it is depicted in a way that seems to confound narrative, split between Vulcan's cave and a fantastical triumphal arch of rock. It is impossible in the context of this "subject" to simply and adequately account for the much looser association of characters in the foreground—Apollo and the Muses singing and dancing to the lyre, Mercury with a syrinx, Pegasus, and the Hippocrene Spring. Homer's account of the story is frequently invoked to solve this dilemma: according to him, Mercury and Apollo were called to witness the lovers' humiliation once they had been ensnared by Vulcan.[62] However, in the same breath Homer also specifies Poseidon's presence, and it is Poseidon who goes on the play an active role in the narrative. Other misalignments similarly militate against the Homeric model.[63]

It has been noted more than once that it is with the scene of the Muses, rather than with the story of Mars and Venus, that the *Parnassus* makes its connection with dynastic and other precedents in the decoration of studioli—including, of course, Leonello's.[64] I suggest, therefore, that the Muses are the starting point of the painting, and that the story of Mars and Venus is in fact the

---

[60] See in particular Wind 1948, 9–20; Tietze-Conrat 1949; Wind 1949; Gombrich 1963; Verheyen 1971, esp. 35–41; Lehmann 1973; Jones 1981; Lightbown 1986, 194–201. Iain Fenlon (1997, 355–58) has offered a musical assessment of the *Parnassus* based on Lehmann's study, which otherwise has not won universal support.

[61] Campbell 2000; Campbell 2004, 117–44.

[62] For example by Wind 1948, 9–10; Gombrich 1963, 197; and Campbell 2000, 79.

[63] For example, Homer specifies a garlanded Venus, and at no point does he locate Vulcan at his forge. A more likely source for Mantegna's depiction of Mars and Venus seems to be Ovid's *Ars Amatoria*.

[64] The point is noted in Christiansen 1992, 421; Fenlon 1997, 356; Campbell 2004, 129.

subject of the Muses' song, conjured into being above them by their singing. Such an arrangement is not at all out of character for the Muses, who according to the ancient writers were known specifically to sing about the gods, and thus to inspire mortal poets to recount their mythologies.[65] The subject of the painting is therefore, in a sense, song itself.

It might be thought that such a conceit was without visual precedent, but in fact one was close at hand, in the *Imagines* of Philostratus, among which we find one that is similar to the *Parnassus* both in narrative conception and in appearance. Whilst the painting clearly does not copy it exactly, it is easy to imagine that one was prominent among the inspirations for the other:

> [Here we see] An Aphrodite, made of ivory: delicate maidens are hymning in delicate myrtle groves. The chorister who leads them is skilled in her art...The type of the goddess is that of Aphrodite goddess of Modesty, unclothed and decorous, and the material is ivory...However, the goddess is unwilling to seem painted, but she stands out as though one could take hold of her.
>
> Do you wish us to pour a libation of discourse on the altar? For of frankincense and cinnamon and myrrh it has enough already, and it seems to me to give out also a fragrance as of Sappho....the artistry of the painter must be praised...because he even makes us hear the hymn. For the maidens are singing, and the chorister frowns at one who is off the key, clapping her hands and trying earnestly to bring her into tune...As to their garments, they are simple and such as not to impede their movements if they should play—for instance, the close-fitting girdle, the chiton that leaves the arm free, and the way they enjoy treading with naked feet on the tender grass and drawing refreshment from the dew; and the flowered decoration of their garments, and the colors used on them—the way they harmonize the one with the other—are represented with wonderful truth...As to the figures of the maidens, if we were to leave the decision regarding them to Paris or any other judge, I believe he would be at a loss how to vote, so close is the rivalry among them in rosy arms and flashing eyes and fair cheeks and in "honeyed voices," to use the charming expression of Sappho.
>
> Eros, tilting up the center of his bow, lightly strikes the string for them and the bow-string resounds with a full harmony and asserts that it

[65] See in particular the passage from Hesiod's *Theogony* discussed in chapter 1 of the present study.

possesses all the notes of a lyre...What, then, is the song they are singing? For indeed something of the subject has been expressed in the painting.[66]

Philostratus describes a group of muse-like female singers, lightly dressed "such as not to impede their movements," "treading with naked feet on tender grass," who occupy "myrtle groves" beneath an altar with an image of Venus, naked and ivory-white, whilst singing her history, to the accompaniment of Eros playing his bow as a lyre. We only know the subject of their song because "something of [it] has been expressed in the painting." Further similarities can easily be found in the descriptive detail—for instance, the Muses are indeed dressed in chitons.

With this interpretation in mind, it is easy enough to see how the painting could have been put to work on behalf of Isabella-the-musician. It manifests and celebrates the power of the ultimate ancient exemplars of female artistic and cultural agency—the Muses, identifying them as, through their song, the ultimate authors of the classical poetic tradition. In poetic tributes Isabella was frequently placed among their number, a "tenth muse," and such might well be the implication of the gap left by Mantegna at the back of the circle of muses— large enough to fit an invisible tenth muse, to whom the adjacent muses even hold out their hands.[67] The painting goes further, identifying the Muses as exemplary singers, and identifying the subject of their exemplary song as love—precisely the subject of the vernacular poetry sung so enthusiastically by Isabella. The choice of the story of Mars and Venus might appear a strange one, evidencing as it does the debauchery of the pagan gods, but according to Ovid it was the best-known (and thus, in a sense, the most exemplary) ancient myth: "the tale was long most noted in the courts of Heaven."[68] It was also the prime gambit in an old rhetorical argument in favor of poetic license: in Boccaccio's words, "if Apelles, or our own Giotto...should represent Venus in the embrace of Mars instead of the enthroned Jove dispensing laws unto the gods, shall we therefore condemn these arts?"[69] And if there is any doubt

[66] Philostratus 1931, 2.1.

[67] On Isabella's adoption of the Muse as a "personal insignia," and her lauding in such terms by court poets, see Verheyn 1971, 44–46; Fletcher 1981, 51; Lightbown 1986, 197–200; San Juan 1991, 71; Campbell 2004, 120 and 124–25 with n24. Lightbown also discusses references to Isabella's habitat as Parnassus. Of course, the comparison of a praiseworthy woman to the muses was an obvious and popular strategy: see, for instance, the correspondence of Cassandra Fedele and Angelo Politian discussed in Jardine 1985, esp. 805–6.

[68] Ovid 1922, 4.189 (the *Metamorphoses*). He tells it also in the *Ars Amatoria* Bk. 2, when he writes similarly "There is a story, most famous over all the world, of Mars and Venus caught by Mulciber's guile"—Ovid 1929, 2.561–62. For more on the exemplarity of the Mars and Venus myth, see Campbell 2000, 78–79.

[69] Osgood 1956, 38—the quote is from Boccaccio's *Genalogia deorum gentilium*. Campbell (2000, 78) also connects this passage of Boccaccio with the *Parnassus*.

as to the decorum of love as a subject for song, we have only to understand that Mantegna has depicted the mother of love, Venus, as "Aphrodite goddess of Modesty, unclothed and decorous" (as Philostratus stipulates). Thus Mantegna's *Parnassus* presents a case for the validity of women's musical and poetic activities, and at the same time asserts the suitability of love as the subject matter for women's song.[70]

Understood in this way, the painting is in effect an enabling emblem of the singing Isabella, and it appears to have been understood in these, or at least very similar, terms by Isabella's contemporaries. Trissino, for instance, appears to use the idea that the *Parnassus* is literally a portrait of Isabella as the frame for the literary "portrait" he paints of her erudition in his *Ritratti* of 1514, describing the painting obliquely:

> Now, seeing that it is a necessary thing, continued Bembo, to number erudition among all the dignified pursuits with which she is equipped, we will make a portrait, which will be of great variety, and of many figures...In it will be all the assets of the Castalian Spring, and of Parnassus; and not one thing only, such as Calliope, Clio, Polyhymnia, or the other wise ones; but that [i.e., the asset, or virtue] of all the Muses, together with that of Mercury and Apollo have to be evident in it; and all those things that the Poets decorate in verses, the historians write in prose, and the Philosophers, now one, now the other, admonish; we find our portrait adorned with these things.[71]

Both Stephen Campbell and Mary Rogers have mentioned the *Parnassus* in discussing this text to different ends, but neither has sought to develop a close connection.[72] However, my interpretation of the painting appears to confirm

---

[70] Isabella was neither the only nor the first person to pursue these objectives—for further examples of attempts to make a case for a decorous feminine discourse on love, see Shephard 2015.

[71] "Hora, perciò che egli è necessaria cosa, seguì il Bembo, che la eruditione a tutte le degne operationi sia maestrevole scorta, uno ritratto faremo, il quale sarà di molta varietà, e di molte figure; tal che forse anchora in questa parte non saremo da la vostra imagine superati. Adunque tutti i beni di Castalia, e di Parnaso facciamola havere; e non una cosa sola, come Calliope, Clio Polymnia, o l'altre sapere; ma quello di tutte le Muse insieme, et appresso di Mercurio, e di Apolline esserli manifesto; e di tutte quelle cose, che i Poeti ornano in versi, gli historici scriveno in prosa, et i Philosophi ne l'uno, e ne l'altro ammoniscono; di queste adorno il nostro ritratto si tuova." Trissino 1524, [21] (the copy I consulted is unpaginated, but I have counted page numbers from the first page of text). Rogers 1988 offers an extended and illuminating discussion of Trissino's work, placing it in the context of contemporary paintings.

[72] Campbell 2004, 200; Rogers 1988, 51–52. Campbell writes in passing that the passage "seems to draw on the imagery of" the *Parnassus*; Rogers similarly mentions that the passage

Trissino's ekphrastic intent: he focuses precisely on the scene of the Muses together with Mercury and Apollo, mentioning the story of Mars and Venus only obliquely as a subject suitable for the Muses' poetic treatment. Offering to the Muses the patronage of Isabella's space, in their usual guise as facilitators of poetry and song, made of her studiolo, in effect, another Helicon.

The Muses and their song are the most obvious, but perhaps not the only strategies of legitimation implemented through the *Parnassus*. It may be no coincidence that the text which I have suggested inspired the painting makes multiple references to Sappho. The ancient lyric poet, famously female and yet taken by later antique writers as the exemplary, even paradigmatic exponent of her genre, would have made a very attractive ancient exemplar for Isabella, as has recently been argued by Stephen Campbell.[73] An association is in fact indicated by Trissino in his final gloss on the "portrait" of Isabella's erudition, continuing on directly from the section quoted above:

> and above all in Poetry she delights, and much on this she dwells; which seems most appropriate, being that she rules over the country of Virgil; and in sum it is such, that if Hipparcha, Anete, Aria and Hypatia; if Sappho, Corinna, Praxilla, with the other six female lyric poets, of which Greece boasts, were all reduced into one, this one still would not constitute an image equal to the one we have assembled.[74]

Though little of her poetry was known at the beginning of the sixteenth century, Sappho's legacy was held in the custody of a large body of references, lauds, and motifs, among which we find several also applied to Isabella.[75] An epigram from the *Greek Anthology* (well known among Mantuan poets in this period), identifying Sappho as the tenth Muse appears to give in words precisely the effect intended by the painting: "Some say there are nine Muses...but how careless,

"immediately calls to mind" the *Parnassus*, suggesting that Isabella is to be loosely identified with Venus in the picture.

[73] Campbell 2004, 199–204. Campbell's basis for the association of the two is an argument that Lorenzo Costa's *Coronation* depicts a coronation of Sappho, but as this identification proceeds from a loosely configured misinterpretation of the many musical aspects of the painting it is not at all convincing. On the other hand, his more general point that the painting is a Coronation of a Woman Poet is well taken.

[74] "e sopra il tutto di Poetica si diletta, e molto in quella si dimora; il che convenevolissimo pare, essendo la patria di Virgilia da questa signoreggiata; et insomma è tale, che se Hipparchia, Anete, Aria, et Hypátia; se Sappho, Corinna, Praxilla, con le altre sei lyrice Donne, di che Grecia si vanta, sosseno tutte in sola ridotte, e quella non anchora bene si potrebbe questa nostra figura assembrare." Trissino 1524, [21–22].

[75] The Renaissance reception of Sappho is conveniently summarized in Reynolds 2000, 81–94, and is separately discussed in Campbell 2004, 199–204.

look again,…Sappho of Lesbos is the tenth."[76] Boccaccio fleshes out Sappho's muse-like persona, claiming that she too "sings upon the lyre / the loves of the gods."[77] The Sapphic phrase "honeyed voices," adopted by Philostratus to describe the singing of his dancing maidens, was elsewhere applied to Sappho herself, who won the epithet "sweet-voiced," a laud echoed in several descriptions of Isabella's singing voice (although also given to other musicians of her period).[78]

Also, classical descriptions of Sappho addressing her songs to her lyre may have inspired the adoption of the same conceit in two sonnets written by Niccolò da Correggio especially for Isabella to sing.[79] Horace, for instance, describes Sappho "complaining to her Aeolian lyre about the girls of her city" (*Carmina* 2.13.21–25). In "Non è in me foco," Isabella similarly addresses her instrument (perhaps in this case a lute) directly, referring to the relief she experiences when "talking" with it from amorous woes:

Non è in me foco, non, non temer, legno;	There is no fire in me, no, have no fear, wood;
se ne le braccia mie spesso io ti toglio,	if I often take you up with my arms,
arder non ti posso io, se ben mi doglio;	I cannot burn you, however much I suffer;
il tuo concento aiuta il basso ingegno.	your harmony helps base talent.
D'ogni passion, d'ogni mio affanno e sdegno	Of every passion, of all my trouble and scorn
mentre teco io ragiono, mi dispoglio,	whilst I talk with you, I am divested,
ed ogni mio pensiero in te raccoglio,	and all my thoughts in you I draw together,
de tutti i pesi mei fido sustegno.	faithful sharer of all my burdens.
Non mi venir tu in questo caso a manco,	Do not fail me in this instance,
ché se questa fortuna io vinco mai,	because (if I ever overcome this fate of mine),
como bon servo ancor ti farò franco;	I will set you free like a good servant;
fra le delizie mie sempre starai,	among my delights you will always be,
e se per aiutarmi ora io ti stanco,	and if in helping me now I tire you,
riposando io, tu ancor riposarai.	I resting, you too will find rest.

In "Conscio fidel" we find Isabella once again commending her instrument for the solace it offers her when she tells it of her sorrows:

---

[76] Translation Reynolds 2000, 70. On knowledge of the Greek (or Palatine) Anthology within Isabella's orbit, see Campbell 2004, 200, with the further references given there.

[77] Boccaccio's Eclogue XII on Sappho is discussed and quoted extensively in translation in Campbell 2004, 202–3.

[78] For instance, in the descriptions written by Trissino and Bembo—see Prizer 1999, 35, and Appendix, Document 5 respectively.

[79] On the sonnets and the reasons for believing them to have been written for Isabella, see Prizer 1999, 36–38. They are published in Benvenuti 1969, at 132–33.

Conscio fidel de tutte le mie doglie,	Faithful confidante of all my pains,
con il qual parlo e piango il mio dolore,	with which I speak and weep my sorrow,
che (se licito è a dir) tanto è minore	that (if one may say so) is so much reduced
quanto il tuo dolce suon parte ne toglie,	when your sweet sound banishes them in part,
per un tuo simile ebbe Orfeo la moglie,	by means of one like you (which calmed the rage of hell) Orpheus had his wife [back]:
che li placò quello infernal furore:	
cusì ancora io placar Fortuna e Amore	thus also by you I hope to calm Fate and Love,
spero, ché onor non li serian mie spoglie.	so that they will not be given my mortal remains as ornament.
In te non si consuma altro che nervo,	In you there is nothing consumed but string,
e no ancor tuo; in me nervo, ossa e polpa	that is not yours; in me nerve, bone and flesh
patiscon tutti, e con il corpo l'alma.	all suffer, and together with the body the soul.
Supporta adunque se di te mi servo,	Be content, then, if I make use of your services,
ché quanto più patirem senza colpa	because the more we suffer blamelessly
più dolce avrem la victoriosa palma.	the sweeter will be the victor's palm.

Perhaps, through Philostratus, we can understand the exemplary Sappho to be another of the legitimizing associations invoked by the *Parnassus*, and (as Sappho was remembered as a lyric poet—that is, as a singer) another with a specifically musical relevance.

The boldness of the *Parnassus*'s statements, however, led to uncomfortable interpretative ambiguities. Filarete had identified the facade of a brothel, not the private room of a princess, as the appropriate spot for a depiction of Venus.[80] Inevitably (and, one suspects, intentionally) the design of the painting led to an implicit association of Isabella with Venus—an association that was occasionally made explicit with revealing results. A surviving verse by Battista Fieri of 1498–99 attempts to calm a dispute with Isabella sparked by an earlier, lost, verse.[81] It seems that Fieri fell into the trap, lauding Isabella in direct association

---

[80] In his *Trattato di architettura* of the 1460s—Filarete 1965, 1:131.

[81] The poem here discussed is given in transcription and translation in Jones 1981, where its relevance to the *Parnassus* is explored at more length. I quote from his text and translation. The association of Isabella with Venus was not limited to Fieri, and is further mentioned or discussed in Elam 1981, 24; Kolsky 1984, 61; San Juan 1991, 73; Campbell 2004, 124–26. Interestingly,

with the Venus in the *Parnassus,* and building the connection further through
the association of Mars with Isabella's husband Francesco. Isabella, it seems, had
rebuked him by explaining that the story was *counter*-exemplary: "Sed tamen
incautus Fabri non viderant Iras / In Marten Ultrices solicitare manus" (care-
lessly he [the poet] had not seen the angry smith / Moving with vengeful hands
against Mars). Jones argues that Fieri's initial interpretation of the painting was
really "wrong," but I am less certain. It seems unlikely that Fieri means it literally
when he claims that he did not notice Vulcan in the painting: more probably he
is using a poetic mode of presentation to indicate that at first he did not understand the "true" significance of Vulcan's presence. In fact, Fieri's poetic apology
is rather playful throughout, appearing to perpetuate the Venusian connection
even as he withdraws it. The poet understood, perhaps, that his mistake was not
primarily one of interpretation, but one of decorum in the public sphere.

Minervan Equivocations

The next paintings installed in the studiolo, finished in 1502 and 1505, seem
to effect a retreat from—or at least a qualification of—the position established
in the *Parnassus.* In my view, they signal a new strategy of poetic association,
visible also in other aspects of the studiolo and grotta: now Isabella places herself alongside Minerva in the struggle against the vices. No doubt they do so
with difficulties such as that precipitated by Fieri, and censure such as that
provoked in 1502, in mind.[82]

In Mantegna's *Pallas Expelling the Vices from the Garden of Virtue* we find
the exemplary goddess and her lieutenants entering a garden at speed, throw-
ing into retreat various dubious and grotesque characters ranging from the
Bacchic to the wholly allegorical. Three of the four Virtues approach the scene
from above in a cloud. An anthropomorphic tree at the left bears the inscription: AGITE, PELLITE SEDIBUS NOSTRIS / FOEDA HAEC VICIORUM
MONSTRA / VIRTUTUM COELITUS AD NOS REDEUNTIUM /
DIVAE COMITES (Come, divine companions in Virtue who are returning to
us from heaven, expel these foul monsters of Vices from our seats). At the far
right, a banner attached to a heavily built stone structure demands: ET MIHI
MATER VIRTUTUM SUCCURRITE DIVI (Gods, save me too, the Mother

Fieri, like Trissino, appears to refer to the *Parnassus* as an image of Isabella: "Ille dolet dictam
Venerem te candida Elisa, / Sed fuerat Vati Iusus, Imago tua" (Fair Isabella, he is sorry to have
called you Venus, but [it was] an image of you [that] had been the source of the poet's fancy).

[82] In this connection, it is interesting to note that Stephen Kolsky has suggested that Mario
Equicola's treatise in defense of women, *De mulieribus,* which features a lengthy appreciation of
Isabella, was composed to rescue her reputation from the inappropriate behavior of her donzelle

Figure 3.3   Gian Cristoforo Romano, portrait medal of Isabella d'Este, 1498, British Museum, London. © British Museum.

of the Virtues). The partisans of Virtue, it seems, are heading across the painting to liberate the Mother of Virtue; and in the process they are shooing away their Vice-ridden opponents, who have taken up residence in her "seat." Among the vices is Venus, depicted wearing the same armband with which she is adorned in the *Parnassus*.

In Perugino's *Combat of Love and Chastity*, Minerva (in accordance with the instructions sent to the artist) has "spezato lo strale d'oro et l'arco d'argento posto sotto li piedi" (broken [Cupid's] golden arrow and cast the silver bow underfoot).[83] Again, the forces of Virtue (in the form of Minerva, Diana, and the nymphs) take to the field against those of Vice (Venus, Cupid, and assorted Erotes and satyrs). Again, on the face of it, we are presented with a violent disavowal of the themes courted in the *Parnassus* and evidenced in Isabella's pastimes—blind Love, that inescapably Petrarchan character, is about to be run through by Minerva herself.[84]

The new Minervan association is also suggested by a medal made for Isabella by Gian Cristoforo Romano in 1498, and displayed in her grotta (Figure 3.3). On the obverse it shows a portrait of Isabella; on the reverse, a

at the Ferrarese festivities in 1502 (Kolsky 1991, 69–70; the suggestion is taken up again in Regan 2005, at 58).

[83] The instruction is published, most recently, in Campbell 2004, 172–73 with n6.

[84] As Campbell points out (2000, 80–81; 2004, 121), the contextual implausibility of this disavowal throws the sincerity of the new direction in Isabella's paintings into doubt. The paintings are actually full of moral ambiguity. Perugino's instructions make it clear that it should not yet be known who will win the battle, and that meanwhile all the background scenes should pertain not to chastity but to lust. Similarly, the other inscription visible in Pallas, whilst apparently perfectly straightforward ("Otia si Tollas Periere Cupidinis Arcus"—Throw out leisure and Cupid's arrows are vanquished), in fact turns out to come from Ovid's tongue-in-cheek *Remedia Amoris* (line 139), at a point where he is advocating military service as a way of avoiding love's torments.

snake and a winged Victory bearing a palm are surmounted by Sagittarius and
a sun.[85] Notwithstanding Luke Syson's objections, the combination can only
indicate Minerva: Nike and the snake Erikthonius are her most characteristic
companions, and Sagittarius is the sign of her father Jupiter, with whom she
was very closely connected.[86] The fact that Minerva is literally absent from
the reverse of the medal can reasonably be taken to imply that she should be
identified with Isabella herself, whose portrait graces the other face.

Finally, the Minerva connection was given an explicitly musical aspect in a
roundel on the marble door surround made for Isabella's studiolo by Romano
some time before 1505 (and later moved into the new studiolo in the Corte
Vecchia).[87] The Goddess is depicted in her warrior's garb but with a book at her
feet. On the surround she is accompanied by three musical muses: Clio with
fame's trumpet; Euterpe with flute, panpipes, and a keyboard instrument; and
Thalia with a lyre. Their intended resonances are indicated through pendant
roundels: Clio is associated with a peacock, symbol of immortality; Thalia with
a monkey (*simia*) dressing up like an actor; Euterpe with the sweet-singing
nightingale. This last, the nightingale, is the only animal to be equipped with
an inscription in Greek: "Hail Procne." Its counterpart, Euterpe, located
directly opposite Minerva high on the doorframe, is similarly distinguished
(Figure 3.4). The keyboard instrument or throne at her right is decorated with
a stack of five mensuration signs evidently intended to recall Isabella's *impresa
delle pause* (discussed below in detail), and Iain Fenlon reports that the stand
to her left bears faintly the inscription "ISAB[ELLA]."[88] Thus Isabella is identified unambiguously with the Muse of music and lyric poetry (that is, of song
in Isabella's vein), who in turn is identified as the privileged companion of
Minerva.

[85] Though the sun makes sense in conjunction with the astrological sign Sagittarius, it was also
a Gonzaga device. In that capacity it had previously appeared on a medal of Ludovico Gonzaga,
Francesco's grandfather—Chambers and Martineau 1981, cat. 15.

[86] The Minervan connection was originally identified by Andrea Norris (1987, 133–36,
esp. 135) but has since been rejected by Luke Syson (1997, 290). Pausanius (1918, 1.24.7—the
Description of Greece) reports both the snake and Nike as important aspects of the statue of
Athena in her temple on the Parthenon: "The statue of Athena is upright, with a tunic reaching
to the feet, and on her breast the head of Medousa is worked in ivory. She holds a statue of Nike
(Victory) about four cubits high, and in the other hand a spear; at her feet lies a shield and near
the spear is a serpent. This serpent would be Erikhthonios." Against the Roman coins adduced
by Syson as evidence for his more convoluted interpretation, set a Vespasianic coin published
by Mattingly (1923–62, 2: pl.22 no.4, also 122 and lii) which is closer in both appearance and
iconography and without doubt shows Minerva. See also the similar, if more conventional, medal
of Minerva made for Ercole just a few years earlier (reproduced in Gundersheimer 1972, fig. 6).

[87] On the door surround, see Campbell 2004, 140–44.

[88] Fenlon 1997, 364–65. Unfortunately, the available images of the doorframe are too poor to
permit a confirmation of the inscription.

Figure 3.4 Giulio Romano, Euterpe tondo from studiolo doorway, ca. 1505, Mantua. Reproduced by permission of the Ministero per i Beni e le Attività Culturali.

Poets writing in praise of Isabella certainly employed Minervan associations in connection with Isabella's pursuit of the arts, and specifically music. Diomede Guidalotti, in a sonnet probably dating from the year of the *Parnassus*'s creation, claims that "Volse di l'arti de Minerva il vanto" (She wanted the best of the arts of Minerva).[89] A later poetic complement offers a pregnant synthesis of Minerva with the *Parnassus* (even a rewriting of the painting). Celio Calcagnini, in a Latin poem written shortly after 1523 in praise of an alabaster organ acquired by Isabella's son Federico, mentions her as "Princeps Palladii magna Isabella chori" (Isabella the great princess of Athena's choir).[90] The word "chori" implies not only singers but dancers, and thus the epithet might easily have been intended to conflate the Muses of the *Parnassus*, singing and dancing beneath Venus, with Isabella's more circumspect representations.[91]

[89] On the dating of the sonnet, see Prizer 1999, 31–32, from which I quote the extract.

[90] Text and translation Prizer 1999, 43–44.

[91] For a similar conflation, see the verse by Baptista Mantuanus given in Campbell 2004, 100–101 and n46.

Minerva's close association with the Muses came on the good authority of Ovid's *Metamorphoses*, where she honors the sisters with a visit (the framing device for several stories in Book 5). Here her resonance with them is as goddess of wisdom, approving the scholarly nature of their pursuits: "felicesque vocat pariter studioque locoque / Mnemonidas" (she deemed the charm of that locality [Helicon] a fair surrounding for the studious days of those Mnemonian Maids).[92] Minerva's introduction to the mythic vocabulary of the studiolo thus served to establish indisputably the type and quality of the recreations enjoyed therein.[93] The goddess's patronage of the arts in which Isabella had a particular interest is also established by Ovid, this time in *Fasti* Book 3, where we learn that she is not only the goddess of painting and sculpture, but also the "dea carminis" (goddess of song).[94]

In Minerva, Isabella may thus have found the ideal character through which to deploy a moral strategy frequently used in the Renaissance to defend music. Musical expertise and ability was only available through the discipline of study. Cortese provides a complete exposition of this view in order to refute the accusation that music prompts lust:

> On the opposite side, however, many agree to resort to it [music] as to a certain discipline that is engaged in the knowledge of concordance and modes.[95]

As the knowledge of musical concordance pertains to the soul and the divine, Cortese continues, to develop (through study) the rational faculties necessary to judge music expertly is tantamount to expertise in morality itself:

> it must be said that music must be sought after for the sake of morals, inasmuch as the habit of passing judgment on what is similar to morals in its rational basis cannot be considered to be different from the habit of passing judgment on the rational basis of morals themselves, and of becoming expert in this latter judgment through imitation.[96]

---

[92] Ovid 1922, 5.267–68.

[93] For further discussion of Renaissance strategies for asserting the chastity of the Muses see Campbell 2004, 126–30.

[94] The relevant passage runs: "spurn her not…thou who dost ply the graving tool and paint pictures in encaustic colours, and thou who dost mould the stone with deft hand. She is the goddess of a thousand works: certainly she is the goddess of song; may she be friendly to my pursuits, if I deserve it." Ovid 1931, 3.829–34.

[95] "contra autem multi eam cantanque disciplinam quandam adhibendam esse volunt, que in symphonie modorumque cognitione versetur." Text and translation Pirrotta 1966, 148 and 152.

[96] "eodemque modo dicendum est, eam morum causa esse expetendam, siquidem consuescere de eo iudicare, quod simile morum rationi sit, nihil aliud videri potest quam consuescere

Filippo Oriolo da Bassano's epic poem *Monte Parnaso*, written ca. 1520 in evident personal cognizance of the musical environment of the North-Italian courts (including Isabella's), offers a more elaborate but closely equivalent moral reading. His Canto XX proceeds directly from a lengthy description of musicians accompanying a dance on Parnassus to warnings against the seductive appearance of women of questionable virtue; in the following canto the poet encounters the Muses dancing, whose vulnerability to similar criticism is obviated by the fact that they give in song an account of the technical aspects of music theory.[97] If music (and dance) can be associated with rational study, their licentious potential is avoided.

This approach to the morality of music was particularly appropriate to the discussion of musical women—because they were particularly open to the kind of censure it combated—and there are multiple examples of its use. For instance, when her Renaissance biographers wanted to rescue Sappho from the damning erotic associations built around her poetry by late Roman writers, they asserted that it was only "with diligent study" that "she ascended the steep slopes of Parnassus."[98] Similarly Johannes Tinctoris, music tutor to Beatrice d'Aragona in late fifteenth-century Naples, praised his student's musicianship on the grounds that "she has given herself most fervently to the study of this science [i.e., music]," with the result that "she delights...not only by her song, but by her judgment."[99]

It seems likely, therefore, that it was with Isabella's Minervan equivocation, and the moral tradition it invoked, in mind that her literati chose the terms of scholarship to describe her interest in music and the other arts. For example, Niccolò Liburnio, in dedicating to Isabella his *Selvette* of 1513, describes her as "scientata" (learned) in the "arti honeste" (honest arts) of "Poesia," "Rhitorica," and "Musica."[100] Equicola, too, describes her as "scientissima" in music in his *Libro de natura de amore*.[101] Also, Bernardo Accolti, in a letter quoted above,

de morum ratione iudicare, in eoque exerceri imitando." Text and translation Pirrotta 1966, 148 and 152.

[97] On the poem see Slim 1965, with excerpts and translation.

[98] This account of Sappho, from Boccaccio's *De mulieribus claris*, is given in transcription and translation in Reynolds 2000, at 86–87. Boccaccio's primary source was the letter from Sappho to Phaon in Ovid's *Heroides*, which certainly does not favor a scholarly reading of the poetess. Ariosto, too, calls Sappho "dotto" in the arts of "le sacre muse" (Orlando Furioso, XX, 1).

[99] "duxit huius scientiae studio se ferventissime dedere...non modo cantu et pronunciatione vehementius gaudeat." Text Tinctoris 1975, 1:69; translation Tinctoris 1967, 6–7—in his *De Natura et Proprietate Tonorum*. This praise follows a discussion of musical judgement richly qualified by the rhetoric of "ratio" over "affectus" (illustrated by the erroneous judgement of King Midas). The whole passage is more fully discussed in Shephard 2015.

[100] Liburnio's work is quoted at more length in transcription and translation in Prizer 1999, 33 and n85.

[101] The description comes in the course of a panegyric on Isabella's grotta contained in the autograph manuscript version of Equicola's work, given in transcription in Kolsky 1989.

acknowledged Isabella's "judgment" of poetry and music alongside her practical abilities. To ensure decorum, it seems, her music and poetry must be associated with *ratio* (reason) and the intellect rather than *affectus* (sentiment) and the body.[102]

Such a moral attuning of music-making appears also to be encoded into Costa's *Coronation*; in fact, his picture seems to encapsulate this view of Isabella's music-making. In the *Coronation* Isabella's musical interests are located very clearly within a grove at the entrance to which is an armed guard—presumably intended to ward off the vices. The characters chosen to represent those interests equally clearly identify them as studious in nature: Pythagoras and Aristoxenus were scholars, authors of influential theories of musical harmony and proportion. Through the person of Aristoxenus, who is in the process of applying his theory to a lute, the studiousness of musicianship is even extended to the lute song patronized by Isabella. The status of this painting as a gift from a neighboring court gives special significance to its particular configuration of Isabella's musicianship, even though it was designed by one of Isabella's own retainers. It is a document of both Isabella's intended musical image, and her success in presenting that image to elite Italian society at large.

Voice and Agency

In this analysis, it appears that Isabella's concern with her musicianship and its moral implications was absolutely central to her strategic self-presentation.[103] That this was so is suggested yet again by the fact that she turned her singing voice into a multivalent and portable sign: the so-called *impresa delle pause* (Figure 3.5).[104] Luzio and Renier date the invention of this impresa to before 1502; Ivy Mumford, aware of further examples of its use, has argued that it may already have been current when Isabella moved to Mantua.[105] Judging from the pride of place afforded it in the heraldic decoration of several pieces from the Este-Gonzaga majolica service, it was among the most important of Isabella's devices.[106]

---

[102] Boethius establishes this opposition influentially during his encounter with Lady Philosophy at the opening of the *Consolation of Philosophy*—see Panizza 1990, 51.

[103] My discussion of the self-conscious design of Isabella's voice in this section brings up several points, problems, and strategies also recently discovered by Suzanne Cusick in the oeuvre of Francesca Caccini (Cusick 2009, esp. 113–53), although, given the social disparity, only a carefully nuanced comparison is possible.

[104] On Isabella's imprese generally, see Mumford 1979; and Praz 1981, 65–66. Mumford discusses the musical impresa at length, giving details of the various decorative uses to which it was put, as do Luzio and Renier (2005, 33–34).

[105] Luzio and Renier 2005, 33–34; and Mumford 1979, 65.

[106] Mumford 1979, esp. 60–62.

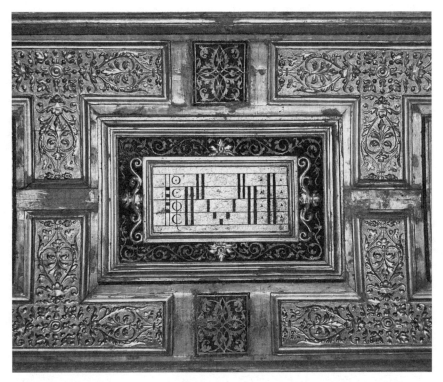

Figure 3.5 Isabella's *impresa delle pause* as it appears on the ceiling of her *grotta* in the Corte Vecchia of the Palazzo Ducale, Mantua. Reproduced by permission of the Ministero per i Beni e le Attività Culturali.

The *impresa delle pause* featured prominently in the decoration of Isabella's private rooms.[107] A barrel-vaulted roof installed in her grotta in 1502 was covered with multiple iterations of the sign. The roof made some years later for the new grotta in the Corte Vecchia bore the impresa conspicuously alongside Isabella's other key devices. In the later apartment the impresa also appeared in a roundel, part of a brief series of devices decorating the walls of a corridor leading to the courtyard garden.[108] In addition, Isabella had a seal bearing the device, which she kept on a writing desk in her grotta.[109] It consists of a short stave on which appear a clef, four mensuration signs, a symmetrical pattern of rests, and a repeat sign.

[107] On the use of the imprese in Isabella's apartments see Mumford 1979, esp. 67–68.

[108] It is visible in the photographs of the corridor published in Brown 2005, figs. 45–46.

[109] No. 184 in the inventory as published in Ferrari 2001: "E più, suso la detta tavola, un calamaro di ferro, nel quale è posto dentro l'oro lavorato alla zimina, con quattro temperatori, una forficina, lavorati alla medema foggia, con due penne dentro, cioè una d'avorio e una di ferro, lavorate alla medema manera, con un polverino et il calamaro lavorati alla detta foggia, con un sigillo legato a modo d'anello ch'imprime le pause, impressa di Madama bona memoria, et con uno horologlino picciolo di cristale da polvere."

The interpretation of imprese in general, and of Isabella's imprese in particu-lar, is a treacherous business.[110] By their nature, imprese often invite a variety of creative readings, rather than a single obvious one, and distinguishing between intended and unintended readings is difficult. Published interpretations of imprese have sometimes failed to take into account the fact that many noble men and women were less than fully versed in the writings of contemporary philoso-phers, and readings of excessive complexity are often unconvincing. Responding to a treatise written by her close associate Mario Equicola on her motto "nec spe nec metu," Isabella herself remarked that the device "cum tanti misteri non fu facto cum quanti lui gli attribuisse" (was not made with as many mysteries as he attributed to it).[111]

Modern interpretations of the *impresa delle pause* have tended towards either improbable Neoplatonic complexity or dismissal, and on the whole I concur with James Haar's distinctly skeptical assessment of their value.[112] Lauriane Fallay d'Este set the tone for several later readings, interpreting the device in the context of Ficinian philosophy as a symbol for the perfect harmony of the spheres. In her view, the clef refers to the Orphic view of music as the "key to the universe"; the various mensuration signs signify a progression (read up the stave) from imperfect to perfect (from duple to triple time); and meanwhile the central rest represents the harmony resulting from the eight other rests orbit-ing around it, which are the celestial spheres; the total being located within the cosmos, represented by the five lines of the stave. The ensemble refers, accord-ing to this view, to Isabella's penetration of the world soul, and her familiarity with Ficino's silent "inspired music."[113] The dismissive approach, on the other

[110] For a helpful introduction to the subject of imprese, see Lippincott 1990.

[111] Quoted in Genovesi 1993, at 85.

[112] Haar 1995, esp. 277–81.

[113] Fallay d'Este 1976. Also in this vein is Genovesi 1993; and, in greatly simplified form as a symbol of balance, Fenlon 1997, 361–62. The most recent interpretation is to be found in Benthem 2009. Benthem argues that Gian Cristoforo Romano's design for the Euterpe tondo in the door-frame must have been "instrumental in the process of the conception of the impresa" (573). This seems improbable, as Benthem himself says that the frame was completed by 1505, whereas Isabella's impresa was in use by at the latest 1502, and probably much earlier. (In fact, the frame was the subject of discussion as early as 1497 [Brown 2005, 45], but the roundels themselves were certainly yet to be made in 1500 and appear to have been installed in the already-fitted doorway later even than 1505; furthermore, they were probably not made by Romano [ibid., 45n57].) The scenario, it appears, is in fact reversed: the sculptor employed the stack of mensuration signs as a reference to the already-established impresa (which he quotes incorrectly), as a symbol of Isabella designed to identify her explicitly with the muse. Otherwise, Benthem's view is similar in spirit to Fallay d'Este's, though not in detail, proceeding from an unexpected reading of the arrangement of rests. He argues that, by a process that involves respelling the rests in terms of breves, both the Latin and Greek alphabets are to be mapped onto Isabella's sign. This represents, for Benthem, the artful combination of "tone, time, and text" for which Isabella, in her muse-like

hand, is well represented by Stephen Campbell, who draws out of the impresa the theme of silence, but almost completely suppresses the self-evidently musical nature of the impresa, finding it insufficiently "philosophically weighty."[114]

In my view, the arrangement of the impresa's various components is visually as much as musically determined—which, given the decorative function of the sign, is not altogether surprising. The stack of mensuration signs after the clef is present, very likely, as much to give the beginning of the stave a visual symmetry with the repeat mark at the end as to convey any musically defined meaning.[115] Similarly, the arrangement of the rests does not appear to have a music-technical significance beyond indicating a lengthy silence; but the rests are placed to form the letter "M" (i.e., Musica). As Iain Fenlon has pointed out, the clef of the impresa is one that would have suited Isabella's voice, and the repeated silence the impresa dictates can therefore be read as hers.[116]

Mario Equicola, in eulogizing Isabella and her grotta, explains the *impresa delle pause* as a symbol of prudence—of knowing when to sing and when to remain silent:

> I remember the very wise Biante to have said, that he often regretted not having remained silent. This the most prudent Isabella d'Este, Marchesa of Mantua, has signified in an ingenious image with all the rests of practical music, which admonish us and those of lively voice, telling them "stay silent at the right time."[117]

persona, was celebrated. Within this system, the set of rests as represented in the finished impresa stands for "n," which Benthem reads as "Nomen," referring to Isabella "shining from heaven in eternity" (576) via the symbolism of the number thirteen (there are thirteen rests).

[114] Campbell 2004, 76–77.

[115] The success of this visual strategy is suggested by the fact that Mumford (or her publisher) gives her image of the impresa upside down—1979, Pl.1. It is also noted in Fallay-d'Este 1976, 84.

[116] Fenlon 1981, 88. By way of comparison, the song "Cantai mentre nel cor," to be discussed later in the present chapter as one sung by Isabella, placed the Cantus line in the neighbouring clef C2 (in Antico's *Canzoni, sonetti, strambotti et frottole. Libro tertio* [Rome 1513]).

[117] "Habia in memoria il sapientissimo Biante di haver parlato, esserse piu volte pentito ne mai de haver taciuto. Questo in figure ingeniosamente ha significato la prudentissima Isabella da Este de Mantua Marchesa [principe deleted] con tucte le pause della musica pratica le quali ci admoniscono et quelli ad viva voce ne dicono 'ad tempo taci'." From the autograph manuscript of Mario Equicola's Libro de natura de amore preserved in the Biblioteca Nazionale Universitaria, Turin, cod. N.III.10, fol. 240r. Text Kolsky 1989, n23. The impresa is ascribed the same significance again elsewhere in the same manuscript (fols. 197r–98r): "La volta in lamnia con le pause del musico concento che ad tempo tacere denota" (The laminated vault with the symmetrical musical rests that signify [that you have to] leave silent time [i.e., sometimes remain silent]). Text Kolsky 1989, 235.

Prudence can be considered the ultimate courtly virtue, consisting for the Renaissance in the judgment required to respond to any situation with the most morally appropriate action (more or less Aristotle's *phronesis*): Castiglione calls it "the knowledge of how to choose what is good."[118] Appropriately, Trissino, in proposing to provide portraits dealing individually with Isabella's embodiment of the virtues, names prudence as the chief among them, "which is the foundation of all the things that guide man to happiness."[119] Prudence and silence were not infrequently equated, although silence was more usually treated in a discourse on speech, rather than song.[120] For instance, in a treatise devoted to silence, the contemporary Ferrarese scholar Celio Calcagnini argued that the prudent man judges his speech or silence to the subject and the occasion, advising that one "should not say anything not to the point or too little fitting...either say something better than silence, or else hold your voice."[121] Somewhat later in the sixteenth century, Stefano Guazzo noted that a woman's silence was particularly praiseworthy, and greatly improved the common opinion of her prudence.[122]

Equicola's interpretation is certainly in accordance with the potential moral anxieties over female musical agency described above: Isabella's voice is morally safe because she knows when not to sing. It is equally in accord with a stock contemporary complaint addressed to musicians; Agrippa, for instance, in his *De vanitatis*, gripes that:

> [music] is the exercise of base men...which have no consideration of beginning nor ending, as it is read of Archabius the trumpeter, to whom men were glad to give more to make him cease, than to make him sing.[123]

[118] "la virtú si po quasi dir una prudenzia ed un sapere eleggere il bene." Text Castiglione 1947, 422; translation Castiglione 1967, 292. On the virtue of prudence in Renaissance Italy, see Fubini 2003, 104–5; and Zuccolin 2007.

[119] "de i quali quello de la Prudentia sarà il primo; la quale è di tutte le cose, che guidano l'homo a la felicità, preparatrice." Trissino 1524, [22].

[120] For an introduction to Renaissance writings on silence, see Patrizi 1998.

[121] The treatise is called *Descriptio silentii*. The full passage runs: "De prudentibus etiam dici solet illud,... [in Greek], id est, Vulpes non garrit. Prudentes enim diligenter omnia potius circunspiciunt, audiunt ac rimantur: omniaque id observant ne quid praeter rem aut parum commodum loquantur. Immo caeteris illud obijciunt,... id est aut dic quippiam silentio melius, aut vocem tene." (Concerning prudent men the following is customarily said, that the fox does not chatter. [For] prudent men observe, listen to, and examine all things diligently [and] more readily; and indeed they all observe this thing, that they should not say anything not to the point or too little fitting. And indeed they object to others the following: either say something better than silence, or else hold your voice.) Calcagnini 1544, 493.

[122] In the well-known *La Civil conversazione* published in 1574: see the passage given and discussed in Patrizi 1998, 415.

[123] "esse illam uilium ac infelicis intemperantisque ingenij hominum exercitium, & qui nec incipiendi, nec finiendi rationem teneant, sicut de Archabio tibicine legitur, qui pluris conducendus

The impresa, then, is conciliatory. It reassures the world that prudent Isabella, though certainly musically accomplished, will not endanger herself and her companions by using her voice inappropriately, and thus inviting opprobrium. As a prominent decorative element in Isabella's private apartment, such a message seems apt.

At her brother's wedding in 1502, Isabella deployed the impresa in another, somewhat different way. At an important moment in the celebrations, she appeared before the eyes of all wearing a "bella camora richamata di quella invencione di tempi e pause" (beautiful camorra adorned with that invention of time signatures and rests).[124] The practice of displaying heraldry, devices, and imprese on items of dress was a common one among the Italian nobility, particularly at events such as jousts and weddings.[125] Such decoration could serve to advertise dynastic connections, as well as to encode aspects of a personality that were thought particularly famous or virtuous. Isabella was certainly well known for her musical interests, and on this camorra displayed them as a defining accomplishment, allied to her prudence. In so doing, she may have envisioned an interaction of those two messages. The visual strategies deployed in her studiolo and grotta suggest that she was aware of the need to negotiate a moral license for her agency in artistic and literary spheres. As I have described, the feminine vices at stake in the discourse against musical women were concerned with the body: vanity and incontinence. In response to the continuing (indeed, increased) need for negotiation within the more public forum of the wedding, I suggest, Isabella sought with her camorra to present upon her body an assertion of the decorum of her musical identity. Isabella may have aimed, with such a message inscribed upon her, to avert the possibility of negative moral judgments stemming from the unusual visibility of her musical accomplishments.

Nonetheless, as Stephen Campbell has argued with respect to her painted decorations, the strategies of self-definition that Isabella's musical impresa enacts are double-edged: though it cannot endorse it openly, it evidences a sympathy with the sensual body.[126] Though in the impresa Isabella's voice is

erat ut desineret, quam conducendus ut caneret." Text Agrippa 1531, fol. 33r; translation Agrippa 1974, fol. 28v. Similarly, though more gently, Castiglione (1967, 96; see also 118): "I should like you to explain how he is to practice [music]...; for there are many things which in themselves are commendable but which are most unseemly when practiced at the wrong time; and on the other hand, there are many things that seem inconsequential but which are greatly esteemed when performed on the appropriate occasion."

[124] Letter of Marchesa Eleanora of Crotone to Marchese Francesco of Mantua, 2 February 1502, transcribed in Luzio and Renier 2005, 34. The event is also recorded by Marino Sanuto in his diary.

[125] See, for instance, the examples given in Welch 2000, 103–4.

[126] Campbell works with this theme throughout Campbell 2004. It particularly colors his interpretation of Mantegna's *Pallas Expelling the Vices from the Garden of Virtue*.

silent, the presence of the staff, clef, and rests indicates unmistakably that her silence unfolds within song. Thus, whilst Equicola could interpret it cautiously as a symbol of prudent silence, the device actually affirms her voice. Paolo Giovio may intend to invoke precisely this irony when he notes in his *Dialogo dell'imprese militari e amorose* that "non merita d'esser passata con silenzio la signora Isabella, Marchesana di Mantova" (the lady Isabella, Marchesa of Mantua, does not deserve to be passed over in silence).[127]

The point is made even clearer when the impresa is placed within the immediate context of Isabella's song—that is, of her poetic interests. In amatory lyric poetry both in antiquity and in Renaissance Italy, silence and the destruction of voice are associated paradigmatically with love: either the debilitating "burning" of proximate desire, or the grief prompted by the absence of the object of desire. Illustrations are supplied in numbers by Petrarch, in whose poetry Isabella took an active interest.

Nancy Vickers has analyzed Petrarch's pointedly "scattered" verse in terms of the destructive encounter of Diana and Actaeon.[128] Actaeon's desire, however unintentionally it is aroused, prompts Diana to turn him into a stag, effectively removing his voice, whereupon he is literally scattered (i.e., torn apart) by his hounds. To preempt a similar silencing at the hands of his Laura, Petrarch dismembers her and scatters her body throughout his verse. Petrarch's verse, according to this reading, sets out specifically to safeguard his poetic voice, and his poetic identity, from the silence and destruction of desire.

Vickers's argument proceeds from an analysis of the famous *canzone* "Nel dolce tempo de la prima etade" (no. 23 in the *Rerum vulgarium fragmenta*), over the course of which Petrarch's voice suffers violence through several bodily metamorphoses: from those that suppress it (he is changed into a rock, at which point the poetic voice turns inward: "E dicea meco '…'"), to those that distort and constrain it (he is turned into a swan, "chiamando con estrania voce," and is dismayed at his inability to sing properly), to those that embody it (his body is destroyed, "e così scossa voce rimasi de l'antiche some"). He is even ordered to silence by his beloved: "dicendo a me: 'Di ciò non far parola'."[129]

What Petrarch called "'l tacito focile d'Amor" (the silent furnace of Love—no. 185 in the *Rerum vulgarium fragmenta*) found more straightforward expression in this sonnet (no. 20):

---

[127] Giovio 1978, 129. Suggestively, the sentence continues "che sempre fu per li suoi onorati costumi magnificentissima"; however, Giovio does not discuss the musical impresa directly.

[128] Vickers 1982.

[129] For an analysis of canzone 23 in terms of love and silence, see Brenkman 1974, esp. 13–18; and Vickers 1982, 97–99.

Vergognando talor ch'ancor si taccia,	Ashamed sometimes that your beauty,
Donna, per me vostra bellezza in rima,	lady, is still silent in my verses,
ricorro al tempo ch' i' vi vidi prima	I recall that time when I first saw it,
tal che null'altra fia mai che mi	such that no one else could ever
piaccia;	please me.
…	…
Piú volte già per dir le labbra	Many times my lips have opened
apersi,	to speak,
poi rimase la voce in mezzo 'l petto;	then voice is stilled in my chest:
ma qual sòn poria mai salir	but what sound could ever climb so
tant'alto?	high?
…	…

The long list of further examples to be found in the *Rerum vulgarium fragmenta* includes nos. 18, 46, 105, 125, 164, 171, 176, and 205 (and my search was by no means exhaustive).

The idea turns up frequently in the poetry set by the frottolists, where its use suggests the status of a stock motif. For instance, in a poem set by Francesco d'Ana and published in 1505, the author complains that "nel tormento la mia lingua tace" (my tongue is silent in its torment). Another, set by Tromboncino, turns on a list of Petrarchan paradoxes provoked by desire, including "tacendo parlo et ragionando taccio" (in silence I speak, and talking I am silent). And in a barzelletta set by Cara, "Mentre io vo per questi boschi," an unhappy lover asks "Ucelin, bel'ucelino, / come sa' tu ben cantar?" (Little bird, pretty little bird, how do you know good singing?), complaining that he, in contrast, is reduced to "angoscioso e amaro pianto" (anguished and bitter weeping).[130] It is impossible that Isabella was not aware of this trope, and therefore it is reasonable to conclude that she was willing to court the implication that her silence, far from evidencing her prudence, was provoked by the Petrarchan love described in the verses she sang.

The various aspects of Isabella's equivocal voice are brought together conveniently in one of the very few frottole that can be identified specifically with one of Isabella's documented musical performances.[131] In December 1514, whilst visiting Naples, Isabella spent an evening in Pozuolo, in the nearby countryside, in the company of Francesco Aquaviva, the Marchese of Bitonto. In May of the following year, Francesco wrote to Isabella to thank her for some

---

[130] The verses set by d'Ana and Tromboncino are given in transcription and translation in Prizer 1991, 13–14. The verse set by Cara is discussed in Prizer 1999, 39–40.

[131] On Isabella's documented musical performances, including the one discussed here, see Prizer 1999, 25–30.

"froctuli et canczoni" she had sent him in settings by Marchetto Cara, but requested one further song called "Cantai," because "de la quale sono affectionatissimo, maxime recordandome de quella sera de Piczolo" (of that I am very affectionate, largely in memory of that evening in Pozuolo). A further letter refers with absolute clarity to a musical performance given by Isabella on that evening. It is not much of a stretch to conclude, as William Prizer has done, that Isabella sang on that occasion a song called "Cantai," and to connect "Cantai" with Castiglione's sonnet "Cantai mentre nel cor," which survives in a setting by Cara.[132]

Cantai mentre nel cor lieto fioria	I sang while in my joyful heart blossomed
de' suavi pensier' l'alma mia spene.	my hope, nourishing sweet thoughts.
Hor che la mancha, e ognor crescon la pene,	Now that it is missing, and the pain grows apace,
conversa al lachrimar la voce mia.	my voice changes to tears.
E'l cor, che ai dolci accenti aprir la via	And my heart, which to sweet words used to open
solea, senza speranza hormai diviene	the way, now without hope has become
de amor toscho albergo, onde convene	the poisoned home of love,
che ciò che indi deriva, amaro sia	so that all which derives from it must be bitter.
Cosi in foscho pensier l'alma ha'n governo	Thus my soul remains in dark thought
che col freddo timor dì e notte a canto	That has cold fear with it day and night
de far minaccia il mio dolor eterno.	To menace my endless sorrow.
Però se provo haver l'anticho canto,	If, nonetheless, I try again that old song,
tinta la voce dal dolor interno	my voice is colored by my internal sorrow
esce in rotti sospir' e duro pianto.	[and] it emerges in broken sighs and hard tears.

Castiglione's sonnet, which in 1514 emerged from Isabella's lips as song, adopts the trope of the voice destroyed by love as a framing conceit. It makes reference to two poems of Petrarch, one of which deploys the same conceit. The first, beginning "Cantai, or piango, et non men di dolcezza / del pianger prendo che del canto presi" (I sang, now I weep, and no less sweetness / do I derive from weeping as I did from song—no. 229), finds Laura still alive; whilst in the second, beginning "Amor, quando fioria / mia spene, e 'l guidardon di tanta

[132] Prizer 1999, 26–28. I supply his translation, slightly altered.

fede" (Love, when flourished / my hopes, and the practice of such fidelity—
no. 324), she is dead. Whether Castiglione's lover suffers from frustrated desire
or lover's grief is unspecified. Either way, the sonnet and Isabella's performance
of it serve to locate the sensuous implication of Isabella's voice-symbol—that
she is silenced not by prudence but by love—in her actual voice. At the same
time, it makes clear the further implication of the impresa that Isabella's silence
is only figurative, and in fact evidences her voice: we know that Isabella's voice
is "broken" not because she is silent—not because it is actually broken—but
because she has sung it.

However, in revealing the subversive face of the voice-as-sign, the verse also
reveals the conciliatory. Prizer notes that the poem is especially appropriate
as the song of a gentlewoman, on account of being "particularly delicate and
courtly." I would add that it achieves this delicacy largely by being, at least
cosmetically, utterly androgynous—it is devoid of the gendered (or sexed)
physical or experiential reference points that so often qualify the relationship
between the lover and the object of their love in courtly poetry.[133] Crucially, as
a result, the speaker is to a certain extent disembodied: their physical existence
is signaled only by heart, soul, voice, and tears. It offers, through that subtle
characteristic, an analogue of the impresa's careful negotiation: the physical
presence of the subject position is overwritten almost entirely by its voice,
which at the same time is concerned to emphasize its silence.

[133] Paula Higgins (1991, 171–72) briefly discusses the importance of the "neutral voice" to
fifteenth-century creative women. See also LaMay 2002, 57–58.

4

Alfonso and the Eloquence
of Bacchus

...and truth has come to be proverbially credited to wine.
Pliny the Elder[1]

Making Alfonso's Studiolo: A Summary

Alfonso began work on improving his private apartment almost as soon as he succeeded to the duchy of Ferrara, Modena, and Reggio in 1505. A continually evolving, but essentially unbroken, program of building and decoration lasted almost until his death. The lion's share of the work concerned a series of structures, all of which predated Alfonso's reign in one form or another, that linked the two ducal residences, the castle and the palace. A ravelin, essentially a part of the castle, projected over the moat, and a "Via Coperta" (covered walkway) proceeded along an arcade over the city's central piazza from the moat to the palace.[2] It was in the Via Coperta and ravelin that Alfonso had made a new apartment, including a room now known as the "studio" and one termed variously "studiolo" or "camerino." The *studio* was decorated with marble reliefs made by Antonio Lombardo, and the studiolo with paintings by Bellini, Titian, and Dosso Dossi. It is this second room that mostly concerns me in this chapter.[3]

---

[1] Pliny 1938, 14.141, referring to the proverb *in vino veritas*.

[2] These building programs have been studied in detail, but the interpretation of the available evidence has been hotly disputed. See Hope 1971; Goodgal 1978; Hope 1987; Goodgal 1987; Brown 1987; Bentini 1998; Ballarin 2002; Borella and Ghinato 2006. A coherent assessment of previous opinion is Bayer 1998; a summary reassessment in light of new archaeological evidence is Borella 2004. Fortunately, the areas of disagreement are of little relevance to the present study.

[3] Some question exists over the use of the term "studiolo" to refer to Alfonso's room. Liebenwein excludes it from his definition, and Shearman points out that Alfonso himself only ever calls it a "camerino" in his correspondence concerning the room with Roman agents (Liebenwein 1988, 2 with n3; Shearman 1987, n4). The word "studio" is used in the court accounts for another

Alfonso's apartment seems to have followed a format not unlike those of his parents.[4] Alongside the studio and studiolo, one of the rooms contained a bed, and may have been his bedroom. Three larger rooms probably served for reception and entertainment. One accessed a balcony, and contemporary correspondence suggests that one was used for dining.[5] There must also have been a private chapel nearby.[6]

The decorations ordered by Alfonso for his rooms were lavish.[7] Following a rebuilding of 1518, decorative marble pavements were installed, and ceilings, part gilded, part painted. Payment records show that Dosso worked on the ceilings with his assistants right through the 1520s, and fragments of his work for two of the rooms survive—two segments of a tondo for the balcony room, and seven rhomboids, probably for the bedroom. A contemporary observer singles out the decoration of the door surrounds for particular mention: "among other things one can see above all the exits of the Camerini heads ancient and modern by sculptors."[8] It may well be that these were made by Lombardo, who was probably at work for Alfonso until his death in 1516. Lombardo's principal contribution was the decoration of the studio in marble, begun perhaps in 1506 and installed from 1508.[9]

room—the room decorated with marble reliefs (though this room was also sometimes called a "camerino"). However, it seems obvious that the "camerino" was modeled closely on Isabella's studiolo, which was referred to as such. We should probably understand the relationship between Alfonso's "camerino" and "studio" along similar lines to that between Isabella's "studiolo" and "grotta." (An uncertainty also attended the nomenclature of Isabella's studiolo, which she also sometimes referred to as a "camerino"—see Verheyen 1971, 2.) Furthermore, Titian (who had been in the room) named it a "studio," and Vasari, in describing its decoration, acknowledged both possibilities, calling it a "stanzino, o vero studio" (little chamber, or rather, study) as well as a "camerino" (see the letter published in Hope 1971, 646; and Vasari 1878–85, 6:474 and 7:433). Paul Holberton (1987 57–59) has shown very clearly that in its aesthetic and recreational vision the room fits closely with the less austere aspects of the studiolo tradition. I therefore think it reasonable to refer to it as a studiolo, and to discuss it as such in this study.

[4] On the apartments of Ercole I d'Este and Eleonora d'Aragona see Tuohy 1996, esp. 72–104.

[5] See the letters published as Hope 1971, Appendix, documents IV and VII. These letters are difficult to interpret because at the time they were written the name "camere dorate" was in the process of creeping from Alfonso's father's old apartment in the palace to Alfonso's new apartment in the Via Coperta. For several reasons to do with the layout of the palace it seems likely that they refer to the newer set of rooms.

[6] See Goodgal 1978, 164–68.

[7] Information and documentation relating to the decoration of the rooms can be found particularly in Campori 1874; Walker 1956; Hope 1971; Goodgal 1978; Hope 1987; Shearman 1987; and Ballarin 2002, vol. 3, with a comprehensive digest of documents.

[8] "fra laltre cose la vederà sopra tuti le ussi depsi Camerini teste antiche e moderne de scolptori." Bernardino de' Prosperi to Isabella, 4 October 1518. Text Hope 1987, 30.

[9] The documents concerning this project can be found in Goodgal 1978, Appendix I, esp. Documents 17–31, discussed at 164–66. On Lombardo's marbles for Alfonso, see in particular Sheard 1993.

Almost all of the surviving evidence concerning paintings made for the walls of the rooms involves those installed in the studiolo. In 1598, in the confusion attendant upon the ejection of the Este dynasty from Ferrara by the Church, Cardinal Aldobrandini requisitioned five large canvases and Cardinal Borghese a frieze in ten parts from the room. From inventories made at the time and a little later, we can match four of the five large paintings with works still in existence today, and we have a relatively large amount of evidence about the appearance of the fifth.[10] We also know a certain amount about the frieze, which was by Dosso and depicted scenes from the *Aeneid*, and five surviving paintings have been identified as its remains.[11] From a slightly later inventory we know that the studiolo, like some other rooms in the Via Coperta, had a painted ceiling. Payments made to Dosso for the decoration of ceilings in the Via Coperta in the 1520s make it very likely that the studiolo ceiling was decorated by him, but no evidence survives as to its appearance.

The four surviving large paintings are the *Feast of the Gods* by Bellini, dated 1514, and three paintings by Titian: the *Worship of Venus, Bacchus and Ariadne,* and the *Bacchanal of the Andrians,* all painted most probably between 1518 and 1524.[12] The Bellini has long been thought to be modeled on a passage from Ovid's *Fasti*. The model for Titian's *Bacchus and Ariadne* has been argued variously to be Catullus or one of two passages from Ovid; and the remaining two paintings are based on extracts from Philostratus's *Imagines*. The missing painting was by Dosso, and was described by Vasari as "una Baccanaria d'huomini" (a Bacchanal of men).[13] Alfonso's dealings with Bellini and Titian are documented variously in the court records and in correspondence.[14] From these sources we also learn of a commission to Michelangelo which may or may not relate to the studiolo, as well as two commissions to Raphael (the subjects of which are known) and one to Fra Bartolomeo which almost certainly did relate to the room; however, as far as is known, none of these artists ever delivered a painting for the studiolo.[15]

[10] These inventories are transcribed and studied in Hope 1971; Goodgal 1978; and Hope 1987.

[11] On these see most recently Christiansen 2000.

[12] A good overview of the process of accumulating the pictures and their significance is Bayer 1998. The only serious attempt to tie them all into a single, entirely coherent program is Marek 1983.

[13] Vasari 1878–85, 6:474. For the various other descriptions of this picture see Hope 1971, 641n4.

[14] See in particular Campori 1874.

[15] On Alfonso's dealings with Michelangelo, see most recently Rosenberg 2000. A summary of Alfonso's relations with Raphael can be found in Shearman 1987, in which John Shearman published documents showing for the first time that Alfonso's relationship with Raphael predated 1517. The relevant documents can now be found conveniently in Shearman 2003.

Figure 4.1 Giovanni Bellini, *The Feast of the Gods*, 1514, oil on canvas, National Gallery of Art, Washington. Image courtesy of the National Gallery of Art, Washington.

The design of the series of large paintings has been connected by some scholars with a letter of 15 October 1511. Mario Equicola, tutor to Alfonso's sister Isabella, writes to his employer from Ferrara to report that his return to Mantua has been delayed:

> It pleases the Lord Duke that I stay here for eight days: the reason is the painting of a room in which there will be six fables or histories. I have already found them and given them to him in writing.[16]

It is widely accepted that the room in question is the studiolo, and that the *Feast of the Gods* might have been one of the "fables or histories" "found" by Equicola. However, the large gap between the completion of that painting and the appearance of the next, the *Worship of Venus*, together with the sudden

[16] "Al S.r. Duca piace che reste qui octo di: la causa e la pictura di una camera nella quale vanno sei fabule overo istorie. Gia le ho trovate et datele in scritto." Text Shearman 1987, n35.

Figure 4.2 Dosso Dossi, *Aeneas at the Entrance to the Elysian Fields*, ca. 1520, oil on canvas, National Gallery of Canada, Ottawa. © National Gallery of Canada.

dominance from 1518 of subjects drawn from Philostratus, have led to a general assumption that the project stalled at the end of 1514 and was re-begun with a new program around 1517.[17]

The discovery by John Shearman of documentation showing that the commission to Raphael for the studiolo, known from letters of 1517–20, had already been issued in 1514 suggests that this view needs revision. Also pertinent are the turbulent political circumstances of the 1510s, which interrupted not only the decorative program of the studiolo but also that of the marble studio, and Alfonso's building projects. During 1509–10, Alfonso was deeply involved in a military campaign against his Venetian neighbors as part of the League of Cambrai. From 1510 until the death of Pope Julius II in 1513, he found himself on the wrong side of a more dangerous struggle, as the Italian community united to throw Alfonso's French allies out of the country. Fighting flared again in 1515, as a new French king sought to recover lost territories.[18] With these events in mind, it is easy to follow a thread through from Equicola's visit,

[17] For example, Holberton 1987, 59.

[18] The standard contemporary history of these wars is that written by Francesco Guicciardini—see Guicciardini 1969, esp. 191–279; the standard modern accounts are Pastor 1911, 6:299–436 and, from the Ferrarese perspective, Gardner 1906, 55–105.

during a lull in the fighting late in 1511, to the completion of the studiolo proj-ect.[19] The point is important because in what follows I work from the view that the design of Alfonso's studiolo decoration was established, more or less, in late 1511, rather than developing on a work-by-work basis as did Isabella's.

Musical elements abound in the paintings made for Alfonso's studiolo. The summer scene of a country picnic with musical entertainment is rehearsed twice, once in the *Feast of the Gods* (Figure 4.1) and again in the *Bacchanal of the Andrians* (Figure 4.8), which features a notated song. Also, in one of the surviving sections of Dosso's frieze of scenes from the life of Aeneas, *Aeneas at the Entrance to the Elysian Fields* (Figure 4.2), we see a group relaxing in a landscape who seem to be reading from books in oblong format: this was the standard format for music partbooks in the early sixteenth century. Behind them, couples are engaged in a dance. Music appears, too, as the identifying attribute of mythical personae. In *Aeneas at the Entrance to the Elysian Fields*, in the wooded landscape to the left, we find two separate lira da braccio play-ers, identifiable via Virgil's text as Orpheus and Musaeus. The *Feast of the Gods*

[19] A similar hiatus punctuated Isabella's decoration projects, relating to the capture of her hus-band Francesco by the Venetians in 1509 and the consequent threat to their state—see Brown 2004, 282.

Figure 4.3 Titian, *Bacchus and Ariadne*, ca. 1520, oil on canvas, National Gallery, London. © The National Gallery, London.

features Pan playing a pipe and Apollo holding a lira da braccio. Finally, in Titian's *Bacchus and Ariadne* (Figure 4.3), Bacchus's maenads and satyrs take up their traditional roles as players of cymbals, tambours, and horns, familiar from late antique sarcophagus reliefs known in the Renaissance.

Music also features prominently in the surviving decoration of other rooms of Alfonso's new apartment. Among Lombardo's marble reliefs from the studio preserved in the Hermitage Museum and the Louvre, one features musical instruments (Figure 4.4), and in fact several of the figures in the set seem to be singing.[20] A female figure in the National Gallery, a fragment of the ceiling tondo from one of the larger rooms in the apartment, also seems to be singing (Figure 4.5).[21] In light of the presence of highly characterized courtly musicians in other ceiling tondi

[20] See the excellent reproductions published in Ceriana 2004, 134–85, esp. 164–66 (some of the reliefs reproduced here were probably not for the studio, but for door surrounds elsewhere in the apartment).

[21] On this painting see Humfrey and Lucco 1998, 187–91.

Figure 4.4 Antonio Lombardo, *Female Faun between Two Tritons*, 1508, marble, The State Hermitage Museum, St. Petersburg.

Figure 4.5 Dosso Dossi, *A Man embracing a Woman*, ca. 1524, oil on panel, National Gallery, London. © The National Gallery, London.

(such as that by Niccolò dell' Abate for the studiolo of Count Giulio Boiardo), one might tentatively suggest that the woman is Dalida de' Puti, a musician first in the employ of Alfonso's wife Lucrezia Borgia and later mistress of his brother Cardinal Ippolito.[22] Finally, one of the rhomboid paintings by Dosso surviving from the ceiling of Alfonso's bedroom shows two singing men, a woman holding a closed

---

[22] On the tondo made by Niccolo dell' Abate see Bernardini 2007, 52–53. On Dalida de' Puti see Prizer 1985, 8–11; Messisbugo 1992, 46; and Prizer 1998, 295–98 and 305–6.

Figure 4.6 Dosso Dossi, *Allegory of Music*, 1520s, oil on canvas, Galleria Estense, Modena. Reproduced by permission of the Ministero per i Beni e le Attività Culturali—Archivio Fotografico della SBSAE di Modena e Reggio Emilia.

partbook, and another partbook lying open and more or less legible on a ledge (Figure 4.6).[23]

Music and Landscape

Alfonso's musical interests were no less substantial than his sister's—although, no doubt on Isabella's model, he seems to have considered patronage of the frottola a feminine preserve, assigning it to his wife Lucrezia Borgia.[24] We know

[23] Images in Humfrey and Lucco 1998, 158–70. To my knowledge the music has not been identified, although Adriano Cavicchi (2004, 84) notes that the text is Italian, suggesting that it is a frottola or early madrigal.

[24] On Lucrezia's music patronage see Prizer 1985, with the additional observations in Shephard 2015. On Alfonso's music patronage see in particular Vander Straeten 1969, 6:94–102; Brown 1975; Lockwood 1976a; Lockwood 1979; Prizer 1980, 14–28; Lockwood 1981, esp. 14–15; Lowinsky 1982; Camiz 1983; Lockwood 1985, esp. 90–91; Prizer 1987; Fenlon

that he played the lute because in 1489 a payment was made for its repair.[25] Correspondence shows that in 1494 Alfonso was taking singing lessons, for which he borrowed a singing method from Isabella.[26] His agent and retainer Girolamo da Sestola taught keyboard instruments, suggesting that Alfonso may have studied them as well.[27] Several documents name him as a player of the viol. In 1499 the instrument maker Lorenzo da Pavia, a regular correspondent of Isabella's, informed Alfonso's sister that the duke was in Venice to order a set of five viols of different sizes, with a view to learning the instrument. Just two months later, in May, Isabella had begun to learn herself, and was planning to play with Alfonso the next time she visited Ferrara.[28] Marino Sanuto records that Alfonso even performed as part of a consort of six viols during the celebrations attendant upon his wedding to Lucrezia Borgia in 1502.[29] Elsewhere we hear that, whilst duke, Alfonso played and sang with members of his personal staff.[30] His early biographers even describe him as a maker of musical instruments—particularly "flauti."[31]

These energetic personal involvements put the lower priority with which Alfonso apparently regarded his chapel choir, in contrast to his father, into perspective.[32] Although Alfonso initially maintained the large choir established by Ercole I as part of a general policy of continuity, his popularity following his successful defense of Ferrara from the pope's armies allowed him to abandon the compensatory strategies of public presentation adopted during his father's troubled reign. Towards the end of the war and after, he turned his attention instead to the development of his spaces for private leisure—a move apparently viewed by his subjects as a just reward for his labors.[33] Alongside the

---

1990; Prizer 1998; Lockwood 1998; Lockwood 2001; Rifkin 2002; Boorman 2006, 274–78 and 285–86; and Cavicchi 2006.

[25] Prizer 1999, 20–21 with n44.

[26] The correspondence is published in Prizer 1999, 17.

[27] Isabella negotiated with Alfonso to borrow Girolamo in the capacity of music teacher more than once in the 1490s—see Prizer 1999, 19–20.

[28] These documents are published in Prizer 1982, 104.

[29] "Al 3.o acto vene una musica de sei viole, assai bona, fra quale vi era il signor don Alfonso." Sanuto 1879–1902, 4:230 (part of the "Ordine di le pompe e spectaculi di le noze de madono Lucrezia Borgia," which occupies 4:222–30).

[30] The evidence in question is that of Angelo Mosti, discussed later in the current chapter. A letter of 1495 mentions that Alfonso's brothers sang together with Ercole in their youth (Lockwood 1972, 113), and there is no reason to doubt that Alfonso did the same.

[31] See the quotations assembled in Camiz 1983, 87.

[32] On Alfonso's dealings with his chapel choir, see in particular Lockwood 1979, 209–11; Prizer 1980, 14–23, 46–52, and Appendix II, Documents 51–58; Shephard 2010b, 55–96; and Shephard forthcoming.

[33] See the excerpt from the encomium on Belvedere by Scipione Balbo given in Fiorenza 2008, 59 and n24; and also Giraldi Cinzio 1556, 154.

preparation of his new apartment, Alfonso took up a venerable Este preoccupation in creating for himself a new rural pleasure palace (*delizia*) on a wooded
island in the Po on the southern outskirts of Ferrara, known as the Boschetto.
The major public project after the war, the revision and rebuilding of sections
of Ferrara's fortifications, supplied the soil for an artificial hill at the north of
the city, on which was built a second villa named Montagnone.[34]

The new directions of Alfonso's extra-musical patronage, although rooted in
Este tradition, were closely in accord with contemporary courtly fashion. In the
early 1500s, following the lead of Jacopo Sannazaro and the Venetian painters
associated with Giorgione, the courts took to their hearts the pastoral mode—a
vision of landscape, founded largely on readings and visualizations of Virgil and
Ovid, which placed shepherds, nymphs, and satyrs in a range of amorous relationships, orbiting around a rural pantheon (Apollo, Bacchus, Ceres, etc.).[35] The pastoral mode played an increasingly important role in court entertainments at Ferrara
under Alfonso, even before the beginning of his reign. The celebrations attendant
upon his wedding in 1502, for example, featured a whole evening of bucolic theatre; and a more properly pastoral drama involving a lovelorn shepherd was performed during the celebrations of the first anniversary of Alfonso's succession.[36]

Although nothing survives of either Montagnone or Boschetto, it is easy
enough to envisage how this pastoral vogue might have inflected their design
and the experience of their delights.[37] A good indication can in fact be found
within the private apartment prepared simultaneously, particularly the studiolo. Drawing on Ovid and Virgil, the room's decoration offered a vision of syl-
van relaxation, showing picnics in lush glades by river banks, and identifying
its patron deities as gods and goddesses of the countryside. It is interesting to
note that these subjects accord more closely with Alberti's advice on the decoration of a villa than with anything he suggests for the urban palace.[38] In effect,

[34] On the *delizie* see Zaniboni 1987; and Fiorenza 2008, 55–63. The villa on the Boschetto,
called Belvedere, was begun in 1513. On Alfonso's alterations to the walls see, in brief, Zaniboni
1987, 24–25.

[35] I am referring to Sannazaro's *Arcadia* (modern edition Sannazaro 1966). On the pastoral
mode in Renaissance Ferrara see Gardner 1906, esp. 49–50; Benvenuti 1979 (discussing the
topos's fifteenth-century Ferrarese roots); Pieri 1982; and Gerbino 2009, 13–100. For an overview of the pastoral mode see Cafritz, Gowing, and Rosand 1988; Freedman 1989; and Hunt
1992.

[36] The bucolic evening in the course of the 1502 entertainments is described on the basis of
Isabella's report to her husband in Gregorovius 1903, 259. The pastoral drama performed dur-
ing the anniversary celebrations, as well as another held in 1508, is described and discussed in
Gerbino 2009, 61–67.

[37] The connection between Belvedere and the vogue for the pastoral is explored at length in
Fiorenza 2008, 49–77.

[38] For Alberti, the rules of decorum in decoration are most relaxed of all in the country villa,
which is "the most lighthearted" of buildings: here, we "are particularly delighted when we see

it seems, Alfonso created a physical setting for his bucolic leisure outside the walls, whilst having the same setting manifested in paint, complete with its classical overtones, within the palace.[39] Such a strategy makes perfect sense in the context of the seasonality of court life: winters at the palace alternated with summers at one of the *delizie*—in Alfonso's reign usually Boschetto.[40]

Alfonso's active musical interests, so far as we can judge, were frequently consonant with this pastoral vein. During the wedding of 1502, a country dance was performed to the accompaniment of the bagpipes; on another occasion, some years later, bagpipes were featured at a banquet held in honor of Lucrezia. As the instrument of the contemporary Italian countryside, the bagpipes were taken up within the pastoral—together with the pipe (*flauto*), which we know Alfonso enjoyed making himself—as the equivalents of the pipes played by Pan and the shepherds of Virgil's *Eclogues*. The anniversary celebrations also featured "pastoral" music, including Apollo playing a "lira" (lyre/lira da braccio), flautists, and a *moresca* danced to the tambourine.[41] Meanwhile, the lute, which Alfonso played, was associated with a more courtly vision of pastoral in paintings such as Giorgione's *Fête champêtre*, via its connection with the shepherd Apollo's lyre.

Further, Alfonso's new pastoral spaces furnished the venues for his music-making. His contemporary biographer, Agostino Mosti, describes musical entertainment during the summer at Boschetto, both in the villa and in its park:

> the Prince himself would [habitually] play the viol in wintertime before dinner, [with] one or another of his valets or private chaplains, and passed thus the time not only before, but also after dinner, singing

paintings of pleasant landscapes or harbours, scenes of fishing, hunting, bathing, or country sports, and flowery and leafy views"—almost all of which could be seen in Alfonso's studiolo, if one includes the Aeneas frieze. Translation Alberti 1988, 299.

[39] Other scholars have also remarked on a close affinity between the decoration of the studiolo and the building of the Boschetto. Several, noting that Boschetto housed a menagerie, have pointed to the large number of animals visible in the studiolo paintings (Fehl 1974a, 69n87; Holberton 1987, 60; Shearman 1987, 215–16; Colantuono 2005, 235–36). Anthony Colantuono (2005, 229ff) has drawn a particularly close connection between Boschetto and Titian's *Bacchanal of the Andrians*, made for the studiolo, which features a river. It is worth noting in this connection that Dosso was engaged in decorating the villa on Boschetto at the same time (1518–19) as he worked on the Via Coperta apartment (Goodgal 1978, 167). For a recent brief but perceptive overview of the importance of landscape in Ferrarese court culture under Alfonso, see Bayer 1998, 43–46.

[40] Charles Rosenberg has proposed a similar reading of the rural vistas prominent in the decoration of the Salone dei Mesi in Palazzo Schifanoia—see Rosenberg 1997, 86.

[41] Gerbino 2009, 62–63; see also 230 on the roots of later pastoral dance in the *moresca*.

two or three motets, French songs, and others, [and] just as [hap-
pened] in summertime at the Villa and at the Boschetto, while they
ate, the musicians sang four or six very dainty songs.[42]

Mosti draws a link between the musical practices of summer and winter, locating the latter implicitly within the private spaces of the palace. Given that the
summer scene of a country picnic with musical entertainment is rehearsed
several times in the decoration of the studiolo, it seems quite possible that it
was considered an appropriate venue for the viol-playing and the singing mentioned—perhaps even that it was designed as such.

We saw in connection with Leonello that the lost fresco decoration of
the villa of Belfiore, described by Sabadino, featured depictions of musical entertainments in the countryside covering several generations of Este
princes, including Ercole I.[43] Although colored with the style of the previous
century, Sabadino's descriptions help to give life to Mosti's brief remark.[44]
Placed in this context, the probable direct connection between the recreation depicted in Alfonso's studiolo and the actual practice of the court
at the *delizie* becomes clearer. The reality of the female recorder players
depicted reclining by a stream in Titian's *Bacchanal of the Andrians* may be
more profound still: an inventory of 1520 notes the presence of three recorders belonging to Ippolito (whose mistress was a professional musician) at
Belfiore.[45]

An indication of the spirit in which such musico-pastoral recreation was
undertaken at the time Alfonso was building his studiolo can be found
in Giorgione's *Fête champêtre* of ca. 1510 (Figure 4.7).[46] In this painting,
a man whose dress identifies him as a contemporary courtier plays his
lute introspectively, whilst enjoying a metaphorical communion with the

---

[42] "il Prencipe [Alfonso I d'Este] stesso averebbe il verno innanzi cena suonato di Viuola,
ma un cotal Cameriere, un Cappellano privato de' suoi, e passato quel tempo non solo avanti,
ma anco dopo la cena, cantato dui o tre mottetti, Canzone Francese, ed altri, come spesse volte
l'istate alla Villa ed al Boschetto mentre si connive i musici averebbono cantato quattro o sei
Canzone molto leggiadre." Solerti 1892, 182.

[43] The section concerning Ercole's court can be found in Gundersheimer 1972, 71.

[44] Descriptions of similar entertainments dating from the end of Alfonso's reign can be found
in Messisbugo 1992.

[45] Lockwood 1985, 98.

[46] The painting is also attributed to Titian, Giorgione completed by Titian, and a follower of
Titian—on the question of its attribution, see Anderson 1997, 308. From among the many published interpretations of this painting, mine is broadly in line with those of Philip Fehl (1957)
and Paul Holberton (1993). For further discussion of the musical aspects of the painting, see
Shephard 2013a, 233–34.

Figure 4.7 Giorgione and/or Titian, *Fête champêtre*, ca. 1510, oil on canvas, Musée du Louvre, Paris. © Bridgeman Art Library.

nymphs and shepherds of Virgil's *Eclogues*.[47] In much the same way that, in Virgil's *Eclogue* 10, the love-grief of the real Roman aristocrat Gallus conjures about him the cast of pastoral characters, the song of the courtier in the *Fête champêtre* (which, doubtless, is about unrequited love in a Petrarchan vein) has conjured forth the nymphs and shepherds latent in the pastoral landscape around him.[48] Holberton notes that the metaphorical presence of nymphs in gardens and landscapes is standard fare in early sixteenth-century writing.[49] Music functions here as the tool that bridges the gap between the real, or human, and the metaphorical, or divine, realms—a role already long ascribed to it in the sphere of religious experience.[50] It seems clear, in this light, that the *Fête champêtre* makes manifest

[47] Some scholars refuse to identify the seated rustic as a shepherd on the basis of his costume, but a comparison with the similarly attired shepherds in Giorgione's slightly earlier *Adoration of the Shepherds* (National Gallery, Washington) overcomes their objection.

[48] It is not important to this point that the courtier is not in fact singing: the achievements of the celebrated lutenist Pietrobono in the previous century had made it possible to hear words in the playing of a lute, as mentioned in chapter 2 above, and after all much of the music played on the lute was arranged from amorous frottole and chansons.

[49] Holberton 1993, 247.

[50] See, for instance, the first, fifth, and sixth prerogatives assigned to music by Gilles Carlier in a treatise of ca. 1470—Cullington 2001, 34–36 and 50–52.

the gently classicizing conception lying behind musico-pastoral leisure. One might conveniently imagine that the man-made drinking fountain in the painting locates us precisely within the groomed nature of a country estate—one whose buildings, perhaps, are those visible in the background.[51] The paintings made for Alfonso's studiolo accomplish a similar task, albeit more obliquely, revealing the depth of their comment upon the duke's musical leisure.

Despite the distinctly secular aspect of the studiolo's decoration, even the motets mentioned by Mosti fit it well. Devotional paintings were featured marginally in the decoration of several Renaissance studioli, private devotion constituting an aspect of the *vita contemplativa*.[52] The motet could sit comfortably also within the pastoral environment, painted or real: from the early 1500s the pastoral mode inflected both religious texts and pictures—in particular small devotional pictures destined (like many motets) for a secular setting.[53] It is interesting to note that what may be the only surviving music manuscript prepared at Alfonso's court, a manuscript of motets mostly by composers in his employ, was copied in octavo partbook format.[54] The tiny size, equivalent to that of Aldus's "pocket" classics and perhaps prompted by the similarly diminutive music publications of Andrea Antico, imports portability—such as one would require when heading out on a summer's day to sing in the gardens of the Boschetto (in the manner of the reclining group in Dosso's *Aeneas in Elysium*).[55] The partbook format perhaps connotes spontaneity and therefore

[51] Cf. David Rosand's brief comments on the relationship between pastoral and leisure in Rosand 1992, 162.

[52] Arguments have been made for the ascription of specific religious paintings to the studioli of Leonello and Federico da Montefeltro—see Clough 1995, 32. Vasari places Titian's *Tribute Money* in Alfonso's studiolo, although if he is correct it was later displaced by mythological paintings—see Hope 1971, 649. For the close connection frequently made between studioli and devotion in general see Boström 1987, 56–58; Liebenwein 1988, 5 and 38; and Thornton 1997, 9–11.

[53] For a recent perceptive analysis of literary and painted Christian pastoral see D'Elia 2005, 9–26. Of course, the motet's presence in a secular setting needs no special justification, and nor does its use as dinner entertainment—see the references given in Shephard 2010a, 109n81.

[54] The manuscript is London, Royal College of Music, Ms. 2037. Only the superius and bassus parts survive. On it see Lowinsky 1968, 3:116–17; Rifkin 2002, esp. n3; and Shephard 2010b, Appendix.

[55] Cf. the letter dated 5 July (i.e., high summer) [1516], published and discussed in Lockwood 1979, 224–34, in which Jean Michel reports to Alfonso's invalid brother Sigismondo that he has been delayed in sending music books "car le Seigneur a esté dehors et les avoir avec luy" (because his Lordship [Alfonso] was away and had them with him). Antico published music partbooks in octavo format, whereas his competitor Petrucci published them in quarto. The most widely used music partbooks in octavo format during the 1520s were therefore Antico's, and included his four volumes of motets.

informality: there would be no need to copy out parts for performance from a sourcebook, as may have been the practice with some choirbooks. It certainly, at octavo size, implies intimacy: more than two to a part would be difficult to manage, and surely one is the intention. The manuscript seems in this analysis to be a natural tool of Alfonso's pastoral musical recreation.

Trouble on Parnassus: Bacchus's Masculine Eloquence

It has become a commonplace of the scholarly tradition that the *Bacchanal of the Andrians* (Figure 4.8) is the most "musical" of the duke's paintings. Erwin Panofsky claimed that it is "unified as well as dynamised by a pervasive rhythm," while David Rosand identifies music as its "organizing principle."[56] The painting has also received attention from eminent musicologists—most particularly Edward Lowinsky, who corresponded on the subject with Panofsky.[57] However, musicological statements on the *Andrians* have been characterized by a reluctance to stray too far into the interpretative territory (and literature) of art historians, whilst art historians have limited themselves in discussion of the musical element to poetic vagueness.

The commission for the painting may have been given immediately after the completion of *Bacchus and Ariadne*, in 1523, and it was probably finished in 1524 or early 1525.[58] As has long been recognized, it is based, like Isabella's *Parnassus* (as I have argued) and *Comus* (as is well established), on a section from the *Imagines* of Philostratus. The relevant ekphrasis describes a picture showing a Bacchanalian festival on the island of Andros:

> The stream of wine which flows on the island of Andros and the Andrians made drunk by the river are the subject of this picture, for the land of the Andrians made rich in wine by Bacchus breaks open and sends (the wine) to them as a river. If you think it is water it is not a large river but if you think it is made of wine then it is large and, of a truth, divine. Were you but to taste it I am sure you would think little of the Nile and the Danube and you might perhaps say that they

[56] Rosand 1987, 85–86; Panofsky 1969, 20–21. The interpretative literature on this painting includes Wind 1948, 60–61; Panofsky 1969, 96–102; Wethey 1969–75, 37–41; Fehl 1974a; Goffen 1997, 107–26; Pedrocco 2001, 140; Jaffé 2003, 106–7; Colantuono 2005.

[57] Panofsky 1969, 101n26; Lowinsky 1982.

[58] Peter Humfrey (Humfrey 2004; Humfrey 2007, 103) has recently suggested on the basis of style that the *Andrians* was painted between the *Worship of Venus* and the *Bacchus and Ariadne*, but the evidence is uncertain, and I retain the conventional view established by Gould (1969, 12).

Figure 4.8   Titian, *Bacchanal of the Andrians*, ca. 1524, oil on canvas, Prado, Madrid.
© Bridgeman Art Library.

would seem better to you if they were smaller, as long as they flowed like this one.

Such things, as I apprehend it, do the Andrians, crowned with ivy and sage, sing to their women and children. Some of them dance on the one and some on the other shore, and others recline on the ground. Perhaps this too may be part of their song, that the river Achelous brings forth reeds and the Peneus in Thessaly has delightful [groves], and Pactolus used to bear flowers, but that this river has the gift to show forth men to be mighty in council, rich, attentive to their friends, and to let them grow beautiful and six foot tall from a small size. For, once a man has drunk his fill of its stream he is equipped to gather all these qualities into one and let them enter into his soul. And perhaps they also sing that this river alone is not waded into by either cattle or horses, but was graciously given by Bacchus to men only to drink from it, and as it is drunk it flows on without ever exhausting its course.

You will have to pay attention to hear that some of them are singing these things, for their [minds] are confused by the wine. But what
you may (readily) see in the picture is the river himself. He is lying
on a bed made of grapes, pours out his source neat, and looks ever so
committed to his desire. And about the river there grow thyrsi, that
is branches wound about with tendrils of vines as they grow by the
water. But if you go beyond the land with the drinking feasts taking
place, there you encounter Tritons with sea-trumpets who dip up
the wine with their trumpets. A part of it they drink and a part they
blow into the air. Some of them are drunk and dance. Bacchus is sail-
ing to the feast on Andros. His ship has already entered the port and
he brings with him satyrs and, together with them, bacchantes and
sileni, and he also brings along Laughter as well as Comus, both very
cheerful gods and great experts at feasting, so that the river's harvest
may be reaped in the sweetest way.[59]

Titian has rendered the text closely, within reason. We have, running
across the foreground, a "stream of wine" which is certainly "not a large
river." Several of the men present possess "crowns of ivy and sage," and two,
at the back left of the main group, "sing to their women and children," who
are also in evidence. We have two people dancing and several reclining on
the ground. The child urinating into the stream dramatizes the assertion
that "as it is drunk it flows on without ever exhausting its course."[60] The
river, personified, "lies on a bed of grapes" on a hill to the right, and "tendrils of vines" wind up the trunk of a tree that "grows by the water." The
sleeping nude at the right foreground, who rests on an urn, is surely the
nymph of the stream overcome by her charge's unusual constituent, an identity that she might well combine with that of Comus, as Harry Murutes has
argued.[61] The scene involving the Tritons has been transposed to a group of
mythically naked men at the left of the picture, their "sea-trumpets" turned
into amphorae and oenochoe. Meanwhile, in the distance, Bacchus's ship
approaches the shore.
    A few elements of the painting appear not to relate directly to the text, but
they may nonetheless have been prompted by Philostratus. About halfway

---

[59] This is Maria Reina Fehl's translation (Fehl 1974b) based on the translation made for
Isabella and later lent to Alfonso.

[60] The urinating child may also be Laughter—see Murutes 1973, esp. 521. If so, it is appropriate that Equicola/Titian should signpost the fact by allowing the child to reveal humorously the
reason for the stream of wine's inexhaustibility.

[61] Murutes 1973, 521–22.

through the second book of the *Imagines*, he offers what seems very like a reprise of the subject of the Andrians' festival, in the description of a painting of an island sacred to Bacchus.[62] This island has been left by Bacchus in the charge of Silenus, who is presumably to be identified with the potbellied figure at the extreme left in Titian's painting. Mention is made of "golden mixing-bowls overturned, and flutes still warm," which feature in the foreground of the *Andrians*. Present also on the sacred island are birds, "for Dionysus provides the vine for all birds," perhaps providing the pretext for Titian's guineafowl (which, with its African associations, is appropriate to a god supposedly raised in Lybia).[63]

Music is present in the painting in the form of the singers, the dancers, and the *flauti*, but its significance for the composition is greater than these motifs alone reveal. The ekphrasis on the Andrians is framed almost entirely in terms of song. Much of the contents of Philostratus's first two paragraphs, describing the central scene and eulogizing the powers of wine, are identified as the song that the Andrians "sing to their women and children." Philostratus makes out that it is through their song that the picture communicates its content to the viewer: "You will have to pay attention to hear that some of them are singing these things, for their [minds] are confused by the wine." In a sense, following Philostratus's conceit, the main scene and theme of Titian's painting emanate from the mouths of the two singers at the back left by the tree line. The ekphrasis indicates very clearly that their song has been inspired by Bacchus's wine.

A close association between Bacchus and music is, of course, strongly in accord with his depiction in antique literary sources. Particularly explicit is Diodorus Siculus, whose *Library of History* was to be found in the Este library in two vernacular translations and would therefore have been especially accessible to Alfonso.[64] According to him, when Dionysus "went abroad he was accompanied by the Muses ... by their songs and dancing and other talents in which they had been instructed these maidens delighted the heart of the god."[65]

---

[62] Philostratus 1931, 2.17.

[63] Anthony Colantuono is therefore wrong to assert that "Titian's portrayal of the Guinea fowl may be inconsistent with a portrayal of the island of Andros" (Colantuono 2005, 234). Colantuono notes (2005, 232–33) that Strabo (*Geography* 5.1.9) mentions the guineafowl as an inhabitant of the islands in the Po, and that Alfonso had the Boschetto stocked with the bird (235). I agree with Colantuono's general argument that elements of the painting are supposed to recall the Boschetto, but I suspect the mechanisms by which that came about were less philologically sophisticated, and less pointedly allegorical, than he makes out.

[64] An inventory of the Este library in the reign of Alfonso's father, Ercole, is published as Appendix II/2 of Bertoni 1903. The two translated copies are listed as nos. 103 and 121; there is also a Latin copy, listed as no. 141.

[65] Diodorus Siculus's comments on Dionysus follow on immediately from the introductory remarks in Book 4 of the *Library of History* (the translation is Diodorus Siculus 1935).

His satyrs, too, were musical, affording the god "great delight and pleasure in connection with their dancings and their goat-songs." Diodorus concludes his remarks on Dionysus by expanding on the musical theme: "There is general agreement also, they say, that he was the inventor of thymelic [i.e., generally, musical] contests, and that he introduced places where the spectators could witness the shows and organized musical concerts; furthermore, he freed from any forced contribution to the state those who had cultivated any sort of musical skill during his campaigns, and it is for these reasons that later generations have formed musical associations of the artists of Dionysus and have relieved of taxes the followers of this profession." Philostratus, not uniquely, combines this common association of Dionysus with music with the literary tradition according to which song is inspired by divine forces, identifying wine as the means of the god's inspiration.

The *Andrians* is the most explicit, but perhaps not the only "song of Bacchus" to be found in Alfonso's studiolo. Several literary sources have been proposed for the *Bacchus and Ariadne* (Figure 4.3), delivered to Ferrara on or shortly before 30 January 1523, including poem 64 of Catullus's *Carmina*, the story of the two lovers as it appears in Ovid's *Fasti* Book 3, and the account in Book 1 of Ovid's *Ars Amatoria*.[66] Among them, the *Ars Amatoria* version, concise but richly visual, offers the most obvious parallel to Titian's picture, with which it shares so many details that one wonders if (and in fact I doubt that) there is any need to involve the other sources directly.[67] Here, again,

[66] On *Bacchus and Ariadne* see in particular Thompson 1956; Gould 1969; Panofsky 1969, 139–44; Wethey 1969–75, 35–37; Lucas and Plesters 1978; Holberton 1986; Goffen 1997, 107–26.

[67] Scholarly opinion (with the exception of Goffen 1997, 118–20, which takes a similar line to me) has recently tended to privilege Catullus among the possible sources, following Holberton's discovery that an edition of the *Carmina* was dedicated to Alfonso in 1520 (Holberton 1986). As I am working from the hypothesis that all of the subjects for the studiolo paintings were designed by Mario Equicola in 1511, I do not hesitate to identify the edition as a reaction rather than a prompt to classical interests developed by the duke in connection with his studiolo. Once the necessary connection between the edition and Alfonso's painting is thus thrown into question, we are at liberty to notice that Catullus's poem relates to Titian's painting hardly at all. Unlike both the Ovidan accounts, it does not mention the moment of the story depicted, and in its wordy and circuitous progress it is littered with extremely lengthy gloss on Ariadne's lament and on the tangential subject of Theseus's adventures. Its several key visual details—especially those in the long description of Ariadne's distress, which Holberton omits from his study—are entirely absent from Titian's picture. The two are in accord only on absolutely conventional aspects of the activities of Bacchus's host, such as the playing of cymbals and tabors, the wearing of snakes, and the tearing apart of animals (Titian does not show a bullock, as Holberton claims and as Catullus requires, but a more standard fawn); references to all of these can be found, for instance, in the passage discussed above from Philostratus's "Islands." In contrast, the several descriptive cues offered by Ovid in the *Ars Amatoria* account are reproduced by Titian faithfully, logically, and in surprising detail.

my concern is not particularly with the story itself, but with the way Ovid chooses to frame it.

In the *Ars Amatoria*, a handbook on love and seduction, the story of Bacchus and Ariadne is introduced with the phrase "Ecce, suum vatem Liber vocat" (Lo! Liber summons his bard): rather like Philostratus's ekphrasis, it is cast within the narrative as a song inspired by Bacchus (or rather, by implication, by wine).[68] Ovid uses the story to introduce advice on the deployment of wine in the seduction of another man's wife. His advice, which immediately follows the story, picks up key motifs in the ancient discourse on wine, already in part familiar from Philostratus:

> When, then, you find yourself at a feast where the wine is flowing freely, and where a woman shares the same couch with you, pray to that god whose mysteries are celebrated during the night, that the wine may not overcloud thy brain. 'Tis then thou mayest easily hold converse with thy mistress in hidden words whereof she will easily divine the meaning. A drop of wine will enable you to draw sweet emblems on the table wherein she will read the proof of the love you have for her. Fix well thine eyes on her and so confirm the message of thy love. Ofttimes, without a word being spoken, the eyes can tell a wondrous tale. When she has drunk, be thou the first to seize the cup, and where her lips have touched, there press thine own and drink. Choose thou the dainties that her fingers have lightly touched, and as thou reachest for them, let thy hand softly encounter hers. Be courteous to her husband too. Nothing could better serve your plans than to be in his good graces.[69]

The whole episode regarding Bacchus and Ariadne in the *Ars Amatoria* is striking not only for its musical frame, but for the purposeful, in fact playful poverty of the moral framework with which the Bacchic song is associated. Although in this case the frame does not become a part of Titian's picture, it seems improbable, given the range of alternatives, that the story's literary context did not influence the choice of source. The painting's subtext is, according to this reading, as a song inspired by Bacchus that offers a model in seduction.

Given the presence of these explicit and implicit painted "Bacchic songs" in Alfonso's studiolo, it is at least highly suggestive that a contemporary musical setting of an ancient text about Bacchic eloquence survives from his court. Around 1520 the composer Adrian Willaert, an employee of first Alfonso's

[68] Ovid 1929, 1.525. On the implications of the word "vates," translated here appropriately as "bard," see chapter 2 of the present study.

[69] Ovid 1929, 1.565–80.

brother Ippolito and then Alfonso himself, made a song out of a section of Horace's fifth epistle, a text which locates the qualities of wine mentioned by Philostratus and Ovid in the context of senatorial leisure (Example 4.1).[70] In high summer, Horace invites a friend to dinner at sunset, entices him with the promise of wine, and reminds him that the following day is a holiday. He continues, "I shall begin the drinking and the scattering of flowers, and shall suffer you, if you will, to think me reckless"; then follow the lines set by Willaert:

> quid non ebrietas dissignat? operta recludit,
> spes iubet esse ratas, ad proelia trudit inertem,
> sollicitis animis onus eximit, addocet artes.
> fecundi calices quem non fecere disertum?

> What a miracle cannot the wine-cup work! It unlocks secrets, bids hopes be fulfilled, thrusts the coward into the field, takes the load from anxious hearts, teaches new arts. The flowing bowl—whom has it not made eloquent?[71]

Willaert's song is known principally from the theoretical discourse that built up around it over the course of the sixteenth century on account of its startling musical technique.[72] Its musical trick lies in the modulation of a single part within the four-voice texture, such that the song ends with an E♭♭ and a D in unison. In theory, the interval is a kind of 7th and should make a discord, but in practice it would almost inevitably come out as an octave. Accordingly, music history has interpreted the song in the context of contemporary music theory, largely ignoring the probability that it was a product of Alfonso's patronage.[73] It offers a clear and concise statement of what one might call the "theology" of Bacchic inspiration employed and implied in the paintings; further, it proceeds from a leisured scenario closely in accord with the scenes depicted therein. It seems almost inevitable that the connection was intended, or at least noted: the song belongs in the studiolo.

---

[70] On the ideologically charged relationship between Renaissance and Roman conceptions of noble leisure, see Vickers 1990. On Roman precedents for the studiolo in particular see Liebenwein 1988, 3–4. On Willaert's employment in Ferrara see Lockwood 1985; and Shephard 2012.

[71] Horace 1926, 1.5.16–9. The extensive and sometimes bad-tempered literature on this song includes Lowinsky 1956–59; Bent 1984, esp. 16–20; Berger 1987, 39–48; Keyser 1992.

[72] See in particular Giovanni Spataro's correspondence, published as Blackburn, Lowinsky, and Miller 1991. The exchange concerning *Quid non ebrietas* involves letters 3, 12–14, 28, 29, 53, and 60.

[73] Spataro claims in a letter of 23 May 1524 to his friend Pietro Aaron that "Son già passati tri anni, et credo ancora che siano più de quattro, che da uno Messer Laurentio Burgomozo

nelle compoſitioni da loro fatte ; il che non apporta ſe non vergogna infi-
nita.

Luca. *Di queſte impertinentie ne ragionaremo un'altra volta à miglior*
propoſito ; per hora attendiamo à queſta Cantilena di M. Adriano, che ve-
ramente fu un belliſſimo penſiero.

Vario. *Fu di merauiglia all'hora, (&) adeſſo farà ſtupire qualch'uno, che più*
non l'ha veduto, nè ſentito nominare ; è vero che forniſce in ſettima, appa-
rente, come voi detto già hauete ; ma ſe noi vorremo con lo intelletto bene
eſſaminarlo, ritrouaremo che la viſta viene ingannata ; & che queſta Can-
tilena fatta da M. Adriano, huomo ſingolare a' noſtri tempi, forniſce in ot-
taua, & non in ſettima, come appare ; & acciò meglio potiate vederla à
voſtro comodo, ecco che vi faccio dono di una Copia, fedelmente dallo
originale di mano di M. Adriano copiata.

F

Ragionamento

Et ſe bene Gio. Spadaro Muſico Bologneſe, di quei tempi, in ʋn ſuo Diſcorſo, ò lettera, già ſcritta l'Anno 1524. à D. Pietro Aaron alli 9. di Settemb. come ʋi moſtrerò di ſua propria mano; Conclude, che l'ultima figurą Cantabile nella graue parte, poſta; forniſca per ʋn Comma Antico più graue di ʋn'ottaua, ilqual Comma è maggiore del Moderno, come potete ʋedere in queſta demoſtratione, & di quanto.

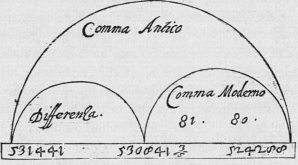

Tuttauia è degno di molta ſcuſa, perche col ſuo Maeſtro, che tutto era Boetiano, tenea per fermo, che l'Antica ſpetie Diatona, che nè ſuoi Tetracordi camina per Tuono e Tuono ambidui ſeſquiottaui, & ʋn Semituono di proportione ſuper 13 partiente 243. foſſe quella ſpetie che ſi Cantaſſe, & Sonaſſe in ogni ſorte d'Inſtromento : & non la Syntona di Tolomeo, che dallo acuto al graue procede per dui Tuoni, ma differenti di proportione l'uno dą l'altro; & ʋn Semituono di proportione ſeſquiquintadecima; erra ne' principij & perciò biſogna che nella Concluſione ſia falſo: & quando ancora haueſſe eſſaminata la Cantilena, ſecondo la Mente di Tolomeo; per la ʋarietà de' Semituoni, & Tuoni, haurebbe fatta ancora la Concluſione falſa; & pur M. Adriano non hebbe mai penſiero di uolere che la Cantilena haueſſe il fine in ſettima; nè più graue, nè più acuto dell'ottaua, ma in ottaua perfetta.

Luca. *Gio. Spataro è ſtato a' ſuoi giorni huomo acutiſſimo nella Muſica, però mi dà l'animo, che ʋedremo qualche coſa notabile, e bella.*

Vario.

Example 4.1 Willaert's "chromatic duo" as it appears in Giovanni Maria Artusi's *L'Artusi overo, delle imperfettioni della moderna musica ragionamenti dui* (Venice, 1600), fols. 21r and 21v. Reproduced by permission of University of Glasgow Library, Department of Special Collections.

The song's unusual construction contributes directly to this connection. Willaert has turned compositional technique to the ends of allegory. The modulating voice of the song, inspired by the "eloquence" of wine, stumbles from hexachord to hexachord, but in the end its blundering reveals a secret of musical notation, a "new art." However, paradoxically, because of the trick, the singer who is actually drunk may well fail to find his way through the song, whose difficulty in performance (according to Giovanni Spataro) defeated even the papal musicians. Thus *Quid non ebrietas* both unlocks and confounds voice, revealing the irony of Bacchic eloquence so obviously implied by the last line of its text: "Whom has the wine-cup not made eloquent?"

The account of Bacchic eloquence given by Philostratus, Ovid, and Horace is not a wholly serious one. Philostratus has his tongue firmly in his cheek when he claims that wine "has the gift to show forth men to be mighty in council, rich, attentive to their friends, and to let them grow beautiful and six foot tall from a small size." Nonetheless, their various transgressions tend towards a single end. Philostratus places his song quite specifically in the mouths of the Andrian men; Ovid's lesson in seduction is cheerfully misogynistic; and Horace's epistle is addressed from one male friend to another. Even the word ἀνδρός (andros) in Greek is the genitive of ἀνήρ, meaning "man."[74] The combination is not casually but pointedly masculine: Bacchus's eloquence is a gift to men, his song sung by a man's voice.

da Mutina, el quale era cantore de la musica secreta de Papa Leone, me fu dicto che da Messer Adriano, musico celeberimo, el quale sta con lo illustrissimo Duca de Ferrara, haveva mandato uno duo a la Beatitudine de Papa Leone, el quale duo finiva in septima" (Already three years have passed, and I believe even more than four, since one Mr Laurentio Burgomozo of Mutina, who was a singer among the private musicians of Pope Leo [X], told me that Mr Adriano [Willaert], celebrated musician, who is with the illustrious Duke of Ferrara, had sent a duo to the Beatitude of Pope Leo, the which duo finishes on a seventh)—Blackburn, Lowinsky, and Miller 1991, letter 12. Thus the "duo" (known contemporaneously in four parts) was sent to Rome ca. 1519–21, and may have been composed around that time. Willaert worked from 1515 for Cardinal Ippolito d'Este, Alfonso's brother. He went to Hungary with Ippolito in October 1517. By August 1519 he had returned, and was apparently in Ferrara without his employer until March 1520. At the Cardinal's death in September 1520 he transferred into the service of Alfonso. As Willaert may have been effectively a free agent at court in 1519 and early 1520, his relationship with Alfonso might easily precede his formal employment; in any case, the Estense of that generation frequently shared retainers unofficially. Though the balance is not clear, it therefore seems more likely that "Quid" was written for Alfonso than for Ippolito. (On Willaert's early employment by the Estense see Lockwood 1985; and Shephard 2012.)

[74] A very similar pun is used in the dedication to Boccaccio's popular *De claris mulieribus*, whose dedicatee was Andrea Acciaiuoli: "when I saw that what Nature has taken from the weaker sex God in His liberality has granted to you, instilling marvellous virtues within your breast, and that He willed you to be known by the name you bear (since in Greek *andres* means 'men'), I felt that you should be set equal to the worthiest of men, even among the ancients"—Boccaccio 1963, Dedication, xxxiii–xxxv.

Such overt masculinity seems natural in the context of Alfonso's studiolo decoration, but, like Isabella's decoration, it may also have had a specific music-ideological end in view. Castiglione, through Signor Gaspare, gave voice in his *Courtier* to the very common view that "music...is most certainly very suited to women...but not to real men": serious interest in music could be considered effeminate.[75] Alfonso may therefore have felt that the masculinity of his musical pastimes needed underlining. In the context of the *Courtier*, the remark is immediately dealt a lengthy classicizing riposte, equivalent (although rather different in character) to the classicizing riposte given in paint and in song in Alfonso's studiolo.

Alfonso's playful assertion of musical masculinity may have had a programmatic as well as a conventional element. When Henry Cornelius Agrippa wanted to satirize and condemn music and the Muses in the 1520s, it was to the musicianship of Bacchus that he turned for ammunition from antiquity:

> Music hath ever been wandering here and there for price and pence, and is the servant of bawdry which no grave, modest, honest, and valiant man ever professed: and therefore the Greeks with a common word called them the Artificers of Father Bacchus, or else (as Aristotle sayeth) *Dionisiaci technitae*, that is the artificers of the Baccanalia, which for the most part, were always used to have lewd customs: leading for the most part, an unchaste Life: partly also in Misery, and Poverty, the which breedeth and increaseth the Vices....And yet for this, these Musicians do much boast...they affirm that the Heavens themselves to sing, yet with voices never heard of any man, except perhaps they have come to the knowledge of those musicians by means of their *Euouae*, or through Drunkenness, or Dreaming.[76]

---

[75] "Allor, il signor Gaspar, La musica penso, disse, che insieme con molte altre vanità sia alle donne conveniente sí, e forse ancor ad alcuni che hanno similitudine d'omini, ma non a quelli che veramente sono; i quali non deono con delizie effeminare gli animi, ed indurgli in tal modo a temer la morte." Text Castiglione 1947, 117; translation Castiglione 1967, 94. For more on this point, see Shephard 2015.

[76] "Hinc Musica ipsa ad precium & stipem semper uagabunda extitit, & lenociniorum clientula, quam nullus unquam professus est uir grauis, modestus, pudicus, fortis. Ideoque Graeci illos communi uocabulo, Liberi patris artifices, siue (ut Aristoteles) Dionysiacos technitas, hoc est, artifices bacchanales appellarunt, qui improbis esse moribus magna ex parte consueuerunt, uitam plurimum traducentes incontinenter, partim etiam cum inopia, quae quidem uitia, & gignit, & auget....Atque tamen hinc plurimum gloriantur Musici isti...ipsos etiam coelos canere affirment, uocibus tamen a nullo unquam mortalium auditis, nisi forte quod Musicis istis per suum euouae, seu per temulentiam, uel insomnium innotuerunt." Text Agrippa 1531, fols. 33r–34r; translation Agrippa 1974, fols. 28v–29v. On Agrippa's *De vanitate* see Keefer 1988, with an assessment of previous opinion.

I suggest that, similarly, Alfonso's Bacchic songs set out to establish a subversive alternative to the patronage of the Muses, conventionally invoked in a studiolo—most recently by Isabella. He set out to inscribe his room in specific response to the musical ideologies usually associated with studioli, and deployed in that context by his sister. However, the duke's purpose, unlike Agrippa's, was not to moralize: none of his literary reference points adopt more than the most gently taunting of tones.

A couple of visual clues in the *Andrians* suggest that Alfonso's response may have been more literal than one might expect. This, the most explicitly musical of the duke's pictures, seems at some points to make contact with its Mantuan equivalent, the *Parnassus*. The design of the two images co-locates the Hippocrene spring and the river of wine—two rather different "sources of eloquence." Furthermore, the *Andrians* contains what looks like a direct quote from the *Parnassus*: the chiton-wearing dancer, whose style of dress is not shared by the other women in the painting, and whose appearance and movement match exactly those of Mantegna's chiton-wearing dancing Muses (Figures 4.10 and 4.11). With the dancer, perhaps, the *Andrians* achieves (though more gently) the trick of satire proposed by Agrippa, and latent in the tradition of depicting the Muse Erato as a bacchante (Figure 4.9).[77] Drawing on the licentious connotations that Isabella sought to evade, it interpolates the supposedly exemplary and inspiring Muses into the Bacchic account of poetic inspiration, revealing and releasing the sensuality of their dance in the *Parnassus* as evidence of their prior debt to the god of wine (of which Diodorus Siculus reminds us in the passage given above).

Such proximities between the siblings' studioli are supported, indeed promoted, by the circumstances under which Alfonso's paintings were made. Quite apart from the interest Alfonso may himself have taken in Isabella's rooms, his paintings were (I have argued) in some sense designed by Mario Equicola, Isabella's personal tutor and a family acquaintance of long standing. His interest in Philostratus, itself an imitation of his sister, was facilitated by the loan of Isabella's vernacular translation of the text, as I mentioned in chapter 3 above. Dosso Dossi, who worked on the studiolo decorations, had previously found employment at the court of Mantua and may have worked there with Lorenzo Costa, who contributed two paintings to Isabella's studiolo.[78] Most tellingly, according to a letter of 22 November 1519, written by

[77] A visual tradition known in Ferrara since the 1460s depicted Erato as a dancing Bacchic musician wearing a chiton, appropriating a figure common on late antique Bacchic sarcophagi. For further examples, see Campbell 2004, figs. 60 and 64; Syson 2002, 55–61.

[78] Fiorenza 2008, 13.

Figure 4.9 Master of the E-Series of the so-called "Tarocchi di Mantegna," *Erato*, 1465, Hamberger Kunsthalle, Hamburg. © bpk | Hamburger Kunsthalle | Christoph Irrgang.

Figure 4.10 Dancing muses, detail from Mantegna, *Parnassus* (Figure 3.1).
© RMN-Grand Palais (Musée du Louvre) / Stéphane Maréchalle.

the Ferrarese courtier and musician Girolamo da Sestola, Dosso and Titian
travelled to Mantua together in that month and inspected Isabella's studiolo.[79]
One might reasonably suppose that the artists' journey was undertaken precisely to facilitate a close visual response. It seems, too, Isabella recognized
that Alfonso's studiolo was undertaken at least partly in discussion with her
own. She kept herself very well informed on the progress of his new apartment, and visited (together with Equicola) almost as soon as it was physically
finished.[80] Further, she demonstrably viewed her studiolo as ripe for emulation: in 1506 she wrote congratulating her husband on the similar rooms he
was preparing in his new Palazzo di San Sebastiano, noting in particular that
he "has learned from the example of my room."[81] Finally, a spirit of artistic

[79] Wethey 1969–75, 39n203. Clifford Brown (1986, 37) gives a similar reading of this visit.

[80] A letter of 13 May 1520 from Mario Equicola in Ferrara to Federico Gonzaga (Isabella's son)
reports that "Madama Illustrissima allogia alle Camere nove del Signor Duca" (My Illustrious
Lady (i.e., Isabella) lodges in the new rooms of the Lord Duke)—text Hope 1971, Appendix,
document X. She had a visit in mind at least as early as September 1518, as we learn from a letter
to her from Obizzo Remo, Alfonso's secretary, of the 16th of that month (Hope 1987, 30).

[81] "ha pur imparato da la mia camara." Text and translation Bourne 2001, 93.

Figure 4.11 Chiton-wearing dancer, detail from Titian, *Bacchanal of the Andrians* (Figure 4.8). © Bridgeman Art Library.

exchange is suggested by the fact that Isabella kept in her studiolo a beech-wood chest of Alfonso's own manufacture.[82]

It appears that the musical ideologies inscribed upon Alfonso's walls established a sophisticated but coherent dialectic with those espoused by his sister. Like those of Isabella and Leonello, his paintings offered, at least on the level of metaphor, to facilitate musico-poetic recreation in a classicizing vein. The nature of that facilitation reveals the parameters and preoccupations of the identity thereby construed. Alfonso's response to his sister was as gendered as her statement: for reasons of basic decorum, Isabella, as a woman, could not have chosen the subjects he chose, and that was partly the point. Perhaps here we detect an element of competition: Alfonso's interests as a performing musician were real and, within a carefully circumscribed circle, public; but their yardstick was inevitably his famous sister, who became a marchesa some fifteen years before he became a duke.[83] In Alfonso's studiolo, in my view, we find an index of the strategies he employed to distinguish his own, masculine, musical personality from that of his sister.

Viewing, Performance, and Identity

The most manifestly musical element of the *Andrians* is yet to be discussed. In the foreground, in front of the reclining women, there is a small scrap of paper bearing the title "Canon," a C1 clef, a c-slash mensuration sign, a series of notes (some with *signa congruentiae*), and a repeat sign (Example 4.2). Beneath the notes is a French text:

> Qui boyt et ne reboyt, Il ne scet que boyre soit

> Who drinks and doesn't drink again, He knows not what drinking is

This canon, in which the single short line of music is to be realized as a multi-voiced and relatively lengthy song, has been the subject of disagreement

---

[82] No. 215 in the inventory of her grotta and studiolo as published in Ferrari 2001: "tre cassette di faggio cornisate, due fatte per maestro Merigo Thedesco, l'altra per il di felice memoria signor Alphonso, duca di Ferrara."

[83] Interestingly, Celio Calcagnini, the most prominent scholar at Alfonso's court, noted in a text circulating in the 1510s that "nulla praeclara ingenia posse ingentes profectus facere, nisi habeant antagonistem (ut Graeci dicunt) qui cum decertent" (no famous talents can enlarge themselves unless they have an antagonist, as the Greeks call it, with whom they can strive)—the text is discussed briefly in Campbell 2005, 639–40, where the relevant passage is given in text and translation as n25.

Example 4.2 Smith's transcription and realization of the canon in the *Andrians*, published in *Renaissance News* 6. Reproduced by permission of the University of Chicago Press.

among scholars.[84] Various resolutions have been proposed: some attractive, some plausible, some completely unworkable. Several key pieces of information are provided in the "score." The c-slash sign suggests that we are in duple meter, which accords with the distribution of the text; the three *signa congruentiae* indicate the moments at which new voices should enter, spaced at intervals of one minim (which is also consonant with the duple meter), and leading to four voices singing together; the repeat marks suggest that the

[84] Musicological discussions of the canon include Smith 1953; Dart 1954; Panofsky 1969, 101n26 (referring to correspondence with Lowinsky); Scherliess 1972; Shinneman 1974;

melody, once sung, should be repeated; and the prominent inclusion of the word "Canon" (literally "rule") suggests that the song's lyric gives some crucial clue as to how to make a realization work. In performance, the first two aspects present no serious problems if the entries arrive at the (perfectly conventional) falling 4th, but as soon as the first voice repeats, the song falls apart in a cacophony of discords.

To overcome the problem, we look to the "rule" for a clue and understand it thus: "Who sings once and doesn't repeat, he knows not how to make the song repeat." The phrase is, read thus, a taunt. It confirms us in our belief that something must change on the repeat, but is extremely reticent about what that thing should be—something to do with knowing "what drinking is." Trial and error reveals that the correct solution is for each singer individually to rise a single scale degree upon their repeat, leading to an infinitely repeatable and (largely) contrapuntally correct four-part song; but even armed with this knowledge, the link is not clear. Lowinsky, who first pointed out that there must be a connection between the "rule" and the resolution, suggested that drinking was thought of as "getting high," but his arguments are not compelling. More likely, I think, the lyric of this song, like the Philostratus and the Horace, is a gently ironic eulogy of the inspiration to eloquence found in wine. It is by following the allegorical cue that the singers are supposed to find their voice, and to successfully perform the song; but by accepting the eloquence of wine they reveal themselves as foolish, because, rising by step, they will eventually overreach their range and find themselves hoarse. The knowledge of "what drinking is" is thus a knowledge of the (light-hearted) Bacchic theology of inspiration that I identified in both Philostratus's and Titian's *Andrians*.

In effect, then, *Qui boyt* is a loose reworking of *Quid non ebrietas*, collapsed to a single line so as to fit into the space of the painting without sacrificing legibility. This observation adds weight to the argument, current in musicology since the 1950s, that Willaert composed the canon for the *Andrians*. Although apparently simple in its means, *Qui boyt* is by no means simple in its effect, and a significant degree of contrapuntal skill (as well as considerable musical curiosity) must have contributed to its conception.[85] A surprising proportion of Willaert's work

Bonicatti 1980; Lowinsky 1982. I largely follow the realization proposed by Smith 1953, whose view was valuably revised and extended by Edward Lowinsky in Panofsky 1969 and Lowinsky 1982. Dart, Scherliess, and Shinneman offer sharply divergent solutions, all of which are clearly wrong for one reason or another; the literature is subjected to thorough review in Lowinsky 1982, and thus I will not bother with individual refutations here. Bonicatti 1980 largely agrees with Lowinsky, in both mechanics and interpretation.

[85] The idea, put forward by Philip Fehl (1987, 124), that Titian wrote the song himself is entirely implausible.

transmitted in Italian sources early in his career makes use of canonic procedures, adding to the case that he possessed both skill and curiosity in unusual measure.[86]

A fascinating role for the canon can be unearthed by applying a suggestion made by both Smith and Lowinsky: that the canon works just as well in performance if two of the four voices read it upside-down (see Example 4.1 for a score).[87] In fact, we can extend this to say that the canon can be performed with any combination of upside-down and normally read voices (i.e., 4+0, 3+1, 2+2, 1+3, 0+4). The music is presented in the painting as if it has been involved in the entertainments of the reclining women, and it is thus upside-down to the viewer. Lowinsky tried to identify two characters in the painting who might have been sitting opposite the ladies to read the music upside-down, but his attempt is not convincing. Instead, in my view, we, the viewers, are the remaining musicians: we read the song upside-down, as it appears to us, whilst the Andrians read it the right way up. The resulting (metaphorical) performance might then involve any combination of viewers and Andrians.[88] The song thus emerges as an interface between the Andrians' world and ours.

The music is here serving as a device to penetrate the picture plane. In this respect it is analogous to the characters termed by Michael Baxandall *festaiuoli*, who play a similar role in many Renaissance paintings—including the others made for Alfonso's room by Titian.[89] The music even occupies a similar position within the picture to its counterparts in the *Worship of Venus* and *Bacchus and Ariadne*. The similarity suggests that the canon, quite likely at about eye-level, is specifically intended to influence and direct the viewer's engagement with the painting. The song draws you into the Andrians' world, and they into yours, offering a cue in the interpretation of the painting.

In conceit, through this mechanism, the painting puts into the viewer's own mouth the ekphrastic power of the song—explanatory both in its relation to Philostratus's musical conceit and in the song's own account of Bacchanalian inspiration. The viewer is himself inspired to sing by and about wine, in imitation

---

[86] For a discussion of the role of canonic techniques in Willaert's early career, see Shephard 2012.

[87] Smith 1953, 52; Lowinsky 1982, 298, 308–9, and 313–14.

[88] Though I have no doubt that the song received a few full performances in the studiolo, it is important to bear in mind that its explanatory force operates largely as a conceit—as a more explicit version of the song of the Muses in the *Parnassus*. It is no more necessary for the viewers to actually sing their parts to experience the conceit than it is for the Andrians to actually sing theirs. Nonetheless, it is worth noting with Gerbino that courtiers sometimes took part in pastoral dramas, with the result that, within the pastoral mode, "A clear distinction between the mental coordinates of the literary world and those of the real world had become (or had been made) almost impossible" (2009, 137).

[89] Baxandall 1972, 72–75. The trick is advocated by Alberti 1972, 82–83. The mechanisms and effects I will proceed to assign to this musical *festaiuolo* are similar to those identified by Randolph Starn for equivalent characters in the *Camera degli Sposi* (Starn 1989, 210–17, esp. 216–17).

of (and in concert with) the Andrians as described by both Philostratus and Titian; and in that song he reveals the picture's significance and the source of its animation in Bacchus's questionable eloquence. In placing the text of the song into the viewer's own voice, it renders the viewer's engagement with the painting a performed ekphrasis, effectively dramatizing Philostratus's conceit. Just as Philostratus encodes the interpretation of his "picture" into the song of the Andrians, so the canon, as a process of viewing, conjures and animates the painting anew in each instance of viewing.

Through this canon and the mechanisms of meaning it interpolates into the painting, Alfonso can be seen to have designed into the *Andrians* a job of mediation that helped him to inscribe his leisured identity upon the room, and upon the experiences available therein. The canon offers a taunt to the uninitiated viewer: it withholds the song, and the painting, as a tantalizingly signifying "secret" (to use Horace's term), to be revealed by someone who knows "what drinking is." In adopting the canon-conundrum as almost a rite of entry, the image refers the viewer inescapably back to a definitive, unlocking view—that of Alfonso. His mediation is necessary to a "correct" viewing of the picture, and through his mediation, the song, and the process of viewing that unfolds through it, the viewer is interpolated into Alfonso's strategy of self-construction.[90]

It is interesting, in this light, to measure the canon against Isabella's musical impresa. For a start, the two look very similar, which may well be intentional (the canon seems to partake of the world of imprese, devices, and emblems as much as it does of any musical genre).[91] In the previous chapter I argued that Isabella's impresa is about voice—its withholding, its assertion, its uncertain morality. I have suggested above that the canon in the *Andrians* is also concerned with voice, its paradoxical release and silencing through wine. Perhaps this is another point on which Alfonso challenges Isabella's claims to agency and identity: in an appropriate paradox, the canon inserts into the silent space of her impresa a song celebrating the moral uncertainty of song that was the very reason for her prudent silence.

---

[90] Stephen Kolsky suggests that a similarly exclusive vision of meaning and its revelation informed Isabella's image-making: Kolsky 1984, 54. My arguments here also bring Alfonso's paintings into close alignment with Mimi Hellman's interpretation of other domestic objects (especially furniture) in eighteenth-century France (Hellman 1999): according to Hellman, "objects were not simply owned, but indeed *performed*" (417), through their design imposing upon the user "aesthetically and socially desirable conduct" (422), making of leisure a kind of work whose object was "the fabrication of elite identity" (416).

[91] On the close relationship between musical puzzles and imprese, devices, and emblems, see Durosoir 1981; and Stras 2005. On the intellectual currency of emblems at Alfonso's court see Fiorenza 2004.

Alfonso's Agency

We are left with a larger question of art and agency. So far I have characterized the *Andrians*, the *Bacchus and Ariadne, Quid non ebrietas,* and the *Andrians'* musical canon as tools designed by Alfonso to help establish in the space of the studiolo his particular vision of classicizing leisure, in friendly competition with that of his sister. But what about Titian and Willaert? What of their agency and prerogative as artists?

The canon is particularly revealing in this respect. Surprisingly, it is difficult to fully integrate *Qui boyt* into the musical logic of the picture and its textual model. It would be tempting to suppose that it is the song sung by the Andrian men "to their women and children," and indeed, as I have argued above, it does serve a function similar to that given to the Andrians' song by Philostratus. But the singing men in the picture are several meters from the music and paying it no attention at all. In fact, as I have noted above, the music seems to be placed for the use of the reclining group, but they too are difficult to resolve into a coherent ensemble for the song. In the foreground there are four recorders, two held by the reclining women and two discarded—by whom? One, lying in the stream, could belong to the reclining nymph, though her participation in any recent activity seems unlikely; the other might have been played by the seated man, or perhaps the man losing his balance in the center was also sitting with the group. Which of these five performers took the four parts of the song? Why would they play it on recorders when its text is so relevant to the import of the painting? How did their performance relate to that of the singing men? Have two conflicting performances been taking place at once?

These problems lead to the unexpected observation that the various protagonists fit together much more comfortably if they are excused from the requirement to relate in some specific and logical way to the notated music. Without the canon, we can very easily see that, as I suggested much earlier, the two men are the Andrians "singing to their women and children," whilst the presence of the "silent" recorders is perhaps inspired by their presence on a very similar Bacchanalian island described elsewhere in the *Imagines*.

In purely visual terms, the canon lies rather unconvincingly in the picture-space, half resting on a fold of a dress and half dangling over the bank towards the stream, in contrast to the more convincing placement of other objects depicted on the ground around it. It has been painted rather thinly over the top of the completed dress and riverbank, which can be seen quite clearly through the paper. Most likely, the canon was added late in the production of the picture, and was not an initial part of Titian's scheme for realizing Philostratus's ekphrasis.

The documented circumstances of Titian's work for Alfonso in the studiolo certainly allow for such an afterthought, and even allow for its instigation by Alfonso himself. Specific evidence survives to attest that, on several occasions, Titian left an appreciable amount of work to complete in situ on his paintings for Alfonso. The evidence reveals explicitly that, whilst working thus in Ferrara, the artist was willing to alter his paintings at Alfonso's request.[92] Court records note his presence in Ferrara from 14 April to 28 June 1524, and yet again from 3 December 1524 to 13 February 1525, the most likely occasions for the delivery of the *Andrians*. As Titian otherwise never incorporated notated music into his pictures, whereas Dosso not infrequently did, it seems likely that here the more celebrated artist was required to accommodate an aspect of Ferrarese taste.[93]

Alfonso's dealings with other artists show a similar eagerness to prompt them to visit in person. Presumably, he preferred to have work done on the spot in Ferrara precisely so that he could supervise it and effect such interventions. This preference probably lies behind the continuing presence at court of Dosso—who was less renowned than Titian, Raphael, and Michelangelo but, according to Vasari, was appreciated by Alfonso for being amiable and pleasant.[94] His musical counterpart, Maistre Jhan, was similarly viewed as a master of the second rank; but judging from his large output of motets, including several mentioning members of the Este family, he must have been a biddable and flattering retainer. Perhaps Jhan was valued similarly for the fact that, unlike "celebrity" musicians such as Josquin and Mouton who visited Ferrara only briefly, he was content to work under the conditions of Alfonso's engaged and interventionist patronage. In his early biography of the duke, Mosti recalls that Alfonso "greatly loved" those courtiers "whom he saw to be solicitous and diligent in their business, and he praised and favored [such men]."[95]

[92] See Campori 1874; Venturi 1928, 103ff; Goodgal 1978, at 176–77; Hope 1987, 26–27. The most detailed documentation concerns *Bacchus and Ariadne*, to which Titian acknowledges that Alfonso may wish to add things once the painting is in Ferrara.

[93] Notated music appears in at least three paintings by Dosso from the 1520s and early 1530s: the *Allegory of Music* (two canons—see Slim 1990); the *Allegory with Pan* (an open part-book); and the rhomboid *Allegory of Music* mentioned earlier. (Cf. the survey of musical elements in Dosso's work offered in Slim 1990, 43–48.) As far as I know, no other painting by Titian at this date features notated music, though some feature music-making (most famously the *Fête Champêtre*, discussed above, and the *Three Ages of Man*); however, in this respect, too, he is exceeded by Dosso.

[94] See Fiorenza 2008, 14.

[95] "il Duca Alfonso si dilettava, e si è sempre dilettato d'uomini virtuosi non meno d'artegiani, che di Cortegiani da spasso amava molto quelli uomini che vedeva solleciti e diligenti alle loro botteghe, e li laudava e favoriva." Solerti 1892, 178.

A scenario not dissimilar to that evidenced for the paintings can be pieced together more circumstantially for *Quid non ebrietas*. The song achieves its association with the *Andrians* and *Bacchus and Ariadne* through the technical tricks of its making: the allegory is not audible in successful performance. Thus the work is meaningless as a product of patronage unless its making—its composition—is as much an object of the patron's interest as its singing; in other words, the performance of the song, like the performance of the paintings, began with its conception. Thus the full range of cultural products here connected with the self-conscious making of Alfonso's musical identity also evidence his related interest in the business of making art—a preoccupation that is perhaps not surprising in light of his reported practical interest in crafts such as founding and pottery (and, of course, making musical instruments).

The corollary of this, and of Alfonso's preference for artists like Dosso and Jhan, is that whilst the duke certainly was also interested in artists of large reputation, he did not participate wholeheartedly in the innovation of the fetishization of the great artist's product (as his dealings with Raphael make clear)—a circumstance that has previously been seen as a stain on his character as a patron.[96] In my analysis, it should be seen instead as a feature of his particular interest in the arts, and as a reflection of his self-conscious and inventively manifested concern to manipulate through art the programmatic requirements of his princely identity.

[96] See in particular Alfonso's rather pragmatic and hard-nosed dealings with Raphael (Shearman 1987); Bellini's *Feast of the Gods* (Bull and Plesters 1990; Goodgal 1987); and Michelangelo (Rosenberg 2000): the last two scholars cited go to great lengths to argue, against the grain of the evidence, that Alfonso bought into the inviolable "hand of the master." The same hard-nosed approach can perhaps be seen in his dealings with Bidon in the 1510s. Probably the most famous singer in Italy during the second decade of the sixteenth century, Bidon left Alfonso's employ around 1513 to work for Leo X. He offered (with some confidence) to return to Alfonso's service in 1517, but Alfonso refused him, accusing him of the "sin of ingratitude," and threatening legal action if he continued to communicate his petitions to the duchy of Ferrara. See Lockwood 1998.

‖ 5 ‖

Conclusions

Living Music at Court

Summary

My analysis of the studioli of Leonello, Isabella, and Alfonso d'Este has revealed a number of features that strongly promote the idea that music belonged in these rooms, indeed was one of the most characteristic activities pursued therein. However, in chapter 1 I specifically set my focus elsewhere, on the musical identities evidenced by studiolo decoration; and I will conclude accordingly.

Leonello's studiolo was housed in the villa of Belfiore, which was by Este tradition a locus for musical entertainments. The evidence published by Cavicchi for the presence of an organ in the room, and Decembrio's comment about keeping a lute in a library, both add weight to the idea that the studiolo itself was a venue for music-making. The revisions made to Guarino's scheme for a decoration of relatively unmusical and morally cautious muses reveal some of the ideological investments made in music at Leonello's court. The *Melpomene* seen by Ciriaco made reference to the ancient practice of performing verse to the accompaniment of the lyre, revealing the classicizing aspect of similar musical practices at the marchese's own court (including those of Pietrobono and, probably, Leonello himself). In the *Euterpe*, on the other hand, music's frequently observed and mythologized seductive powers were brought to the fore, courting an ambivalent moral position and pointing towards an aspect of Leonello's own poetics. These "erotic" poetics are revealed especially in two medals: one reimagining Guarino's version of Calliope as a putto, the other identifying Eros as Leonello's musical muse. These clues suggest that Leonello identified himself as an Ovidian *vates* (in playful contradiction of the Virgilian *vates* proposed by Guarino), a theory apparently confirmed by his own surviving poetry. Within the humanist view of music that likely pertained under

Guarino's instruction, music and poetry amounted to the same thing, and therefore these new conclusions about Leonello's poetics are musical as much as they are literary. They may have a particular bearing on our understanding of the musician Pietrobono's role at Leonello's court: it was his professional duty to offer the facilitatory services of a Muse, and he may have been thought literally to embody that role within Leonello's particular conception.

Leonello's identity emerges from this analysis as fundamentally musical. His efforts to manifest his classical learning and interests seem quite different from those of the dryly humanist Leonello found in Decembrio, drawing instead on a rich reading of classical verse and a wide-ranging appreciation of the classical significance of music. As a poet, and in his studiolo, the marchese saw himself in communion with a musical Muse who, like Ovid's, had undergone an erotic transformation—and whose character served to design and furnish an important part of his leisured identity. Pietrobono, whose role and reputation could be designed in much the same way as his conceptual counterpart, may have served a similar purpose. In this light, the caution of Guarino's Muses might be read not as a response to accusations leveled against him, but as an attempt to refashion morally problematic aspects of the "humanist" identity of his noble student. The fact that Leonello's paintings reflect substantial alterations to the scheme highlight the disjunction of priorities and objectives that could so easily exist between a prince and the literary personalities vying for his patronage.

The situation for Isabella is in some respects turned on its head. For her, the musical idiom of solo song to instrumental accompaniment may have carried similar connotations of antiquity, and in that respect it belonged alongside the other contents of her studiolo and grotto. However, for her, active participation in a musical practice that served to manifest pretensions to humanist and poetic agency was problematic. In contrast to Leonello, far from ignoring the moral representations of her literary retainers, it was only through collaboration with them that the marchesa could publicly establish the legitimacy of her pastime. The decoration of her studiolo served to construct for her a musical identity within which her classicizing musico-poetic practice was asserted to be decorous. In the *Parnassus* this was achieved through an association with the Muses, who sang of the loves of the classical gods, and also with Sappho; in later paintings she adopted a more morally cautious association with Minerva, who stood for the rational and moral learning involved in musical expertise. Isabella's *impresa delle pause*, meanwhile, can be read as a tool with which she could design the moral contours of her singing voice. In its silence, symbolized by rests, Equicola identified the prudence to know when song was appropriate and decorous and when it was not; although, covertly, the impresa also affirms her voice, and can be read to conceal a playful reference to Petrarchan desire. Isabella's camorra decorated with the sign, seen in this light, looks like an attempt to present an image of metaphorically disembodied musicianship, deployed against moral concerns over public female musicianship that centered on sexual incontinence and vanity.

Alfonso's musical identity saw something of a return to the playful and morally ambiguous musical classicism of his uncle Leonello, subjected to a newly flamboyant articulation. Alfonso's diverse and active secular musical interests can usefully be understood in the context of the courtly vogue for the pastoral mode, in which music enjoyed an invocatory relationship with the countryside and its mythological inhabitants. Alfonso's pastoral was playful and Ovidian, bringing with it the close association of music and the erotic already familiar from Leonello; and it was through these connections that his music made contact with the classicizing (if not always exactly humanist) aspect of courtly culture. The *Andrians, Bacchus and Ariadne*, and the song *Quid non ebrietas* served to establish Bacchus as a transgressive alternative to the Muses as a source of musico-poetic inspiration, through the mechanism of the god's wine. In establishing Bacchus as the patron of his musicianship, Alfonso may well have been reacting, purposefully but with wit and humor, to the musical identity and ideologies put forward by his sister, undermining Isabella's moral assertions through the less decorous musical associations of the god of wine, contrasting her silent impresa with his own unconcernedly bucolic voice. Isabella was already widely renowned as a noble musician, and so perhaps the duke needed both to make room for his own accomplishments, and to validate them as aspects of masculine nobility. Finally, Alfonso appears to have made an intervention in the design of the *Andrians* to encode into it, through the mechanism of the song *Qui boyt*, a viewing experience that pointed both outwards to the duke's own musical identity, and inwards to the interpretation of the painting; and which served to place the duke's voice in the viewer's mouth. Such a style of patronage is very much in keeping with the broader sweep of his activities.

Taken as a whole, these three case studies point very clearly to the considerable significance and priority given to music within the leisured privacy of two generations of the Este family. They reveal that music operated at a striking level of integration with other aspects of courtly culture, moving between symbol and practice without any sense of disjunction. Among these integrations, they show music to enjoy significances within what one might call courtly (rather than scholarly) humanism that feature only on the fringes in Gafori or Tinctoris. For the nobles I have discussed, music entered into a collaboration with literary and visual culture, and with the vogue for the antique, to manufacture and manipulate the image of a prince at leisure. Their studioli served as focal points in that enterprise, as well-appointed settings for the performance of the living image. Within these parameters, or rather with these mechanisms, the prince could situate himself within a web of moral and ideo-logical discourses—concerned with rule, virtue, strength, education, civility, decorum—establishing his relationship to norms and ideals, both conceptual and embodied. To the extent that these norms and ideals were not uniformly fixed or stable, but tied to the contestable opinion of peers and subjects, the prince could also use music and its collaborators to negotiate the boundaries assigned to his identity and his agency. No doubt this holds true well beyond the Este dynasty; but perhaps for the Este, whose small state struggled to assert itself politically or militarily against the likes of Milan, Venice, Naples, or even Florence, the instrumental deployment of culture had a particular urgency. In the remainder of this chapter, I will expand on what I think have been the principal themes of this study.

Decorated Space and Musical Meaning

In this book I have been considering music not just as a sonic event but as an interpreted act—the prompt of discussion, thought, and measured reaction. It is not least in this respect that music has a place in the private spaces of the Renaissance palace: over the course of the fifteenth century, the contents of private libraries migrated from the pages of books to the walls in pigment; and thus the paintings I have discussed were designed specifically to offer their audience the kind of more-or-less elevated discussion associated with literary culture—albeit in a mode more appropriate to the prince than to the philologist. The established musical discourses into which our paint-ings have strayed have included the Pythagorean harmony of the spheres, the supposed psychological and physical effects of music, the decorum of musical performance, music as espoused by the Roman orators, the accord between music and poetry, and, most importantly, the multivalent relation-ship between music and love. However, such views were not simply the sub-jects of entertaining conversation, but existed in a vital relationship with actual music-making.

I have aimed to show how the paintings made for Leonello, Isabella, and Alfonso were designed to locate their private space within these discourses in order to throw a particular light upon their patrons' musical recreation. Such recreation is thereby given meanings in productive accord with the ideo-logical and representational strategies of the prince. The inscription of what is essentially a musical aesthetic or ideology onto a space turns that space into a venue: that is, a space which supplies (even imposes) the means to understand the acts performed within it. To that extent, the business of making identi-ties through music operated most potently in the manipulation both of the music-making itself, and of its interpretative frame. To ignore the frame, and its charged musicality, is to fail to understand the music's full range of significance within its context.

Such an understanding of Renaissance space—the "venue"—is far from ahistorical. It was a commonplace of Renaissance discussions of decoration that it should be directly appropriate to the use of the space decorated. For instance, in Filarete's treatise on architecture, the fictional patron for whom the author is building a city—the duke—surveys his new buildings in detail and declares that their decorations should be "relevant to the place." He goes on to assign subjects appropriate to each location: good judges in the hall of the podestà; wise counselors of Rome in the hall of the Palazzo del Commune; the inventors of the arts in the guildhall; and Venus and Priapus above the entrance to the brothel.[1] Decorations, according to Filarete and others, should instruct and manipulate those inhabiting their space, giving meaning to and commenting upon their presence and above all their actions. By this measure the studioli of Leonello, Isabella, and Alfonso were musical spaces, indeed spaces for music, in every meaningful respect.

Objects in Performance

It is striking to reflect that painting was going on in Ferrara for Alfonso's Via Coperta apartment, and for the studiolo in particular, almost until the end of Alfonso's reign. Between them, Titian and Dosso may have been at work there on the project for three years or more during the long decade 1519–29.[2] Similarly, Leonello's studiolo was still incomplete at his death; and Isabella's was in development from her arrival in Mantua in 1490 until about 1530. One can hardly help but conclude that part of the service they required of their artists, part of the delight of their private space, was the performance of making.

Direct evidence of such spectatorship is not lacking in the annals of the Estense. At the villa of Belriguardo in 1493, Ercole spent days cooped up in his room designing frescoes with his painter Ercole de' Roberti—to the frustration of his court, as his secretary Siverio Siveri reported to Duchess Eleonora.[3]

[1] Filarete 1965, 1:129–31. The treatise is entitled *Trattato di architettura* and dates from the 1460s.

[2] This calculation is based on the evidence presented for the contribution of Dosso and its interpretation in Hope 1971, 643–44, and the evidence presented concerning Titian's visits to Ferrara and its interpretation in Hope 1987, 26–27 (with footnotes).

[3] See the letter published in transcription and translation and discussed at length in Gundersheimer 1976.

Later, the process of painting the designs up on the wall in Belriguardo became part of the court's after-dinner entertainment.[4]

Similar, if sometimes less explicit, notices implicate the protagonists of this study. Leonello, for instance, was closely enough involved in his project to correspond with his tutor about the depiction of the Muses, and remained closely enough involved for some of the finished paintings to represent a demonstrably Leonellian revision to the program. Particularly interesting, although not directly related to his studiolo, is Alfonso's famous encounter with Michelangelo on the scaffolding in the Sistine Chapel, reported to Isabella on 9 July 1512:

> And the Lord Duke went into the vault with many people then everyone little by little left the vault and the Lord Duke stayed there with Michelangelo because he could not sate his desire to look at the figures and sufficiently praise them... and he [Alfonso] made talk [with Michelangelo] and offered money and he has a promise to make him one.[5]

Meanwhile, on 4 October 1518 Bernardino de' Prosperi reported to Isabella on the close attention with which Alfonso was supervising building work, including the private apartment, the fortifications, and the new villa known as Montagnone. Isabella's own close involvement in the decoration of her studiolo, and her practice of welcoming visiting artists to her court, are well known.

Whilst the performance of making is usually read as an aspect of the artist's self-fashioning, its spectating appropriated the performance also to the identity of the patron.[6] I noted in chapter 1, with the help of Vergerio and Alberti, that the prince is never entirely beyond the observation of his followers. We only know of Ercole's and Alfonso's spectatorship because it was reported by their courtiers to absent family members: by Siverio to Eleanora d'Aragona, and by Grossino and Bernardino to Isabella. Siverio is able to comment on the painters' work in Belriguardo, and thus he must have watched alongside Ercole. Grossino notes that "many people" accompanied Alfonso to the Sistine Chapel, and thought that information would

---

[4] See the letter published in Franceschini 1993, 80 (Document 81), and discussed in Welch 2004, 28.

[5] "Et il Signor Ducha ando in sula volta con più persone tandem ogni uno apocho apocho sene vene giu dela vollta et il Signor Ducha resto su con Michel Angello che non si poteva satiare di guardare quelle figure et assai careze li... et li fece parlare e proferire dinarij et li ha in promesso de fargiello." Text Shearman 1987, n37.

[6] On the performance of making and the artist's identity, see in particular Campbell 1996; and Welch 2004.

be of interest to Isabella. Isabella, in turn, dealt with Costa (who would soon become a permanent fixture in Mantua) through the Bentivoglio. In fact, a studiolo in progress was a thing of sufficient interest and value to be included on the itinerary of a famous visitor, as when Leonello played host to Ciriaco d'Ancona. The audience for the ruler's spectatorship was varied and substantial.

Aligning music with this kind of context is a more complex task. Competent musicianship was a more widespread feature of the nobility than skill in drawing or painting. At the same time, the composition of notated music was, like painting, largely a professional preserve. The existence of multiple modes of musical making—notated composition, improvisation, and performance—and the fluidity of their boundaries make for a degree of confusion. What performance constitutes the "making" and what the finished product? What might one spectate, what might one use, and how does it pertain to identity? The possibilities are various.

In the case of Leonello and Pietrobono, employing (so far as can be discerned) a partly improvised performing style, the elements are to a significant extent bound together in the moment of performance. Evidence of a patron wishing to observe a process of composition, pertaining to the later practice associated with Isabella, is close at hand, to place alongside my remarks in this vein on *Quid non ebrietas* in chapter 4. On 13 September 1514 Isabella's son, Federico Gonzaga, who two years earlier had been Alfonso's guide on his visit to the Sistine chapel, wrote to Marchetto Cara from a country estate:

> Having been this morning here in Gonzaga to the market, I have found several beautiful things newly composed but still not finished at the printer and because of their novelty I was not able to leave and let them finish printing.... In this month I pray you and wish you to stretch your talent and apply all your art to make some beautiful song on it, but because above all I desire that you make the song not so much bizarre as excellent and that you won't be distracted by other thoughts and duties, you will make me very grateful if you come here to stay with me in pleasure... To your comforts I offer myself always.[7]

[7] "Essendo stato questa matina qua in Gonzaga sul mercato, ho ritrovato alcune belle cose novamente composte ma non anchor finite dal stampatore e per la novità lor non ho potuto partir di lassarle finir de stampare.... In questo mezo vi prego vogliati affaticar l'ingegno vostro et ponervi tutta l'arte per far qualche bel canto sopra, me perchè summamente desidero che faciati il canto di bizaria in excellentia et che non siati distratto da altri pensieri et fastidij, mi fareti gran gratia ad venir qui ad star con me in piacer...Alli comodi vostri me offero sempre." Text Prizer 1980, Appendix I, Document 100.

Federico asks that the frottolist come to stay with him whilst he "makes" music for some new poems. It seems very likely that such a practice was a primary feature of daily life in Isabella's studiolo.

The musical environments of the studioli of Leonello, Isabella, and Alfonso more generally serve similarly to draw attention to musical making. Leonello identifies himself as a divinely inspired *vates*, whose poetry is dictated to him as song by an Erotic Muse; meanwhile, in his *Euterpe* musical harmony is forged by a blacksmith. Isabella's *impresa delle pause* and her song *Cantai mentre nel cor* address her own problematic music-making—making now deferred to the act of musical performance. Her *Parnassus* and Alfonso's *Andrians* offer alternative sources of musical inspiration, whilst *Quid non ebrietas* and *Qui boyt* play with the hazards of Bacchic inspiration. In the case of all three nobles, it is striking to note that they patronized relatively little music in which they could not themselves participate.[8] Evidently their direct involvement, as far as possible at every stage and mode of the making of music, as with painting, was central to its role at their courts.

The *Parnassus* and the *Andrians* introduce a key aspect of music's efficacy in constructing identities. In chapter 3 I argued that the *Parnassus* shows the Muses conjuring forth the subject of their song. In chapter 4, I discussed the way Titian and Willaert dealt with Philostratus's conceit that framed the painting he described as a song. The song *Qui boyt* placed the force of this conceit in the voice of the patron himself. Music in these chapters was found to possess invocatory power—the ability to make manifest that of which one sings. In performance (in making) music represents, and in representing it brings into being.

This closely resembles the ontology (or perhaps rather the phenomenology) of musical performance found in Castiglione and Ficino in chapter 1 above, according to whom music has the capacity to manifest in the listener the states of mind it imitates. It resembles, too, the widely articulated status accorded visual making. For example, Alberti famously claimed that through painting "the absent are made present," and Castiglione envisaged his wife and child interacting with his portrait during his physical absence from the family home. In an analysis of these and many similar instances, Patricia Simons has recently concluded that Renaissance portraiture, at least, "performatively shapes its world": that life as represented in paint enjoys an instrumental relationship with "real" life.[9]

---

[8] Leonello even sang with his chapel choir—see Lockwood 1984, 44–45.

[9] Simons 1995. For more on the relationship between music and portraits, see Shephard 2010a, 99–110.

Voice and Agency

Throughout this study I have made frequent reference to the patron's "voice." For Hesiod, the poet's voice finds its source and origin in the Muses. Leonello's voice, in the 1444 medal, is given to him by Eros, playing with the significance of *vates*. Isabella's *Parnassus* foregrounded the Muses' powerful voices, and by extension her own "honeyed voice"; but, meanwhile, her *impresa delle pause* dealt subtly with the moral difficulties surrounding a woman's voice and its bodily origin. Alfonso posited an alternative source for the poet-musician's voice in Bacchus, but his paintings and his songs also highlight the hazards of the Bacchic voice. *Qui boyt* turned the duke's own voice into a mediating act of visual interpretation.

In these cases the word "voice" operates in two ways. First, the word refers to an actual singing voice, and to the patron's practice of active musical participation. Second, it serves as a metaphor for something like "agency"—both the patron's cultural agency and their ability to design and manifest an identity. As the *impresa delle pause* demonstrates, concerned as it is with the negotiation of voice as a symbol for and an aspect of agency, there are several respects in which these two meanings are closely related. In chapter 1 I argued, with the help of Perinbanayagam, that being is an act of authorship, entailing the writing of the self as a text. As my discussion of performance above suggests, song carried a part of that text, fully endowed with music's ontological force. The patron's song and the patron's self could thus be tied inextricably to one another. Such a conception of voice allows us to see song as a means for a patron to establish his coordinates within his ideological and relational contexts.

The song *Qui boyt* nicely encapsulates this point, whilst revealing another nexus in the relationship between voice and identity. The act of singing *Qui boyt*, through its ekphrastic content and through its equivalence to the song of Philostratus's Andrians, constitutes a metaphorical authoring of the painting in which it appears; meanwhile, I have suggested that it literally owes its place in the *Andrians* to the agency of the duke. Voice refers not only to the patron's authorship of himself, but also to his authorship of his surroundings (what I have called his "cultural agency"). Here the patron admits mediation: in most circumstances, it is others who do the actual making (be it musical, literary, architectural, visual, or material). Filarete describes the ideal situation, as the duke for whom he is preparing an ideal city walks around the site explaining his vision, or discusses drawings in the palace, setting the agenda with judgment and discretion, but responding to the advice of the man who must actually carry out the project. The project is the duke's, and it is to him that its fame will principally attach—in fact, the influence of his authorship extends even to the identity of the scholar or artisan who will benefit from his patronage.

Concern with authorship and the circumstances of its mediation is prominent in all three studioli here studied. As a literary space in which some of the
writing is on the wall in paint, and some hangs in the air as song, all attuned
to the writing of the self, perhaps authorship is an inevitable studiolo topic.
Leonello sought to connect his own musico-poetic authorship with the intervention of the Muses; although, in so doing, he invited an intermediation from
Guarino that he ultimately sought to conceal and subvert. The cases of Isabella
and Alfonso are directly opposed in this respect—a fact of which evidently
both were aware. For Isabella, authorship was problematic, something to be
negotiated through references to the Muses or Minerva, and to be dissembled
via a displacement of her voice from body to silent sign. For her, mediation was
essential: her agency found expression through the authorship of a coterie of
public men, from which distance it could safely be reflected back upon her as
an aspect of her (re)presentation. She did not literally make her paintings or
her medals, but (as we see in several letters) it was upon her "ingegno" that the
praise of her peers devolved.[10] Similarly, though as a musician she performed
in an improvisatory tradition, she almost certainly relied on the agency of men
in her employ for the authorship of the music, the praise for which then effectively divulged upon her. Alfonso, on the other hand, apparently took pleasure in the materiality of direct authorship. His early biographers are happy
to acknowledge that he made things with his own hands, and I have already
discussed the extent of his involvement in decoration and building projects.
The subjects chosen for his studiolo paintings seem to reflect a self-conscious
delight in his relative moral freedom, founded in the masculinity they are at
pains to assert.

Imaging the Prince

I have said that the princes here considered were numbered among the images
to be viewed and admired within their studioli. Such is most explicitly the
case for Isabella, whose female companion wrote of "being in the image of she
who on earth I rightly worship" whilst attending the marchesa in her grotta.
Similarly, contemporaries appear to have treated the paintings made for
Isabella's studiolo as compound and indirect portraits. Alfonso was also "seen" in
his private apartment: Equicola, for example, saw him there reading Philostratus.

---

[10] The subject of *ingegno* in general, and the relationship between the artist's and the patron's
ingegno in particular, have recently been considered at length in Syson and Thornton 2001, 91
and 135–81. An example of the praise of Isabella's ingegno being prompted by an artist's work on
her behalf is discussed by Syson and Thornton at 120.

In terms of its hermeneutics, the scenario of a prince in a studiolo is closely akin to a portrait of a prince surrounded by props and attributes—Ciriaco certainly configured the organ in Leonello's studiolo as among the marchese's praiseworthy attributes.

As a princely attribute, music was both a solution and a problem. Greenblatt has described identity in the Renaissance as a matter of "firm and decisive identification with normative structures," and music certainly played a range of roles in the ideals and codes that governed the behavior of ruling men and women.[11] As a symbol, music could stand for a good education, a healthy soul, and even fair government (through the metaphor of "harmony"). The musically active prince could be praised for his proficiency, cultivation, and knowledge of the liberal arts; he could be compared to Achilles and Apollo, and named a friend of the Muses. However, he could also be labeled a lackey and a degenerate, his prudence called into question; and, worst of all, he could be called effeminate. For the noble lady, the danger lay in being thought incontinent and vain.

The musical attributes with which our three rulers were framed in their studioli were evidently chosen carefully to invoke the most suitable and helpful connotations in the prince's living portrait, and to avoid the negative. However, in doing so, Leonello, Isabella and Alfonso appear to have arrived at quite different solutions. In the studioli of Isabella and Alfonso, the extent to which these choices were shaped by gender is particularly apparent. The reason for this distinction is evident. Several aspects of music and music-making were conventionally connected with the erotic, and sexual (or sexualized) behavior was a central factor in the definition of approved gender roles.

A pair of sonnets by Pietro Aretino will usefully set the tone for our analysis of the musical gendering of the princely "portraits" found in Alfonso and Isabella's studioli. The poems, known from a letter of 1537, were written in response to Titian's portraits of Francesco Maria della Rovere, Duke of Urbino, and his duchess Eleonora Gonzaga (Isabella's daughter).[12] Aretino itemizes the virtues and qualities with which each is endowed. Titian's painting of the duke "reveals the victories held within his heart," giving him a heroic aspect, through the "awesomeness between his brows," the "fiery spirit in his eyes," and his breastplate and "ready arms" in which "courage burns."[13] By contrast, in the duchess's portrait can be discerned "harmony," Eleonora's "gentle spirit"

---

[11] Greenblatt 1986, 35.

[12] Text and translation of these poems (which I have followed) can be found in Rogers 1986, 303–4, where they are also discussed at 297. In addition, see Simons 1994, 173–75.

[13] "scopre le palme entro al suo cuor sparte.... Egli ha il terror fra l'uno e l'altro ciglio, / l'animo in gli occhi... Nel busto armato e ne le braccia pronte / arde il valor."

and modest "simplicity"; she is "humble in deed" and "chaste."[14] Further, the decorum of her appearance is praised: "honesty dwells in her attire, / modesty veils and honors her bosom and her hair."[15] Finally, Aretino is able to detect her "prudence" and "good counsel," which prompt her to "fair silence."[16] This is precisely the clearly and normatively gendered praise that noblemen and women of the period would hope to prompt through their image-making, describing their success in embodying contemporary ideals.

I argued in chapter 3 that in Isabella's studiolo and grotta she was engaged in constructing an identity of images which, to a significant extent, sought to design, explain and even hide her bodily existence and her agency. In the place of corporeality and action, her musical images assert her modest virtue, her prudence, and her silence, veiling and qualifying the realities of her musical activities. The musical attributes with which she was framed ultimately cast her musicianship as Minervan—that is, chaste and studious, existing in a secluded grove (such as that depicted in Costa's *Coronation*), guarded from the forces of vice.

Alfonso, on the other hand, I found to use music to reach out from his studiolo "portrait," asserting himself over his viewer, even forcing them to sing with his voice. This approach I found reflected in the exaggerated princely agency of his cultural activities in general. His musicianship was identified very clearly as Bacchanalian—that is, vigorous, physical, and eroticized. In the light of Aretino's poem, we could reasonably read his musical identity as a claim to powerful, virile masculinity; and in fact his efforts to distinguish his approach from the effeminate musicianship of the unmanly, and the musical femininity of his sister, suggest that Alfonso himself consciously sought to configure his studiolo and its music in these terms.

We might make a comparison here with a literal portrait of the duke painted by Titian, in which an enormous canon projects forward from his body at about groin height, threatening a violent and monstrous imposition of his masculinity upon the viewer (in an odd parallel with the other kind of canon in the *Andrians*). Giraldi, in describing a different portrait of Alfonso, gives us some indications as to how we should understand this image, stressing its masculine potency:

> This face of Alfonso, dark in color, of impressive form, and severe, with lively eyes, and with nose honestly bent down to the bottom, with

[14] "la concordia, che regge in Lionora / le ministre del spirito gentile…Seco siede modestia in atto umile."

[15] "Onestà nel suo abito dimora, / Vergogna il petto e il crin le vela e onora."

[16] "Prudenza il valor suo guarda, e consiglia / nel bel tacer."

beard, and grey hair, such [features] show signs of heroic strength, and of tenacious spirit, that so resemble the living Duke ... [representing] the martial valor of Alfonso[17]

The canon in Titian's portrait obviously indicates Alfonso's military prowess, but it also refers to the potency of his artisan pastimes: he cast canon himself, in the same spirit in which he made *flauti*, and intervened in his artists' work.

Leonello's musical attributes, like those of Alfonso, play with the erotic in ways that would have been uncomfortable for a woman. The subject position adopted in his verse is that of the unrequited male lover of Petrarchan and pastoral verse; and for him, it seems, musicianship was inextricably connected with the person of Eros. However, Leonello's musical masculinity was constructed within a rather different mode of classicism to that invoked by Alfonso. Whilst Alfonso draws a connection with virile Bacchic abandon, appropriate to the more Ovidian courtly "humanism" of the early sixteenth century, Leonello's musical eroticism is clothed in the Ciceronian reserve that was fashionable among the early humanist scholars.

The conceit of the inhabited studiolo as princely "portrait," replete with meaningful musical attributes that served to frame and shape the ruler's identity, is a suitable one with which to end. Very likely it closely approximates the way in which the patrons involved viewed the business of equipping and using a studiolo. It was a room for leisure, certainly, but for leisure with purpose, in which the space, its decoration, and its owner combined to produce an image defining the owner's often subtle and multivalent identification with contemporary ideals and standards of princely behavior, suitable to be viewed by selected retainers, courtiers, relatives, and guests. I hope I have demonstrated the importance of the role played by music in producing that image, and I hope that in the process I have offered some new models and directions for research into the relations between music and visual culture in Renaissance Italy.

---

[17] "Questo volto d'Alfonso di color bruno, di ciera terribile, et severa, con occhi vivi, et con naso honestamente chinato giu in fondo, con barba, et capegli canuti, quali mostrano segni d'heroica fortezza, et d'animo costante, che tanto somiglia al Duca vivo, fu per commissione del Duca Hercole amorevol figliuolo ritratto co' suoi colori da Girolamo da Carpi Ferrarese, degno d'esser paragonato à pittori antichi, per rappresentare il martiale valor di Alfonso, et la eccellente industria del pittore." Giraldi Cinzio 1556, 113. This text opens his biographical sketch of Alfonso.

BIBLIOGRAPHY

Abramov-van Rijk, Elena. *Parlar Cantando: The Practice of Reciting Verses in Italy from 1300 to 1600*. Bern: Peter Lang, 2009.

Agrippa, Henry Cornelius. *Henrici Cornelii Agrippae ab Nettesheym, splendidissimae nobilitatis Viri, & armatae militiae Equitis aurati, ac LL. Doctoris, sacrae Caesareae Maiestatis à Consilijs, & archiuis Indiciarij, de Incertitudine & Vanitate Scientiarum & Artium, atque excellentia Verbi Dei, declamatio*. Paris: Jean Pierre, 1531.

———. *Of the Vanitie and Uncertaintie of Artes and Sciences*. Translated by James Sanford, and edited by Catherine M. Dunn. Northridge: California State University, 1974.

Ahern, Charles F., Jr. "Ovid as Vates in the Proem to the Ars amatoria." *Classical Philology* 85 (1990): 44–48.

Alberti, Leon Battista. *De Re Aedificatoria*. Paris: Berthold Rembolt, 1512.

———. *On Painting and On Sculpture: The Latin Texts of De Pictura and De Statua*. Edited and translated by Cecil Grayson. London: Phaidon, 1972.

———. *On the Art of Building in Ten Books*. Translated by Joseph Rykwert, Neil Leach, and Robert Tavernor. Cambridge, MA: MIT Press, 1988.

Anderson, Jaynie. "Il Risveglio dell'Interesse per le Muse nella Ferrara del Quattrocento." In *Le Muse e il Principe: Arte di Corte nel Rinascimento Padano*, edited by Alessandra Mottola-Molfino and Mauro Natali, 2 volumes, 2:165–85. Modena: F. C. Panini, 1991.

———. *Giorgione: The Painter of Poetic Brevity*. Paris: Flammarion, 1997.

Anselmi Parmensis, Georgii. *De Musica*. Edited by Giuseppe Massera. Florence: Olschki, 1961.

Austern, Linda Phyllis, and Inna Naroditskaya, ed. *Music of the Sirens*. Bloomington: Indiana University Press, 2006.

Austin, J. L. *How to Do Things with Words*. Oxford: Clarendon Press, 1962.

Babb, Warren, trans., and Claude V. Palisca ed. *Hucbald, Guido and John on Music: Three Medieval Treatises*. New Haven: Yale University Press, 1978.

Ballarin, Alessandro. *Il Camerino delle Pitture di Alfonso I*. 6 volumes. Cittadella: Bertoncello, 2002.

Baruffaldi, Girolamo. *Rime Scelti de Poeti Ferraresi, Antichi e Moderni*. Ferrara: Per gli eredi di Bernardino Pomatelli, 1713.

Baxandall, Michael. "A Dialogue on Art from the Court of Leonello d'Este: Angelo Decembrio's De Politia Litteraria Pars LXVIII." *Journal of the Warburg and Courtauld Institutes* 26 (1963): 304–26.

———. "Guarino, Pisanello and Manuel Chrysoloras." *Journal of the Warburg and Courtauld Institutes* 28 (1965): 183–204.

———. *Painting and Experience in Fifteenth Century Italy*. Oxford: Clarendon Press, 1972.

Bayer, Andrea. "Dosso's Public: The Este Court at Ferrara." In *Dosso Dossi: Court Painter in Renaissance Ferrara*, edited by Peter Humfrey and Mauro Lucco, 27–54. New York: Metropolitan Museum of Art, 1998.

Beichner, Paul E. *The Medieval Representative of Music, Jubal or Tubalcain?* Notre Dame: Mediaeval Institute, University of Notre Dame, 1954.

Bent, Margaret. "Diatonic *Ficta.*" *Early Music History* 4 (1984): 1–48.

Bentini, Jadranka. "From Ercole I to Alfonso I: New Discoveries about the *Camerini* in the Castello Estense of Ferrara." In *Dosso's Fate: Painting and Court Culture in Renaissance Italy*, edited by Luisa Ciammitti, Steven Ostrow, and Salvatore Settis, 359–65. Los Angeles: Getty Research Institute for the History of Art & the Humanities, 1998.

Benthem, Jaap van. "'La prima donna del mondo:' Isabella d'Este's Musical Impresa, its Conception, and an Interpretation." In *Uno gentile et subtile ingenio: Studies in Renaissance Music in Honour of Bonnie J. Blackburn*, edited by M. Jennifer Bloxam, Gioia Filocamo, and Leofranc Holford-Strevens, 569–76. Turnhout: Brepols, 2009.

Benvenuti, Antonia Tissoni. *Niccolò da Correggio: Opere*. Bari: Laterza, 1969.

———. "Schede per una Storia della Poesia Pastorale nel Secolo XV: La Scuola Guariniana a Ferrara." In *In Ricordo di Cesare Angelini: Studi di Letteratura e Filologia*, edited by Franco Alessio and Angelo Stella, 96–131. Milan: Il saggiatore, 1979.

Berger, Karol. *Musica Ficta: Theories of Accidental Inflections in Vocal Polyphony from Marcheto da Padova to Gioseffo Zarlino*. Cambridge: Cambridge University Press, 1987.

Bernardini, Maria Grazia. *The Estense Gallery of Modena: A Guide to the History and the Art Collections*. Milan: Silvana Editoriale, 2007.

Berti, Luciano. *Il Principe dello Studiolo: Francesco I dei Medici e la Fine del Rinascimento*. Florence: Edam, 1967.

Bertoni, Giulio. *La Biblioteca Estense e la Coltura Ferrarese ai Tempi del Duca Ercole Primo (1471–1505)*. Turin: Loescher, 1903.

———. "Un Copista del Marchese Leonello d'Este (Biagio Bosoni da Cremona)." *Giornale Storico della Letteratura Italiana* 72 (1918): 96–106.

———. "Il Cieco di Ferrara e Altri Improvvisatori alla Corte d'Este." *Giornale Storico della Letteratura Italiana* 94 (1929): 271–8.

Blackburn, Bonnie J., Edward E. Lowinsky, and Clement A. Miller, ed. *A Correspondence of Renaissance Musicians*. Oxford: Clarendon Press, 1991.

Boccaccio, Giovanni. *Concerning Famous Women*. Translated by Guido A. Guarini. New Brunswick: Rutgers University Press, 1963.

Boethius, Anicius Manlius Severinus. *Theological Tractates and The Consolation of Philosophy*. Translated by H. F. Stewart, E. K. Rand, and S. J. Tester. Cambridge, MA: Harvard University Press, 1973.

———. *Fundamentals of Music*. Translated by Calvin M. Bower, and edited by Claude V. Palisca. New Haven: Yale University Press, 1989.

Bolzoni, Lina. "L'Invenzione' dello Stanzino di Francesco I." In *Le Arti del Principato Mediceo*, 255–99. Florence: Studio per edizioni scelte, 1980.

Bonicatti, Maurizio. "Tiziano e la Cultura Musicale del Suo Tempo." In *Tiziano e Venezia: Convegno Internazionale di Studi, Venezia, 1976*, 461–77. Vicenza: Neri Pozza, 1980.

Boorman, Stanley. *Ottaviano Petrucci: A Catalogue Raisonne*. Oxford: Oxford University Press, 2006.

Borella, Marco. "Lo 'Studio de preda marmora fina' Sopra la Via Coperta di Alfonso III duca." In *Il Camerino di Alabastro: Antonio Lombardo e la Scultura all'Antica*, edited by Matteo Ceriana, 111–18. Milan: Silvana, 2004.

Borella, Marco, and Angela Ghinato, ed. *Il Castello per la Città: Il Progetto della Via Coperta*. Ferrara: Italia Tipolitografia, 2006.

Boskovits, Miklos. "Ferrarese Painting about 1520: Some New Arguments." *The Burlington Magazine* 120, no. 903 (1978): 370–85.

Boström, Hans-Olof. "The Studiolo: Background and Tradition." *Nationalmuseum Bulletin* 40, no. 2 (1987): 53–68.

Bourne, Molly. "Renaissance Husbands and Wives as Patrons of Art: The Camerini of Isabella d'Este and Francesco Gonzaga." In *Beyond Isabella: Secular Women Patrons of Art in Renaissance Italy*, edited by Sheryl E. Reiss and David G. Wilkins, 93–123. Kirksville: Truman State University Press, 2001.

Brenkman, John. "Writing, Desire and Dialectic in Petrarch's 'Rime 23'." *Pacific Coast Philology* 9 (1974): 12–19.

Brown, Beverly Louise. "On the Camerino." In *Bacchanals by Titian and Rubens: Papers Given at a Symposium in Nationalmuseum, Stockholm March 18–19, 1987*, edited by Görel Cavalli-Björkman, 43–56. Stockholm: Nationalmuseum, 1987.

Brown, Clifford M. *"Lo insaciabile desiderio nostro de cose antique*: New Documents on Isabella d'Este's Collection of Antiquities." In *Cultural Aspects of the Italian Renaissance: Essays in Honour of Paul Oskar Kristeller*, edited by Cecil H. Clough, 234–53. Manchester: Manchester University Press, 1976.

———. "Public Interests and Private Collections: Isabella d'Este's *Apartamento della Grotta* and Its Accessibility to Artists, Scholars and Public Figures." In *Akten des XXV. Internationalen Kongresses für Kunstgeschichte*, edited by Hermann Fillitz and Martina Pippal, 9 volumes, 4:37–41. Vienna: Böhlau, 1986.

———. "Digest of the Correspondence Concerning the Paintings Commissioned for the *Studiolo* in the Castello (1496–1515)." In *The Cabinet of Eros: Renaissance Mythological Painting and the Studiolo of Isabella d'Este*, Stephen J. Campbell, 280–301. New Haven: Yale University Press, 2004.

———. *Isabella d'Este in the Ducal Palace in Mantua: An Overview of her Rooms in the Castello di San Giorgio and the Corte Vecchia*. Rome: Bulzoni, 2005.

Brown, Clifford M., and Anna Maria Lorenzoni. "The Grotta of Isabella d'Este." *Gazette des Beaux-Arts* 89 (1977): 155–71; and 91 (1978): 72–82.

Brown, Howard Mayer. "A Cook's Tour of Ferrara in 1529." *Rivista Italiana di Musicologia* 10 (1975): 216–41.

———. "Women Singers and Women's Songs in Fifteenth-Century Italy." In *Women Making Music: The Western Art Tradition*, edited by Jane Bowers and Judith Tick, 62–89. Urbana: University of Illinois Press, 1986.

Bryce, Judith. "Performing for Strangers: Women, Dance, and Music in Quattrocento Florence." *Renaissance Quarterly* 54 (2001): 1074–107.

Bull, David, and Joyce Plesters. *'The Feast of the Gods:' Conservation, Examination and Interpretation*. Washington: National Gallery of Art, 1990.

Butler, Judith. *Gender Trouble: Feminism and the Subversion of Identity*. New York: Routledge, 1990.

Cafritz, Robert C., Lawrence Gowing, and David Rosand, ed. *Places of Delight: The Pastoral Landscape*. London: Weidenfeld & Nicolson, 1988.

Calcagnini, Celio. *Caelii Calcagnini Ferrariensis, Protonotarii Apostolici, Opera aliquot*. Basel: Per Hier. Frobenium et Nic. Episopium, 1544.

Calogero, Elena Laura. " 'Sweet Alluring Harmony:' Heavenly and Earthly Sirens in Sixteenth- and Seventeenth-Century Literary and Visual Culture." In *Music of the Sirens*, edited by Linda Phyllis Austern and Inna Naroditskaya, 140–75. Bloomington: Indiana University Press, 2006.

Camiz, Franca Trinchieri. "Due Quadri Musicali del Dosso." In *Frescobaldi e il Suo Tempo nel Quarto Centenario della Nascita*, 85–91. Venice: Marsilio, 1983.

Campbell, Stephen J. *"Pictura and Scriptura*: Cosmè Tura and Style as Courtly Performance." *Art History* 19 (1996): 267–95.

———. *Cosmè Tura of Ferrara: Style, Politics and the Renaissance City, 1450–1495*. New Haven: Yale University Press, 1997.

———. "Mantegna's *Parnassus*: Reading, Collecting and the *Studiolo*." In *Revaluing Renaissance Art*, edited by Gabriele Neher and Rupert Shepherd, 69–88. Aldershot: Ashgate, 2000.

———. "Giorgione's *Tempest*, Studiolo Culture, and the Renaissance Lucretius." *Renaissance Quarterly* 56 (2003): 299–332.

———. *The Cabinet of Eros: Renaissance Mythological Painting and the Studiolo of Isabella d'Este*. New Haven: Yale University Press, 2004.

———. "Eros in the Flesh: Petrarchan Desire, the Embodied Eros, and Male Beauty in Italian Art, 1500–1540." *Journal of Medieval and Early Modern Studies* 35 (2005): 629–62.

Campori, Giuseppe. "Tiziano e gli Estensi." *Nuova Antologia* 1, no. 27 (1874): 583–620.

Cappelli, Antonio. "La Biblioteca Estense nella Prima Meta del Secolo XV." *Giornale Storico della Letteratura Italiana* 14 (1889): 1–30.

Cartwright, Julia. *Isabella d'Este, Marchioness of Mantua, 1474–1539: A Study of the Renaissance.* 2 volumes. Hawaii: University Press of the Pacific, 2002.

Castiglione, Baldassare. *Il Libro del Cortegiano del Conte Baldesar Castiglione.* Edited by Vittorio Cian. 4th edition. Florence: Sansoni, 1947.

———. *The Book of the Courtier.* Translated by George Bull. London: Penguin, 1967.

Cavicchi, Adriano. "Idee e Proposte sull'*Allegoria della Musica* con alcuni Appunti per la Coeva Scena Estense." In *L'Età di Alfonso I e la Pittura del Dosso*, edited by Gianni Venturi, 83–92. Modena: Franco Cosimo Panini, 2004.

Cavicchi, Camilla. "Maistre Jhan alla Corte degli Este (1512–1538)." PhD diss., University of Bologna, 2006.

———. "La Musica nello Studiolo di Leonello d'Este." In *Prospettive di Iconografia Musicale*, edited by Nicoletta Guidobaldi, 129–52. Milan: Mimesis, 2007.

Celenza, Christopher S. "Creating Canons in Fifteenth-Century Ferrara: Angelo Decembrio's 'De politia litteraria' 1.10." *Renaissance Quarterly* 57 (2004): 43–98.

Ceriana, Matteo, ed. *Il Camerino di Alabastro: Antonio Lombardo e la Scultura all'Antica* Milan: Silvana, 2004.

Chambers, David, and Jane Martineau, ed. *Splendours of the Gonzaga.* London: Victoria & Albert Museum, 1981.

Cheles, Luciano. *The Studiolo of Urbino: An Iconographic Investigation.* University Park, PA: Pennsylvania State University Press, 1986.

Christiansen, Keith. "The Studiolo of Isabella d'Este and Late Themes." In *Andrea Mantegna*, edited by Jane Martineau, 418–26. London: Royal Academy of Arts, 1992.

———. "Dosso Dossi's Aeneas Frieze for Alfonso d'Este's *Camerino*." *Apollo* 151 (2000): 36–45.

Cicero, Marcus Tullius. *De Finibus Bonorum et Malorum.* Translated by H. Rackham. 2nd edition. London: W. Heinemann, 1931.

Cieri Via, Claudia. "Il Luogo nella Mente e della Memoria." In Wolfgang Liebenwein, *Studiolo: Storia di uno Spazio Culturale*, edited by Claudia Cieri Via and translated by Alessandro Calefano, VII–XXX. Modena: Panini, 1988.

Clough, Cecil. "Federigo da Montefeltro's Private Study in his Ducal Palace of Gubbio." *Apollo* 86, no. 68 (1967): 278–87.

———. "Federigo da Montefeltro's Patronage of the Arts, 1468–1482." *Journal of the Warburg and Courtauld Institutes* 36 (1973): 129–44.

———. "Art as Power in the Decoration of the Study of an Italian Renaissance Prince: The Case of Federico da Montefeltro." *Artibus et Historiae* 16, no. 31 (1995): 19–50.

Colantuono, Anthony. "Tears of Amber: Titian's *Andrians*, the River Po and the Iconology of Difference." In *Phaethon's Children: The Este Court and Its Culture in Early Modern Ferrara*, edited by Dennis Looney and Deanna Shemek, 225–52. Tempe: Arizona Center for Medieval and Renaissance Studies, 2005.

Cullington, J. Donald, ed. and trans., with Reinhard Strohm. *'That liberal and virtuous art:' Three Humanist Treatises on Music.* Newtownabbey: University of Ulster, 2001.

Cusick, Suzanne G. *Francesca Caccini at the Medici Court: Music and the Circulation of Power.* Chicago: University of Chicago Press, 2009.

D'Elia, Una Roman. *The Poetics of Titian's Religious Paintings.* Cambridge: Cambridge University Press, 2005.

Dart, Thurston. "Smith's Titian Canon." *Renaissance News* 7 (1954): 17.

Dean, Trevor. *Land and Power in Late Medieval Ferrara: The Rule of the Este, 1350–1450.* Cambridge: Cambridge University Press, 1987.

Decembrio, Angelo Camillo. *De Politia Litteraria.* Edited by Norbert Witten. Munich: K. G. Saur, 2002.

Dennis, Flora. "Music." In *At Home in Renaissance Italy*, edited by Marta Ajmar-Wollheim and Flora Dennis, 228–43. London: V&A, 2006.

————. "Unlocking the Gates of Chastity: Music and the Erotic in the Domestic Sphere in Fifteenth- and Sixteenth-Century Italy." In *Erotic Cultures of Renaissance Italy*, edited by Sara F. Matthews-Grieco, 223–45. Aldershot: Ashgate, 2010.

————. "When is a Room a Music Room? Sounds, Spaces and Objects in Non-courtly Italian Interiors." In *The Music Room in Early Modern France and Italy*, edited by Deborah Howard and Laura Moretti, 37–49. Oxford: Oxford University Press, 2012.

Diodorus Siculus. *Library of History*. Translated by C. H. Oldfather. Cambridge, MA: Harvard University Press, 1935.

Dunkerton, Jill, Ashok Roy, and Alistair Smith. "The Unmasking of Tura's 'Allegorical Figure:' A Painting and its Concealed Image." *The National Gallery Technical Bulletin* 11 (1987): 5–35.

Durosoir, Georgie. "Musique et Langage Emblématique." In *Emblèmes et Devises au Temps de la Renaissance*, edited by Marie Thérèse Jones-Davies, 5–8. Paris: J. Touzot, 1981.

Einstein, Alfred. *The Italian Madrigal*. Translated by Alexander H. Krappe, Roger H. Sessions, and Oliver Strunk. 3 volumes. Princeton: Princeton University Press, 1948.

Elam, Caroline. "Mantegna at Mantua." In *Splendours of the Gonzaga*, edited by David Chambers and Jane Martineau, 15–25. London: Victoria & Albert Museum, 1981.

Elwert, Theodor W. *Versificazione Italiana dalle Origini ai Giorni Nostri*. Florence: Le Monnier, 1973.

Eörsi, Anna K. "Lo Studiolo di Lionello d'Este e il Programma di Guarino da Verona." *Acta Historiae Artium Accademiae Scientarum Hungaricae* 21 (1975): 15–52.

Ettlinger, L. D. "Muses and Liberal Arts: Two Miniatures from Herrad of Landsberg's Hortus Deliciarum." In *Essays in the History of Art Presented to Rudolf Wittkower*, edited by Douglas Fraser, Howard Hibbard and Milton J. Lewine, 29–35. London: Phaidon, 1967.

Fabiański, Marcin. "Federigo da Montefeltro's 'Studiolo' in Gubbio Reconsidered. Its Decoration and Its Iconographic Program: An Interpretation." *Artibus et Historiae* 11, no. 21 (1990): 199–214.

Fallay d'Este, Lauriane. "Un Symbole Néo-Platonicien: La Devise du Silence au Studiolo d'Isabelle d'Este." In *Symboles de la Renaissance*, edited by Daniel Arasse, 79–88. Paris: Presses de l'Ecole normale supérieure, 1976.

Fallows, David. *Galfridus and Robertus de Anglia: Four Italian Songs*. Lustleigh: Antico Edition, 1977.

————. "Prenez sur moi: Ockeghem's Tonal Pun." *Plainsong and Medieval Music* 1 (1992): 63–75.

————. "Leonardo Giustinian and Quattrocento Polyphonic Song." In *L'Edizione Critica tra Testo Musicale e Testo Letterario*, edited by Renato Borghi and Pietro Zappalà, 247–60. Lucca: Libreria musicale italiana, 1995.

Falvo, Joseph D. "Urbino and the Apotheosis of Power." *Modern Language Notes* 101 (1986): 114–46.

Fehl, Maria Reina. "The Italian Translation of Philostratus by Demetrius Moscus." In Philip Fehl, "The Worship of Bacchus and Venus in Bellini's and Titian's Bacchanals for Alfonso d'Este," *Studies in the History of Art* 6 (1974b): 89–92.

————. "Four 'Imagines' by the Elder Philostratus in the Translation Prepared by Demetrius Moscus for Isabella d'Este." In *Ekphrasis und Herrscherallegorie: Antike Bildbeschreibungen im Werk Tizians und Leonardos*, Michaela Marek, 123–37. Worms: Wernersche Verlagsgesellschaft, 1985.

Fehl, Philip. "The Hidden Genre: a Study of the *Concert Champêtre* in the Louvre." *Journal of Aesthetics and Art Criticism* 16 (1957): 153–68.

————. "The Worship of Bacchus and Venus in Bellini's and Titian's Bacchanals for Alfonso d'Este." *Studies in the History of Art* 6 (1974a): 37–95.

————. "Imitation as a Source of Greatness: Rubens, Titian and the Painting of the Ancients." In *Bacchanals by Titian and Rubens: Papers Given at a Symposium in Nationalmuseum, Stockholm March 18–19, 1987*, edited by Görel Cavalli-Björkman, 108–24. Stockholm: Nationalmuseum, 1987.

Feldman, Martha. "The Courtesan's Voice: Petrarchan Lovers, Pop Philosophy and Oral Traditions." In *The Courtesan's Arts: Cross-Cultural Perspectives*, edited by Martha Feldman and Bonnie Gordon, 105–23. Oxford: Oxford University Press, 2006.

Fenlon, Iain. "The Gonzaga and Music." In *Splendours of the Gonzaga*, edited by David Chambers and Jane Martineau, 87–94. London: Victoria & Albert Museum, 1981.

———. "Gender and Generation: Patterns of Music Patronage Among the Este, 1471–1539." In *The Court of Ferrara and its Patronage, 1441–1598*, edited by Marianne Pade, Lene Wange Petesen and Daniela Quarta, 213–32. Modena: Edizioni Panini, 1990.

———. "Music and Learning in Isabella d'Este's Studioli." In *La Corte di Mantova nell'Età di Andrea Mantegna, 1450–1550*, edited by Cesare Mozzarelli, Robert Oresko, and Leandro Ventura, 353–67. Rome: Bulzoni, 1997.

Ferrari, Daniela. "L'Inventario delle gioie'." In *Isabella d'Este: La Primadonna del Rinascimento*, edited by Daniele Bini, 21–43. Modena: Il Bulino, 2001.

Filarete. *Treatise on Architecture: Being the Treatise by Antonio di Piero Averlino, known as Filarete*. Translated and edited by John R. Spencer. 2 volumes. New Haven: Yale University Press, 1965.

Findlen, Paula. *Possessing Nature: Museums, Collecting and Scientific Culture in Early Modern Italy*. Berkeley: University of California Press, 1994.

Fiorenza, Giancarlo. "Dossi Dossi and Celio Calcagnini at the Court of Ferrara." In *Artists at Court: Image-Making and Identity 1300–1550*, edited by Stephen J. Campbell, 176–87. Boston: Isabella Stewart Gardner Museum, 2004.

———. *Dosso Dossi: Paintings of Myth, Magic and the Antique*. University Park, PA: Pennsylvania State University Press, 2008.

Fletcher, J. M. "Isabella d'Este, Patron and Collector." In *Splendours of the Gonzaga*, edited by David Chambers and Jane Martineau, 51–63. London: Victorian & Albert Museum, 1981.

Foucault, Michel. *The Archaeology of Knowledge*. Translated by A. M. Sheridan Smith. London: Tavistock Publications, 1972.

Franceschini, Adriano. *Artisti a Ferrara in Età Umanistica e Rinascimentale: Testimonianze Archivistiche Parte II, Tomo II: dal 1493 al 1516*. Ferrara: Gabriele Corbo, 1993.

Freedman, Luba. *The Classical Pastoral in the Visual Arts*. New York: P. Lang, 1989.

Fubini, Riccardo. *Humanism and Secularization: From Petrarch to Valla*. Translated by Martha King. Durham: Duke University Press, 2003.

Gaffurius, Franchinus. *De Harmonia Musicorum Instrumentorum Opus*. Translated by Clement A. Miller. Neuhausen-Stuttgart: American Institute of Musicology, 1977.

Gallico, Claudio. "Poesie Musicali di Isabella d'Este." *Collectanea Historiae Musicae* 3 (1962a): 109–19.

———. "Un 'Dialogo d'amore' di Niccolò da Correggio Musicato da Bartolomeo Tromboncino." *Studien zur Musikwissenschaft* 25 (1962b): 205–13.

———. "Civiltà Musicale Mantovana Intorno al 1500." In *Atti del VI Convegno Internazionale di Studi su Rinascimento*, 243–49. Florence: Sansoni, 1965.

———. "Musica nella Ca' Giocosa." In *Vittorino da Feltre e la Sua Scuola: Umanesimo, Pedagogia, Arti*, edited by Nella Giannetto, 189–98. Florence: Olschki, 1981.

Gallo, F. Alberto. *Music in the Castle: Troubadours, Books and Orators in the Italian Courts of the Thirteenth, Fourteenth and Fifteenth Centuries*. Translated by Anna Herklotz and Kathryn Krug. Chicago: University of Chicago Press, 1995.

Gardner, Edmund G. *Dukes and Poets in Ferrara: A Study in the Poetry, Religion and Politics of the Fifteenth and Early Sixteenth Centuries*. London: Constable, 1904.

———. *The King of Court Poets: A Study of the Work, Life and Times of Lodovico Ariosto*. London: Constable, 1906.

Genovesi, Adalberto. "Due Imprese Musicali di Isabella d'Este." *Atti e Memorie: Accademia Virgiliana da Mantova* 61 (1993): 73–102.

Gerbino, Giuseppe. *Music and the Myth of Arcadia in Renaissance Italy*. Cambridge: Cambridge University Press, 2009.

Gibbons, Felton. *Dosso and Battista Dossi: Court Painters at Ferrara*. Princeton: Princeton University Press, 1968.

Giovio, Paolo. *Dialogo dell'Imprese Militari e Amorose*. Edited by Maria Luisa Doglio. Rome: Bulzoni, 1978.

Giraldi Cinzio, Giovanbattista. *Commentario delle Cose di Ferrara, et de Principi da Este*. Translated by Lodovico Domenichi. Venice: Giovanni de' Rossi, 1556.

Godwin, Joscelyn, ed. *The Harmony of the Spheres: A Sourcebook of the Pythagorean Tradition in Music*. Rochester: Inner Traditions International, 1993.

Goffen, Rona. *Titian's Women*. New Haven: Yale University Press, 1997.

Goffman, Erving. *The Presentation of Self in Everyday Life*. London: Allen Lane, 1969.

Goldthwaite, Richard. "The Empire of Things: Consumer Demand in Renaissance Italy." In *Patronage, Art and Society in Renaissance Italy*, edited by F. W. Kent and Patricia Simons, 153–75. Oxford: Clarendon Press, 1987.

Gombrich, Ernst. "An Interpretation of Mantegna's *Parnassus*." *Journal of the Warburg and Courtauld Institutes* 26 (1963): 196–8.

Goodgal, Dana. "The Camerino of Alfonso I d'Este." *Art History* 1 (1978): 162–90.

———. "Titian Repairs Bellini." In *Bacchanals by Titian and Rubens: Papers Given at a Symposium in Nationalmuseum, Stockholm March 18–19, 1987*, edited by Görel Cavalli-Björkman, 17–24. Stockholm: Nationalmuseum, 1987.

Gould, Cecil. *The Studio of Alfonso d'Este and Titian's 'Bacchus and Ariadne': a Re-Examination of the Chronology of the Bacchanals and of the Evolution of One of Them*. London: National Gallery, 1969.

Grafton, Anthony. "Boethius in the Renaissance." In *Boethius: His Life, Thought and Influence*, edited by Margaret Gibson, 410–15. Oxford: Blackwell, 1981.

Grafton, Anthony T., and Lisa Jardine. "Humanism and the School of Guarino: A Problem of Evaluation." *Past and Present* 96 (1982): 51–80.

Gravelle, Sarah Stever. "The Latin-Vernacular Question and Humanist Theory of Language and Culture." *Journal of the History of Ideas* 49 (1988): 367–86.

Greenblatt, Stephen. *Renaissance Self-Fashioning: From More to Shakespeare*. Chicago: University of Chicago Press, 1980.

———. "Fiction and Friction." In *Reconstructing Individualism: Autonomy, Individuality and the Self in Western Thought*, edited by Thomas C. Heller, Morton Sosna, and David E. Wellbery, 30–52. Stanford: Stanford University Press, 1986.

Gregorovius, Ferdinand. *Lucrezia Borgia, According to Original Documents and Correspondence of her Day*. Translated by John Leslie Garner. New York: D. Appleton, 1903.

Guicciardini, Francesco. *The History of Italy*. Translated and edited by Sidney Alexander. New York: Macmillan, 1969.

Guidobaldi, Nicoletta. "Court Music and Universal Harmony in Federico da Montefeltro's Studiolo in Urbino." *Hamburger Jahrbuch für Musikwissenschaft* 12 (1994): 111–20.

———. *La Musica di Federico: Immagini e Suoni alla Corte di Urbino*. Florence: Olschki, 1995.

———. "Un Microcosmo Musicale nel Castello di Federico da Montefeltro a Gubbio." In *Trent'Anni di Ricerche Musicologiche: Studi in Onore di F. Alberto Gallo*, edited by Patrizia Dalla Vecchia and Donatella Restani, 413–27. Rome: Torre d'Orfeo, 1996.

———. "Le Mythe du 'Nouvel Orphée' dans Deux Portraits Musicaux de Giovanni Boldù." In *La musique, de tous les passetemps le plus beau: Hommage a Jean-Michel Vaccaro*, edited by G. Chaix, 195–206. Paris: Klincksieck, 1998.

Gundersheimer, Werner. *Art and Life at the Court of Ercole I d'Este: The De triumphis religionis of Giovanni Sabadino degli Arienti*. Geneva: Droz, 1972.

———. *Ferrara: The Style of a Renaissance Despotism*. Princeton: Princeton University Press, 1973.

———. "The Patronage of Ercole I d'Este." *Journal of Medieval and Renaissance Studies* 6 (1976): 1–18.

———. "Women, Learning and Power: Eleonora of Aragon and the Court of Ferrara." In *Beyond their Sex: Learned Women of the European Past*, edited by Patricia Labalme, 43–65. New York: New York University Press, 1984.

Haar, James. "Music as a Visual Language." In *Meaning in the Visual Arts: Views from the Outside*, edited by Irving Lavin, 265–84. Princeton: Princeton University Press, 1995.

———. "Petrucci's 'Justiniane' Revisited." *Journal of the American Musicological Society* 52 (1999): 1–38.

Handschin, Jacques. "Anselmi's Treatise on Music Annotated by Gafori." *Musica Disciplina* 2 (1948): 123–42.

Haraszti, Emile. "Pierre Bono Luthiste de Mathias Corvin." *Revue de Musicologie* 31 (1949): 73–85.

———. "La Technique des Improvisateurs de Langue Vulgaire et de Latin au Quattrocento." *Revue Belge de Musicologie* 9 (1955): 12–31.

Havelock, Eric A. *The Muse Learns to Write: Reflections on Orality and Literacy from Antiquity to the Present.* New Haven: Yale University Press, 1986.

Hellman, Mimi. "Furniture, Sociability and the Work of Leisure in Eighteenth-Century France." *Eighteenth-Century Studies* 32 (1999): 415–45.

Hesiod. *Theogony and Works and Days.* Translated by M. L. West. Oxford: Oxford University Press, 1988.

Higgins, Paula. "Parisian Nobles, A Scottish Princess, and the Woman's Voice in Late Medieval Song." *Early Music History* 10 (1991): 145–200.

Hill, George Francis. *A Corpus of Italian Medals of the Renaissance Before Cellini.* 2 volumes. Florence: Studio per edizioni scelte, 1984.

Holberton, Paul. "Battista Guarino's Catullus and Titian's Bacchus and Ariadne." *Burlington Magazine* 128, no. 998 (1986): 347–50.

———. "The Choice of Texts for the Camerino Pictures." In *Bacchanals by Titian and Rubens: Papers Given at a Symposium in Nationalmuseum, Stockholm March 18–19, 1987,* edited by Görel Cavalli-Björkman, 57–66. Stockholm: Nationalmusem, 1987.

———. "The *Pastorale* or *Fête champêtre* in the Early Sixteenth Century." In *Titian 500,* edited by Joseph Manca, 245–62. Washington: National Gallery of Art, 1993.

Holford-Strevens, Leofranc. "Sirens in Antiquity and the Middle Ages." In *Music of the Sirens,* edited by Linda Phyllis Austern and Inna Naroditskaya, 16–51. Bloomington: Indiana University Press, 2006.

Hope, Charles. "The 'Camerini d'Alabastro' of Alfonso d'Este." *Burlington Magazine* 114 (1971): 641–50 and 712–21.

———. "The Camerino d'Alabastro. A Reconsideration of the Evidence." In *Bacchanals by Titian and Rubens: Papers Given at a Symposium in Nationalmuseum, Stockholm March 18–19, 1987,* edited by Görel Cavalli-Björkman, 25–42. Stockholm: *Nationalmuseum,* 1987.

Horace [Quintus Horatius Flaccus]. *Satires, Epistles, Ars Poetica.* Translated by H. Rushton Fairclough. London: Heinemann, 1926.

Humfrey, Peter. "Titian's *Bacchanals* for Duke Alfonso's *Camerino*: a Re-Examination of the Chronology." In *L'Età di Alfonso I e la Pittura del Dosso,* edited by Gianni Venturi, 179–85. Modena: Franco Cosimo Panini, 2004.

———. *Titian: The Complete Paintings.* London: Ludion, 2007.

Humfrey, Peter, and Mauro Lucco. *Dosso Dossi: Court Painter in Renaissance Ferrara.* New York: Metropolitan Museum of Art, 1998.

Hunt, John Dixon, ed. *The Pastoral Landscape.* Washington: National Gallery of Art, 1992.

Jaffé, David, ed. *Titian.* London: National Gallery, 2003.

Jardine, Lisa. "'O Decus Italiae Virgo,' or The Myth of the Learned Lady in the Renaissance." *The Historical Journal* 28 (1985): 799–819.

Jones, Roger. "'What Venus Did with Mars:' Battista Fieri and Mantegna's *Parnassus.*" *Journal of the Warburg and Courtauld Institutes* 44 (1981): 193–98.

Jones, Ann Rosalind. "Surprising Fame: Renaissance Gender Ideologies and Women's Lyric." In *The Poetics of Gender,* edited by Nancy K. Miller, 74–95. New York: Columbia University Press, 1986.

———. *The Currency of Eros: Women's Love Lyric in Europe, 1540–1620.* Bloomington: Indiana University Press, 1990.

Kallendorf, Craig W., ed. and trans. *Humanist Educational Treatises.* Cambridge, MA: Harvard University Press, 2002.

Kaske, Carol V., and John R. Clark, trans. and ed. *Marsilio Ficino: Three Books on Life*. Binghamton, NY: Medieval & Renaissance Texts & Studies in conjunction with the Renaissance Society of America, 1989.

Keefer, Michael H. "Agrippa's Dilemma: Hermetic 'Rebirth' and the Ambivalences of *De vanitate* and *De occulta philosophia*." *Renaissance Quarterly* 41 (1988): 614–53.

Kelso, Ruth. *Doctrine for the Lady of the Renaissance*. Urbana: University of Illinois Press, 1956.

Keyser, Dorothy. "The Character of Exploration: Adrian Willaert's 'Quid non ebrietas'." In *Musical Repercussions of 1492: Encounters in Text and Performance*, edited by Carol E. Robertson, 185–207. Washington: Smithsonian Institute Press, 1992.

King, Catherine. "Mnemosyne and Calliope in the 'Chapel of the Muses,' San Francesco, Rimini." *Journal of the Warburg and Courtauld Institutes* 51 (1988): 186–87.

Kirkbride, Robert. *Architecture and Memory: The Renaissance Studioli of Federico da Montefeltro*. New York: Columbia University Press, 2008.

Kohl, Benjamin G., and Ronald G. Witt, ed. *The Earthly Republic: Italian Humanists on Government and Society*. Philadelphia: University of Pennsylvania Press, 1978.

Kolsky, Stephen. "Images of Isabella d'Este." *Italian Studies* 39 (1984): 47–62.

———. "An Unnoticed Description of Isabella d'Este's Grotta." *Journal of the Warburg and Courtauld Institutes* 52 (1989): 232–35.

———. *Mario Equicola: The Real Courtier*. Geneva: Droz, 1991.

Koortbojian, Michael, and Ruth Webb. "Isabella d'Este's Philostratos." *Journal of the Warburg and Courtauld Institutes* 56 (1993): 260–67.

Kristeller, Paul Oskar. "Music and Learning in the Early Italian Renaissance." In *Renaissance Thought and the Arts: Collected Essays*, 142–62. Princeton: Princeton University Press, 1990. (Originally published in *Journal of Renaissance and Baroque Music* 1 [1947]: 255–74.)

LaMay, Thomasin. "Madalena Casulana: *my body knows unheard of songs*." In *Gender, Sexuality and Early Music*, edited by Todd Borgerding, 41–71. New York: Routledge, 2002.

Lehmann, Phyllis Williams. "The Sources and Meaning of Mantegna's *Parnassus*." In *Samothracian Reflections: Aspects of the Revival of the Antique*, Phyllis Williams Lehmann and Karl Lehmann, 59–180. Princeton: Princeton University Press, 1973.

Leppert, Richard D. *Music and Image: Domesticity, Ideology and Socio-Cultural Formation in Eighteenth-Century England*. Cambridge: Cambridge University Press, 1988.

Lichtenstein, Jacquiline. "Making Up Representations: The Risks of Femininity." *Representations* 20 (1987): 77–87.

Liebenwein, Wolfgang. *Studiolo: Storia di uno Spazio Culturale*. Edited by Claudia Cieri Via and translated by Alessandro Calefano. Modena: Panini, 1988.

Lightbown, Ronald. *Mantegna*. Oxford: Phaidon Christie's, 1986.

Lippincott, Kristin. "The Frescoes of the Salone dei Mesi in the Palazzo Schifanoia in Ferrara: Style, Iconography and Cultural Context." 2 volumes. PhD diss., University of Chicago, 1987.

———. "The Genesis and Significance of the Fifteenth-century Italian Impresa." In *Chivalry in the Renaissance*, edited by Sydney Anglo, 49–84. Woodbridge: Boydell, 1990.

Lockwood, Lewis. "Music at Ferrara in the Period of Ercole I d'Este." *Studi Musicali* 1 (1972): 101–31.

———. "Pietrobono and the Instrumental Tradition at Ferrara in the Fifteenth Century." *Rivista Italiana di Musicologia* 10 (1975): 115–33.

———. "Josquin at Ferrara: New Documents and Letters." In *Josquin des Prez*, edited by Edward E. Lowinsky, 103–37. Oxford: Oxford University Press, 1976a.

———. "Dufay and Ferrara." In *Dufay Quincentenary Conference*, edited by Allan W. Atlas, 1–25. Brooklyn: Brooklyn College Dept. of Music, 1976b.

———. "Jean Mouton and Jean Michel: New Evidence on French Music and Musicians in Italy, 1505–1520." *Journal of the American Musicological Society* 32 (1979): 191–246.

———. "Musicisti a Ferrara all'Epoca dell'Ariosto." *Quaderni della Rivista Italiana di Musicologia* 5 (1981): 7–29.

———. *Music in Renaissance Ferrara 1400–1505: The Creation of a Musical Centre in the Fifteenth Century*. Oxford: Clarendon Press, 1984.

————. "Adrian Willaert and Cardinal Ippolito I d'Este: New Light on Willaert's Early Career in Italy, 1515–21." *Early Music History* 5 (1985): 85–112.

————. "A Virtuoso Singer at Ferrara and Rome: The Case of Bidon." In *Papal Music and Musicians in Late Medieval and Renaissance Rome*, edited by Richard Sherr, 224–39. Oxford: Clarendon Press, 1998.

————. "Bruhier, Lupus and Music Copying at Ferrara: New Documents." In *Essays on Music and Culture in Honour of Herbert Kellman*, edited by Barbara Haggh, 150–60. Turnhout: Brepols, 2001.

Lorenzetti, Stefano. "'Quel celeste cantar che mi disface:' Immagine della Donna ed Educazione alla Musica nell'Ideale Pedagogico del Rinascimento Italiano." *Studi Musicali* 23 (1994): 241–61.

————. *Musica e Identità Nobiliare nell'Italia del Rinascimento: Educazione, Mentalità, Immaginario*. Florence: Olschki, 2003.

Lowinsky, Edward E. "Willaert's Chromatic 'Duo' Reexamined." In *Music in the Culture of the Renaissance and Other Essays*, edited by Bonnie J Blackburn, 681–98. Chicago: University of Chicago Press, 1989. (Originally published in *Tijdschrift voor Muziekwetenschap* 18 [1956–59]: 1–36.)

————. *The Medici Codex of 1518: A Choirbook of Motets Dedicated to Lorenzo de' Medici, Duke of Urbino*. 3 volumes. Chicago: University of Chicago Press, 1968.

————. "Music in Titian's Bacchanal of the Andrians: Origin and History of the Canon Per Tonos." In *Music in the Culture of the Renaissance and Other Essays*, edited by Bonnie J Blackburn, 289–350. Chicago: University of Chicago Press, 1989. (Originally published in *Titian, His World and His Legacy*, edited by David Rosand, 191–282. New York: Columbia University Press, 1982.)

Lucas, Arthur, and Joyce Plesters. "Titian's Bacchus and Ariadne." *National Gallery Technical Bulletin* 2 (1978): 25–47.

Lucian of Samosata. *Lucian, Volume III*. Translated by A. M. Harmon. London: Heinemann, 1921.

Luzio, Alessandro. *I Precettori d'Isabella d'Este: Appunti e Documenti*. Ancona: A. Gustavo Morelli Edit., 1887.

Luzio, Alessandro, and Rodolfo Renier. *La Coltura e le Relazioni Letterarie di Isabella d'Este Gonzaga*. Edited by Simone Albonico. Milan: Edizioni Sylvestre Bonnard, 2005. (Originally a series of articles in *Giornale Storico della Letteratura Italiana* 1899–1903.)

MacCarthy, Evan. "Music and Learning in Early Renaissance Ferrara, c.1430–1470." PhD diss., Harvard University, 2010.

Machiavelli, Niccolò. *Il principe*. Edited by L. Arthur Burd. Oxford: Clarendon Press, 1891.

————. *The Prince*. Translated by N. H. Thomson. New York: Quality Paperback Book Club, 1992.

Marek, Michaela. "Alfonso I d'Este e il Programma del Suo Studiolo." In *Frescobaldi e il Suo Tempo nel Quarto Centenario della Nascita*, 77–83. Venice: Marsilio, 1983.

Mattingly, Harold. *Coins of the Roman Empire in the British Museum*. 6 volumes. London: British Museum, 1923–62.

Mattingly, Garrett. *Renaissance Diplomacy*. Boston: Houghton Mifflin, 1955.

McIver, Katherine A. "Maniera, Music and Vasari." *The Sixteenth Century Journal* 28 (1997): 45–55.

————. "Pastoral Pleasures, Sensual Sounds: Paintings of Love, Music and Morality in Sixteenth-Century Italy." In *Music, Sensation and Sensuality*, edited by Linda Phyllis Austern, 285–98. New York: Routledge, 2002.

McKinnon, James W. "Jubal vel Pythagoras: Quis Sit Inventor Musicae?" *The Musical Quarterly* 64 (1978): 1–28.

Mengozzi, Stefano. "'Clefless' Notation, Counterpoint and the fa-Degree." *Early Music* 36 (2008): 51–64.

Messisbugo, Cristoforo da. *Banchetti, Composizioni di Viviande e Apparecchio Generale*. Edited by Fernando Bandini. Vicenza: Neri Pozza Editore, 1992.

Moretti, Laura. "The Function and Use of Musical Sources at the Padua 'Court' of Alvise Cornaro in the First Half of the Cinquecento." *Journal of the Alamire Foundation* 2 (2010): 37–51.

Mottola-Molfino, Alessandra, and Mauro Natali, ed. *Le Muse e il Principe: Arte di Corte nel Rinascimento Padano.* 2 volumes. Modena: Franco Cosimo Panini Editore, 1991.

Mumford, Ivy L. "Some Decorative Aspects of the Imprese of Isabella d'Este (1474–1539)." *Italian Studies* 34 (1979): 60–70.

Murutes, Harry. "Personifications of Laughter and Drunken Sleep in Titian's *Andrians.*" *Burlington Magazine* 115 (1973): 518–25.

Nagy, Gregory. *Poetry as Performance: Homer and Beyond.* Cambridge: Cambridge University Press, 1996.

Newman, J. K. *The Concept of Vates in Augustan Poetry.* Brussels: Latomus, 1967.

Norris, Andrea S. "Gian Cristoforo Romano: The Courtier as Medallist." In *Italian Medals,* edited by J. Graham Pollard, 131–41. Washington: National Gallery of Art, 1987.

Osgood, Charles G., trans. and ed. *Boccaccio on Poetry: Being the Preface and the Fourteenth and Fifteenth Books of Boccaccio's 'Genealogia deorum gentilium' in an English Version.* 2nd edition. Indianapolis: Bobbs-Merrill, 1956.

Ovid [Publius Ovidius Naso]. *Heroides and Amores.* Translated by Grant Showerman. London: W. Heinemann, 1914.

———. *Metamorphoses.* Translated by Brookes More. Boston: Cornhill, 1922.

———. *The Art of Love, and Other Poems.* Translated by J. H. Mozley. London: Heinemann, 1929.

———. *Fasti.* Translated by James George Frazer. London: Heinemann, 1931.

———. *Amores I.* Translated by John Barsby. Oxford: Clarendon, 1973.

Palisca, Claude V. *Humanism in Italian Renaissance Musical Thought.* New Haven: Yale University Press, 1985.

———. "Boethius in the Renaissance." In *Music Theory and its Sources,* edited by André Barbera, 259–80. Notre Dame: University of Notre Dame Press, 1990.

Panizza, Letizia. "Italian Humanists and Boethius: Was Philosophy For or Against Poetry?" In *New Perspectives on Renaissance Thought: Essays in the History of Science, Rhetoric and Philosophy,* edited by John Henry and Sarah Hutton, 48–67. London: Duckworth, 1990.

Panofsky, Erwin. *Problems in Titian, Mostly Iconographic.* London: Phaidon, 1969.

Pasco-Pranger, Molly. "'Vates operosus:' Vatic Poetics and Antiquarianism in Ovid's Fasti." *The Classical World* 93 (2000): 275–91.

Pastor, Ludwig. *The History of the Popes, From the Close of the Middle Ages.* 3rd edition. 12 volumes. London: Keegan Paul, 1899–1953.

Patrizi, Giorgio. "Pedagogie del Silenzio: Tacere e Ascoltare come Fondamenti dell'Apprendere." In *Educare il Corpo, Educare la Parola: Nella Trattatistica del Rinascimento,* edited by Giorgio Patrizi and Amadeo Quondam, 415–24. Rome: Bulzoni, 1998.

Pausanias. *Description of Greece.* Translated by W. H. S. Jones and H. A. Omerod. London: Heinemann, 1918.

Pedrocco, Filippo. *Titian.* Translated by Corrado Federici. New York: Rizzoli, 2001.

Perinbanayagam, R. S. "How to Do Self with Things." In *Beyond Goffman: Studies on Communication, Institution and Social Interaction,* edited by Stephen Riggins, 315–40. Berlin: Mouton de Gruyter, 1990.

Perry, Jon Pearson. "A Fifteenth-Century Dialogue on Literary Taste: Angelo Decembrio's Account of Playwright Ugolino Pisani at the Court of Leonello d'Este." *Renaissance Quarterly* 39 (1986): 613–43.

Petrarca, Francesco. *The Life of Solitude.* Translated by Jacob Zeitlin. Urbana: University of Illinois Press, 1924.

Peverada, Enrico. "Un Organo per Leonello d'Este." *L'Organo* 28 (1994): 3–30.

Philostratus the Elder. *Elder Philostratus, Younger Philostratus, Callistratus.* Translated by Arthur Fairbanks. London: Heinemann, 1931.

Pieri, Marzia. "La Scena Pastorale." In *La Corte e lo Spazio: Ferrara Estense,* edited by Giuseppe Papagno and Amedeo Quondam, 2 volumes, 2:489–525. Rome: Bulzoni, 1982.

Pindar. *Olympian Odes and Pythian Odes.* Translated by William H. Race. Cambridge, MA: Harvard University Press, 1997.

Pirrotta, Nino. "Music and Cultural Tendencies in 15th-Century Italy." *Journal of the American Musicological Society* 19 (1966): 127–61.

———. "The Oral and Written Traditions of Music." Translated by Lowell Lindgren. In *Music and Culture in Italy from the Middle Ages to the Baroque: A Collection of Essays*, 72–79. Cambridge, MA: Harvard University Press, 1984. (Originally published in *L'Ars Nova Italiana del Trecento*, edited by F. Alberto Gallo, 431–41. Certaldo: Centro di studi sull'Ars nova italiana del Trecento, 1970.)

———. "New Glimpses of an Unwritten Tradition in Words and Music." In *Words and Music: The Scholar's View; A Medley of Problems and Solutions Compiled in Honour of A. Tillman Merritt*, edited by Laurence Berman, 271–91. Cambridge, MA: Department of Music, Harvard University, 1972a.

———. "Ricercare e Variazioni su 'O Rosa Bella'." *Studi musicali* 1 (1972b): 59–77.

———. "Before the Madrigal." *Journal of Musicology* 12 (1994): 237–52.

Pirrotta, Nino, and Elena Povoledo. *Music and Theatre from Poliziano to Monteverdi*. Translated by Karen Eales. Cambridge: Cambridge University Press, 1982.

Pius II. *Commentaries*. Edited in translation by Margaret Meserve and Marcello Simonetta. 2 volumes. Cambridge, MA: Harvard University Press, 2003.

Pliny the Elder [Gaius Plinius Secundus]. *Natural History*. Translated by H. Rackham. 10 vols. London: Heinemann, 1938.

Pliny the Younger [Gaius Plinius Caecilius Secundus]. *Letters, Books 8–10; Panegyricus*. Translated by Betty Radice. Cambridge, MA: Harvard University Press, 1969.

Praz, Mario. "The Gonzaga Devices." In *Splendours of the Gonzaga*, edited by David Chambers and Jane Martineau, 65–72. London: Victoria and Albert Museum, 1981.

Prizer, William F. *Courtly Pastimes: The Frottole of Marchetto Cara*. Ann Arbor: UMI Research Press, 1980.

———. "Isabella d'Este and Lorenzo da Pavia, 'Master Instrument-Maker'." *Early Music History* 2 (1982): 87–127.

———. "Isabella d'Este and Lucrezia Borgia as Patrons of Music: The Frottola at Mantua and Ferrara." *Journal of the American Musicological Society* 38 (1985): 1–33.

———. "The Frottola and the Unwritten Tradition." *Studi Musicali* 15 (1986): 3–37.

———. Review of *Music in Renaissance Ferrara 1400–1505: The Creation of a Musical Centre in the Fifteenth Century* by Lewis Lockwood. *Journal of the American Musicological Society* 40 (1987): 95–105.

———. "Games of Venus: Secular Music in the Late Quattrocento and Early Cinquecento." *Journal of Musicology* 9 (1991): 3–56.

———. "Music in Ferrara and Mantua at the Time of Dosso Dossi: Interrelations and Influences." In *Dosso's Fate: Painting and Court Culture in Renaissance Italy*, edited by Luisa Ciammitti, Steven Ostrow, and Salvatore Settis, 290–308. Los Angeles: Getty Research Institute for the History of Art & the Humanities, 1998.

———. "Una 'Virtù molto conveniente a madonne:' Isabella d'Este as a Musician." *Journal of Musicology* 17 (1999): 10–49.

Propertius, Sextus. *Elegies*. Translated by G. P. Goold. Cambridge, MA: Harvard University Press, 1990.

Quintilian [Marcus Fabius Quintilianus]. *Institutio Oratoria, Books I-III*. Translated by H. E. Butler. London: W. Heinemann, 1920.

Raggio, Olga. "The Liberal Arts Studiolo from the Ducal Palace at Gubbio." *The Metropolitan Museum of Art Bulletin*, n.s., 53, no. 4 (1996): 3–35.

———. *The Gubbio Studiolo and Its Conservation*. 2 volumes. New York: Metropolitan Museum of Art, 1999.

Ramis de Pareia, Bartolomeo. *Música Práctica*. Edited by Clemente Terni. Madrid: Joyas Bibliográficas, 1983.

———. *Musica Practica*. Translated by Clement A. Miller. Neuhausen-Stuttgart: American Institute of Musicology, 1993.

Rawski, Conrad H., ed. and trans. *Petrarch: Four Dialogues for Scholars*. Cleveland: Press of Western Reserve University, 1967.

———. "Petrarch's Dialogue on Music." *Speculum* 46 (1971): 302–17.

Rebhorn, Wayne. *Courtly Performances: Masking and Festivity in Castiglione's 'Book of the Courtier'*. Detroit: Wayne State University Press, 1978.

Reese, Gustave. "Musical Compositions in Renaissance Intarsia." *Bulletin of the American Academy of Arts and Sciences* 19 (1965): 74–97.

Regan, Lisa K. "Ariosto's Threshold Patron: Isabella d'Este in the *Orlando Furioso*." *Modern Language Notes* 120 (2005): 50–69.

Remington, Preston. "The Private Study of Federigo da Montefeltro: A Masterpiece of XV Century Trompe-l'Oeil." *The Metropolitan Museum of Art Bulletin* 36 (1941): 1–13.

Reynolds, Margaret. *The Sappho Companion*. London: Chatto & Windus, 2000.

Rifkin, Joshua. "Jean Michel, Maistre Jhan and a Chorus of Beasts: Old Light on Some Ferrarese Music Manuscripts." *Tijdschrift van de Koninklijke Vereniging voor Nederlandse Muziekgeschiedenis* 52 (2002): 67–102.

Ripa, Cesare. *Iconologia*. New York: Garland, 1976.

Robathan, Dorothy M. "Diodorus Siculus in the Italian Renaissance." *Classical Philology* 27 (1932): 84.

Rogers, Mary. "Sonnets on Female Portraits from Renaissance North Italy." *Word and Image* 2 (1986): 291–305.

———. "The Decorum of Women's Beauty: Trissino, Firenzuola, Luigini and the Representation of Women in Sixteenth-Century Painting." *Renaissance Studies* 2 (1988): 47–88.

Rosand, David. "An Arc of Flame: On the Transmission of Pictorial Knowledge." In *Bacchanals by Titian and Rubens: Papers Given at a Symposium in Nationalmuseum, Stockholm March 18–19, 1987*, edited by Görel Cavalli-Björkman, 81–92. Stockholm: Nationalmuseum, 1987.

———. "Pastoral Topoi: On the Construction of Meaning in Landscape." *Studies in the History of Art* 36 (1992): 161–77.

Rosenberg, Charles M. "Courtly Decorations and the Decorum of Interior Space." In *La Corte e lo Spazio: Ferrara Estense*, edited by Giuseppe Papagno and Amedeo Quondam, 2 volumes, 2:529–44. Rome: Bulzoni, 1982.

———. *The Este Monuments and Urban Development in Renaissance Ferrara*. Cambridge: Cambridge University Press, 1997.

———. "Alfonso I d'Este, Michelangelo and the Man who Bought Pigs." In *Revaluing Renaissance Art*, edited by Gabriele Neher and Rupert Shepherd, 89–100. Aldershot: Ashgate, 2000.

Rubsamen, Walter H. *Literary Sources of Secular Music in Italy c.1500*. Berkeley: University of California Press, 1943.

———. "The Justiniane or Viniziane of the 15th Century." *Acta Musicologica* 29 (1957): 172–84.

San Juan, Rose Marie. "The Court Lady's Dilemma: Isabella d'Este and Art Collecting in the Renaissance." *Oxford Art Journal* 14 (1991): 67–78.

Sannazaro, Jacopo. *Arcadia and Piscatorial Eclogues*. Translated by Ralph Nash. Detroit: Wayne State University Press, 1966.

Sanuto, Marino. *I Diarii di Marino Sanuto*. Edited by Federigo Stefani. 58 volumes. Venice: Visentini, 1879–1902.

Sarchi, Alessandra. "The Studiolo of Alberto Pio da Carpi." In *Drawing Relationships in Northern Italian Renaissance Art: Patronage and Theories of Invention*, edited by Giancarla Periti, 129–52. Aldershot: Ashgate, 2004.

Scher, Stephen K. "An Introduction to the Renaissance Portrait Medal." In *Perspectives on the Renaissance Medal*, edited by Stephen K. Scher, 1–25. New York: Garland, 2000.

Scherliess, Volker. *Musikalische Noten auf Kunstwerken der Italienischen Renaissance bis zum Anfang des 17 Jahrhunderts*. Hamburg: Verlag der Musikalienhandlung, 1972.

Schrade, Leo. "Renaissance: The Historical Conception of an Epoch." In *De Scientia Musicae Studia atque Orationes*, 311–25. Bern: Paul Haupt, 1967. (Originally published in *Kongress-Bericht: Internationale Gesellschaft fur Musikwissenschaft Utrecht 1952*, 19–32. Amsterdam: G. Alsbach, 1953.)

Sheard, Wendy Stedman. "Antonio Lombardo's Reliefs for Alfonso d'Este's *Studio di Marmi*: Their Significance and Impact on Titian." In *Titian 500*, edited by Joseph Manca, 315–58. Washington: National Gallery of Art, 1993.

Shearman, John. "Alfonso d'Este's Camerino." In *'Il se rendit en Italie:' Etudes Offerts à André Chastel*, 209–30. Rome: Edizioni dell'Elefante, 1987.

———. "The Vatican Stanze: Functions and Decoration." In *Art and Politics in Renaissance Italy: British Academy Lectures*, edited by George Holmes, 185–240. Oxford: Oxford University Press, 1993a.

———. "The Apartments of Julius II and Leo X." In *Raphael in the Apartments of Julius II and Leo X*, edited by Guido Cornini et al., 15–37. Milan: Electa, 1993b.

———. *Raphael in Early Modern Sources*. 2 volumes. New Haven: Yale University Press, 2003.

Shephard, Tim. "Constructing Identities in a Music Manuscript: the Medici Codex as a Gift." *Renaissance Quarterly* 63 (2010a): 84–127.

———. "Alfonso I d'Este: Music and Identity in Ferrara." PhD diss., University of Nottingham, 2010b.

———. "Voice, Decorum and Seduction in Florigerio's *Music Lesson*." *Early Music* 38 (2010c): 361–67.

———. "Finding Fame: Fashioning Adrian Willaert c.1518." *Journal of the Alamire Foundation* 4 (2012): 12–35.

———. "Leonardo and the Paragone." In *The Routledge Companion to Music and Visual Culture*, edited by Tim Shephard and Anne Leonard, 229–37. New York: Routledge, 2013a.

———. "Musical Spaces: The Politics of Space in Renaissance Italy." In *The Routledge Companion to Music and Visual Culture*, edited by Tim Shephard and Anne Leonard, 274–80. New York: Routledge, 2013b.

———. "A Mirror for Princes: The Ferrarese Mirror Frame in the V&A and the Instruction of Heirs." *Journal of Design History* 26 (2013c): 104–14.

———. "Noblewomen and Music in Italy, ca.1430–1520: Looking Past Isabella." In *Gender, Age and Musical Creativity*, edited by Lisa Colton and Catherine Howarth. Aldershot: Ashgate, 2015.

———. "The Meaning of Giving in Renaissance Italy: Musical Exchanges in Florence and Ferrara." In *Sources of Identity: Makers, Owners and Users of Music Sources Before 1600*, edited by Lisa Colton and Tim Shephard. Turnhout: Brepols, forthcoming.

Shinneman, Dalyne. "The Canon in Titian's *Andrians*: a Reinterpretation." In Philip Fehl, "The Worship of Bacchus and Venus in Bellini's and Titian's Bacchanals for Alfonso d'Este," *Studies in the History of Art* 6 (1974): 93–95.

Simons, Patricia. "Alert and Erect: Masculinity in Some Italian Renaissance Portraits of Fathers and Sons." In *Gender Rhetorics: Postures of Dominance and Submission in History*, edited by Richard C. Trexler, 163–86. Binghamton: Medieval & Renaissance Texts & Studies, 1994.

———. "Portraiture, Portrayal, and Idealization: Ambiguous Individualism in Representations of Renaissance Women." In *Language and Images of Renaissance Italy*, edited by Alison Brown, 263–311. Oxford: Clarendon Press, 1995.

Slim, H. Colin. "Musicians on Parnassus." *Studies in the Renaissance* 12 (1965): 134–63.

———. "Dosso Dossi's Allegory at Florence about Music." *Journal of the American Musicological Society* 43 (1990): 43–98.

Smith, Gertrude. "The Canon in Titian's Bacchanal." *Renaissance News* 6 (1953): 52–56.

Solerti, A. "La Vita Ferrarese nella Prima Metà del Secolo Decimosesto Descritta da Agostino Mosti." *Atti e Memorie della R. Deputazione di Storia Patria per le Provincie di Romagna*, 3rd ser., 10 (1892): 164–203.

Starn, Randolph. "Seeing Culture in a Room for a Renaissance Prince." In *The New Cultural History*, edited by Lynn Hunt, 205–32. Berkeley: University of California Press, 1989.

Stras, Laurie. "'Al gioco si conosce il galantuomo:' Artifice, Humour and Play in the *Enigmi Musicali* of Don Lodovico Agostini." *Early Music History* 24 (2005): 213–86.

Syson, Luke. "Reading Faces: Gian Cristoforo Romano's Medal of Isabella d'Este." In *La Corte di Mantova nell'età di Andrea Mantegna, 1450–1550*, edited by Cesare Mozzarelli, Robert Oresko, and Leandro Ventura, 281–94. Rome: Bulzoni, 1997.

———. "Tura and the 'Minor Arts:' The School of Ferrara." In *Cosmè Tura: Painting and Design in Renaissance Ferrara*, edited by Stephen Campbell et al., 31–70. Boston: Isabella Stewart Gardner Museum, 2002.

Syson, Luke, and Dora Thornton. *Objects of Virtue: Art in Renaissance Italy*. London: British Museum, 2001.

Thompson, Graves H. "The Literary Sources of Titian's *Bacchus and Ariadne*." *The Classical Journal* 1 (1956): 259–64.

Thornton, Dora. *The Scholar in his Study: Ownership and Experience in Renaissance Italy*. New Haven: Yale University Press, 1997.

Tietze-Conrat, Erica. "Mantegna's Parnassus: A Discussion of a Recent Interpretation." *The Art Bulletin* 31 (1949): 126–30.

Tinctoris, Johannes. *The Art of Counterpoint*. Translated by Albert Seay. Rome: American Institute of Musicology, 1961.

———. *Concerning the Nature and Propriety of Tones*. Translated by Albert Seay. Colorado Springs: Colorado College Music Press, 1967.

———. *Opera Theoretica*. Edited by Albert Seay. 2 vols. Rome: American Institute of Musicology, 1975.

Tornabuoni de' Medici, Lucrezia. *Sacred Narratives*. Edited and translated by Jane Tylus. Chicago: University of Chicago Press, 2001.

Trissino, Giangiorgio. *I Ritratti*. Rome: Lodovico de gli Arrighi, e Lautitio Perugino, 1524.

Tuohy, Thomas. Review of *Le Muse e il Principe: Arte di Corte nel Rinascimento Padano*, edited by Alessandra Mottola-Molfino and Mauro Natali. *Apollo* 134 (1991): 425–26.

———. *Herculean Ferrara: Ercole d'Este, 1471–1505, and the Invention of a Ducal Capital*. Cambridge: Cambridge University Press, 1996.

Vander Straeten, Edmond. *La Musique aux Pays-Bas Avant le XIXe Siècle*. 8 volumes in 4. New York: Dover, 1969.

Vasari, Giorgio. *Le Vite de' Piu Eccellenti Pittori Scultori ed Architettori Scritte da Giorgio Vasari, Pittore Aretino, con Nouve Annotazioni e Commenti di Gaetano Milanesi*. Edited by Gaetano Milanesi. 9 volumes. Florence: G. C. Sansoni, 1878–85.

Venturi, Adolfo. *Storia dell'Arte Italiana*. Part XI, volume 3. Milan: Ulrico Hoepli, 1928.

Verheyen, Egon. *The Paintings in the 'Studiolo' of Isabella d'Este at Mantua*. New York: New York University Press, 1971.

Vicentino, Nicola. *Ancient Music Adapted to Modern Practice*. Translated by Maria Rika Maniates. New Haven: Yale University Press, 1996.

Vickers, Brian, ed. *Arbeit, Musse, Meditation: Betrachtungen zur Vita Activa und Vita Contemplativa*. Zurich: Verlag der Fachvereine, 1985.

———. "Leisure and Idleness: The Ambivalence of *Otium*." *Renaissance Studies* 4 (1990): 1–37 and 107–54.

Vickers, Nancy J. "Diana Described: Scattered Woman and Scattered Rhyme." In *Writing and Sexual Difference*, edited by Elizabeth Abel, 95–110. Brighton: Harvester, 1982.

Waddington, Raymond B. "Pisanello's *Paragoni*." In *Perspectives on the Renaissance Medal*, edited by Stephen K. Scher, 27–45. New York: Garland, 2000.

Walker, John. *Bellini and Titian at Ferrara*. London: Phaidon, 1956.

Webb, Ruth. "The Transmission of the Eikones of Philostratos and the Development of Ekphrasis from Late Antiquity to the Renaissance." PhD diss., Warburg Institute, 1992.

Weil-Garris, Kathleen, and John F. d'Amico. "The Renaissance Cardinal's Ideal Palace: A Chapter from Cortesi's *De cardinalatu*." In *Studies in Italian Art and Architecture, 15th through 18th Centuries*, edited by Henry A. Millon, 45–123. Rome: American Academy in Rome, 1980.

Welch, Evelyn. *Art in Renaissance Italy, 1350–1500*. Oxford: Oxford University Press, 1997.

———. "New, Old and Second-Hand Culture: The Case of the Renaissance Sleeve." In *Revaluing Renaissance Art*, edited by Gabriele Neher and Rupert Shepherd, 101–20. Aldershot: Ashgate, 2000.

———. "Public Magnificence and Private Display: Giovanni Pontano's 'De splendore' (1498) and the Domestic Arts." *Journal of Design History* 15 (2002): 211–22.

———. "Painting as Performance in the Italian Renaissance Court." In *Artists at Court: Image-Making and Identity, 1300–1550*, edited by Stephen J. Campbell, 19–32. Boston: Isabella Stewart Gardner Museum, 2004.

———. *Shopping in the Renaissance: Consumer Cultures in Italy, 1400–1600*. New Haven: Yale University Press, 2005.

Wethey, Harold E. *The Paintings of Titian*. 3 volumes. London: Phaidon, 1969–75.

Wheeler, Graham. "Sing, Muse...: The Introit from Homer to Apollonius." *The Classical Quarterly* 52 (2002): 33–49.

Wind, Edgar. *Bellini's Feast of the Gods*. Cambridge, MA: Harvard University Press, 1948.

———. "Mantegna's *Parnassus*: A Reply to Some Recent Reflections." *Art Bulletin* 31 (1949): 224–31.

Winternitz, Emmanuel. "Quattrocento Science in the Gubbio Study." *The Metropolitan Museum of Art Bulletin*, n.s., 1 (1942): 104–16.

———. *Musical Instruments and their Symbolism in Western Art*. London: Faber & Faber, 1967.

Witten, L. C. "Apollo, Orpheus and David." *Journal of the American Musical Instrument Society* 1 (1975): 5–55.

Woodward, William Harrison. *Studies in Education during the Age of the Renaissance, 1400–1600*. Cambridge: Cambridge University Press, 1906.

Zaniboni, Mario. *Gli Estensi nelle Loro Delizie: Ferrara Medievale e Rinascimentale, Mura, Torrioni, Castelli e Delizie*. Ferrara: Giovanni Vicentini, 1987.

Zarri, Gabriella. *La Religione di Lucrezia Borgia: Le Lettere Inedite del Confessore*. Rome: Roma nel Rinascimento, 2006.

Zuccolin, Gabriella. "Princely Virtues in *De Felici Progressu* of Michele Savonarola, Court Physician of the House of Este." In *Princely Virtues in the Middle Ages, 1200–1500*, edited by Pieter Bejczy István and Cary J. Nederman, 237–58. Turnhout: Brepols, 2007.

INDEX